Series editor G G Chowdhury

Information Systems

iResearch Series

Series Editor: G. G. Chowdhury, Professor of Information Science and Head of the Department of Mathematics and Information Sciences at Northumbria University in Newcastle, UK.

This peer-reviewed monograph series supports the vision of the iSchools and creates authoritative sources of information for research and scholarly activities in Information Science. Each book in the series focuses on a specific aspect or emerging topic of information studies, provides a state-of-the-art review of research in the chosen field and addresses the issues, challenges and progress of research and practice.

Editorial board

Series editor G G Chowdhury

Information Systems

Process and practice

Edited by

Christine Urquhart, Faten Hamad,
Dina Tbaishat, Alison Yeoman

facet
publishing

Published by Facet Publishing,
7 Ridgmount Street, London WC1E 7AE
www.facetpublishing.co.uk

Facet Publishing is wholly owned by CILIP: the Library and Information Association.

British Library Cataloguing in Publication Data
A catalogue record for this book is available from the British Library.

ISBN 978-1-78330-241-3 (paperback)
ISBN 978-1-78330-242-0 (hardback)
ISBN 978-1-78330-243-7 (e-book)

First published 2018

Text printed on FSC accredited material.

Typeset from editors' files in 11/14pt Garamond and Frutiger by Flagholme Publishing Services.
Printed and made in Great Britain by CPI Group (UK) Ltd, Croydon, CR0 4YY.

Contents

List of tables and figures

Tables

Figures

Series editor's foreword

Facet's iResearch series began its journey in 2015 with the aim of publishing unique titles blending theory and research on a specific aspect or an emerging topic in information science. Design and evaluation of information systems and services has remained an area of study and research in many cognate disciplines ranging from computing and information systems, information and library studies, to business management, and so on. Each discipline aims to address a set of unique challenges as they are seen from their disciplinary background and perspectives. This results in research that often fails to take a holistic view of information systems including technologies, people and context. This second title in the iResearch series - edited by Urquhart, Hamad, Tbaishat and Yeoman - aims to address this challenge by bringing together different viewpoints and perspectives of information systems design and evaluation from the contributors' own diverse and yet complimentary areas of teaching and research interests. Quite rightly, in her introduction to the book, Urquhart points out that this title sits within the design and architecture theme of the iResearch series and it aims to encourage information researchers to think critically about the possible connections that can be made between different topics of study in information in order to design, develop and evaluate the most effective and efficient information systems and services. Hence this is not just another book on information architecture that focuses on content architecture alone; the research and development activities reported in this book also cover the other end of the spectrum concerned with service evaluation, performance management and library assessment.

This book, containing 14 chapters written by academics and researchers from different research backgrounds and viewpoints, offers a significant contribution to research and practices in the architecture, design and evaluation of online information systems and services.

Professor Gobinda Chowdhury
Series editor

About the authors

Editors

Christine Urquhart was a full-time member of staff in the Department of Information Studies, Aberystwyth University, UK (1993-2009). Since retiring from full-time teaching she has continued to pursue her research interests. These include information behaviour and information systems research, and the value and impact of information services. She is the lead author for two Cochrane systematic reviews (including one on nursing record systems) and has worked with SaraDunn Associates on several social care information projects. For five years she was Director of Research in the Department at Aberystwyth and devised the research training programmes for doctoral research. She was a member of the 2014 QAA subject benchmark panel for the library, archives, records and information management group.

Dr Faten Hamad is an assistant professor in the Library and Information Science Department, University of Jordan, with a specialisation in computer science and information science. She obtained her PhD degree in information science from Aberystwyth University in 2013. She is currently a member of a committee responsible for preparing one of the new mandatory university courses - learning and scientific research skills - one course among the new university proposed course bundle. She is responsible for teaching modules related to information retrieval, digital libraries and web design. Her current research interests include information retrieval, database performance evaluation and systematic reviews, social media, health informatics and e-services.

Dr Dina Tbaishat is an Assistant Professor at the University of Jordan, Library and Information Science Department. She teaches information technology courses as she has a computer information systems background. She completed a Masters degree in software engineering, where systems analysis and requirements engineering courses sparked her interests in business process modelling. Therefore her PhD in information studies at Aberystwyth University investigated business process modelling in academic libraries. Her research efforts focus on modelling processes using different methods such as Riva and Architecture of Integrated Information Systems (ARIS), in an attempt to streamline processes and possibly improve them. She is also interested in the use of social networks in the educational environment.

Alison Yeoman was awarded her PhD while working as a research officer in the Department of Information Studies, Aberystwyth University, UK. She worked on a range of projects relating to information behaviour (particularly in the context of health), use of electronic resources (including user evaluations of website accessibility), communities of practice, and virtual learning environments. Since leaving Aberystwyth, she has expanded her research interests into social care and the third sector while also working as a senior learning development advisor for Bath Spa University.

Contributors

Dr Sally Burford is an associate professor in knowledge and information studies in the Faculty of Arts and Design at the University of Canberra, Australia, and teaches postgraduate coursework and research students. She is the Associate Dean Education within the Faculty. Sally's research is in the area of knowledge and information practice - specifically, the practice of web information architecture and how social media is incorporated into existing information practices. She is also researching in digital mobility, in particular mobile health. Sally is a member of the News and Media Research Centre at the University of Canberra. Alongside her research, Sally has considerable industry experience in managing online environments, especially online education and large enterprise websites.

Catherine M. Burns is Professor in Systems Design Engineering at the University of Waterloo, Canada, where she directs the Advanced Interface Design Lab and the Centre for Bioengineering and Biotechnology. Catherine's research is in human factors engineering where she is well known for her work in cognitive work analysis, ecological interface design and developing decision support systems. She has contributed over 250 publications and is the co-author of seven books in this area. She is a fellow of the Human Factors and Ergonomics Society.

Karen Colbron is digital content manager at Jisc, working with libraries and archives to make their digital collections visible and discoverable on the web for learning, teaching and research. Following a postgraduate diploma in information studies at Northumbria University, UK, she has worked extensively in public broadcasting in the UK and USA for over 25 years. She is an Emmy Award-nominated archivist who specialises in preserving and creating web access to digitised collections, including the only extant copy of the public radio coverage of the 1963 March on Washington for jobs and freedom, famous for Martin Luther King Jr's speech 'I have a dream'. Her research interests focus on training and guidance on online resource discovery. Additionally, she is interested in digital access issues relating to monographs.

Adam Euerby is Senior Product Designer at FairVentures Lab, an innovation research and development initiative of Fairfax Financial Holdings Ltd, Canada. In his current position he explores future applications of emerging technologies and works with Fairfax companies to further develop their internal innovation practices. Previously, he worked as a product design manager and product designer at D2L Inc., an education-based start-up out of the Waterloo Region in Canada. Adam graduated from the University of Waterloo with a Masters of Applied Science in Systems Design Engineering focused in human factors, where he explored how social networking technologies could support active and productive communities of practice in a range of contexts.

Dr Fernando Loizides is Lecturer of Computer Science and Informatics at Cardiff University, UK. His research lies in information interaction, human–computer interaction and digital libraries, focusing on information seeking, information architecture and user experience, with a special interest in user interfaces and emerging interactive technologies. He has applied development experience and is involved in several research and industrial projects with companies including the European Patent Office, Microsoft, Nokia, Department for Education UK, Cyprus Broadcasting Channel and the Federal Department of Antiquities.

Aekaterini Mavri is a researcher at the Cyprus Interaction Lab and a full-time member of the special teaching staff at the Department of Multimedia and Graphic Arts at Cyprus University of Technology. She has worked as a digital designer in the industry for several years and she is currently teaching modules related to digital design, user experience design and web design and development. Her research interests focus on instructional models and methods that can encourage collaboration and active learning through technological interventions, particularly in web design and development. She is also interested in information architecture, visual presentation and interactive behaviour relating to the design, development and evaluation of semi-structured document triage interfaces for text-heavy environments, such as digital libraries.

Paula Ormandy holds the Chair in Long Term Conditions Research at the University of Salford. She has many years of experience in executing and leading on research funded projects and service evaluations across various healthcare settings. Her research interests focus on patient experience, information needs research and information provision to facilitate self-management in clinical practice for people managing a long-term condition. She is the British Renal Society Vice President for Research and chair of the Research Committee. She is currently examining digital skills training to re-engage people with chronic kidney disease back into the labour market and the use of social media for patient and public involvement in research.

Cristina Vasilica is a Post-Doctoral Research Fellow in Digital and Social Media in Healthcare. Her background is in IT service development working in the industry before embarking on her PhD, which evaluated the impact of social media on patients' information provision, networking and communication. Her research interests focus on creating digital tools, which embed sustainable engagement strategies in the healthcare and educational context. She explores the expansion of digital/social media and emerging technologies across different contexts, combining technical understanding with theoretical constructs to impact on real life information provision, individual engagement in health and social care. For example: a social media approach to respond to the needs of patients with IgA nephropathy or digital marketing to promote health messages.

CHAPTER 1

Introduction

Christine Urquhart

1.1   Introduction

This book attempts to bridge some of the gaps between discrete areas of research that information professionals could use to design helpful and effective information systems and services. We know the problem of silo thinking, and it can be hard to make the connections, to see patterns and the big picture across different research cultures, or even within one broad discipline. An editorial in *MIS Quarterly* (Goes, 2013) points out that information systems research has many streams, many different ways of thinking and doing research. This variety is healthy and probably unavoidable if the broad discipline is to grow and flourish. We are not alone in library and information science and information systems research in facing challenges in deciding how to do research or evaluate practice. It helps to have different perspectives on a problem. Different viewpoints can help to formulate a research question that can be answered, help decide on appropriate methods to use and help to discuss the findings in relation to the existing evidence.

As a group of editors, we have diverse areas of research and teaching interests, covering information retrieval, health information research, knowledge translation and evidence-based practice, information behaviour research, systems analysis and business process analysis. Our teaching and research experience has helped us realise that there are problems with communication across different silos. For example, information architecture within the library and information science field has often been the study of content management. Information seeking may be accommodated for navigation tools, but the activities, processes and workflows that might accompany an information systems architecture may be less obvious. Information behaviour research often seems separate from research on the design of information systems. The context that is so important in information behaviour research may come into personal support and services to support the information systems (hence much of the work on information literacy) but information behaviour research may not contribute directly to information systems design as much as it could. Information behaviour research often focuses on information seeking, and less attention is given to the use of information, and the processes involved in this. Within library and information services themselves, the library assessment literature discusses performance measurement and change management strategies, but there is little published on ways of looking at the process architecture of a library service, and how this may or may not relate to the business aims of the organisation.

This book belongs with the design and architecture theme of the iResearch series. We are trying to encourage students and practitioners to think about the possible connections that can be made. Information professionals graduating from information or knowledge management, or information studies degree schemes may find themselves working at that point where technology, people and information meet. It is interesting – but also challenging and requires integration of much that may have been learnt on different modules during a degree scheme. Our aim is to provide a critical analysis, with supporting case studies of library and information service and systems architecture – in a very broad interpretation of the term architecture. As the book belongs with the iResearch series, we have emphasised methods of enquiry wherever possible, to help students and practitioners choose suitable ones to use for their own investigations.

After this introduction, Section 1.2 outlines an approach to blending science, engineering and design for effective systems, and Section 1.3 explains the function of the commentaries in the book. Section 1.4 argues that the multidisciplinary approach taken in this book may help recent graduates to find employment in the future. Section 1.5 outlines the structure of the book.

1.2   Blending science, engineering and design

While working on this book I read *The New ABCs of Research* by Shneiderman (2016), which comforted me that the approach we were trying to take was a good way to go. In the book Shneiderman discusses the need for different disciplines to collaborate and, perhaps more importantly, the need to combine applied and basic research. He takes this further than the usual problems of the academic perspective of what is important to research and the practitioner perspective of not finding that type of research immediately useful. Shneiderman suggests that there are three streams to blend: science, engineering and design. Science, the basic research, helps us understand the world. We have a considerable body of research on information behaviour research, for example. Engineering, the second strand, is about using technologies, developing new technologies to make things, systems and services that work safely and effectively. Library management systems need to be secure, we want them to cope with the load placed on them, and we want to upgrade them without too many problems. We need health information systems to improve individual interactions with the health services, and to make the work of health professionals more effective. Design, the third strand, is about fresh thinking. Designers need to be open-minded, to entertain a range of possibilities. Human–computer interaction research exemplifies the design approach, integrating ideas from a range of disciplines to produce beautiful and functional interfaces that people will want to use. Large collaborative projects need those three strands of science, engineering and design in order to do research to produce effective solutions to problems.

Large collaborative projects may be the ideal approach, but many practitioners and academics may not have the resources or the time to set up projects on this scale. This book aims to demonstrate a variety of ways of thinking and research approaches that can be applied in large collaborative research, but also in smaller projects. Goes (2013) points out that in the information systems field, different programmes are offered by faculties across the USA. The same could be said for library and information science programmes in the UK. As part of the initial market research for the book, I looked at the outline content of many undergraduate and postgraduate programmes in librarianship, information science, information management, information studies and information systems. The results were confusing, as the same module title, e.g. Information Architecture, may offer completely different content in different institutions. Sometimes it seemed that the technology component of a programme was boxed within one particular module or two, with little apparent impact on other modules. There might be modules that stress the importance of working with users, the human aspects of service delivery, but few modules that really deal with design, and methods to make the lives of users easier through better information systems and services. We often focus on what information should be provided, but sometimes forget how the information work gets done - the workflows and the business processes.

1.3   Function of the commentaries

We were aware that this book required some stitching together of the chapters, to help readers appreciate some of the connections. That is why the chapters have commentaries to provide some cross referencing to other material in the book and further information on the approaches described in the chapters. For example, we do not aim to be another book on information architecture, but we refer to some of the advice given by leading practitioners. We cannot discuss in detail how to undertake object-oriented analysis and design, but we consider some of the methods, such as use cases, that designers and users can employ to help in discussions about system design. Similarly, we show how business process analysis methods operate, but for further advice there are other textbooks and websites that should be used as well.

The introductions to each chapter help readers appreciate how a particular chapter fits into the structure of the book.

1.4   Future proofing your degree studies

In a book examining the future of the professions, Susskind and Susskind (2015, 264) consider future roles for people who now class themselves as 'professionals', arguing that there will be a decline in the demand for the traditional professions and the conventional professional worker. Some of the future roles that they suggest fit neatly (and quite coincidentally) into the content of this book. For example, one future role suggested is that of process analyst (discussed in chapters 5-8), another is the moderator in virtual communities (Chapter 12), and another is the R&D worker, who keeps up to date with specialist areas of knowledge, and appropriate technologies to provide practical expertise in new ways (see chapters 13 and 14 for ways of collecting clinical data, and working with the evidence, using and developing tools for systematic review support for better policy decisions). Other future roles include the designers who will provide online services that are intuitive, simple to use, and designed for people with varying degrees of knowledge (chapters 2-4, 9 and 10).

We cannot make recommendations on how you should try to steer your career, but we hope that the book gives you some ideas on what might be possible, and some of the methods and techniques that you might need to learn to get you where you want to go.

1.5   The structure of the book

The book aims to take a holistic interpretation of information architecture, but to move beyond the view of information architecture that focuses on content architecture alone. We aim to be relevant to the other end of the spectrum, those concerned with service evaluation, performance management and library assessment. To do that we need to look at methods, research approaches and research evidence that consider the workflow and the processes going on in library and information services, and other organisations.

Chapter 2 provides an overview of information architecture, the various approaches and emphases of information architecture, the development of pervasive information architecture, information and knowledge organisation, and information behaviour and how they may influence design of navigation and visualisation. Chapter 3 takes the information and knowledge organisation one step further, and looks at methods of taxonomy testing for information architecture, with an overview of taxonomy development, and discussions of case studies from the literature on taxonomy testing in library and information services. We move from the detail of taxonomy to thinking about the big picture of organisational website design in Chapter 4. Sally Burford discusses her research using grounded theory on practising web information architecture in large organisations. She describes the components of owning information architecture (the governance), negotiating information architecture (the human exchanges in design and changes), enacting information architecture (those implementing, improvising and acting on the website), and the knowing of information architecture (where and how learning takes place).

Chapter 5 introduces some of the methods and techniques for process analysis that are discussed in more detail in chapters 6-8. Chapter 5 explains how to describe the functionality from the user perspective using use case diagrams, and how use case descriptions consider the steps of the interaction between system users and the high-level functions, the use cases. The chapter goes on to describe the principles of process analysis and how to derive a process architecture for an organisation or part of an organisation. Chapter 6 provides more guidance on process modelling with the Riva technique. Chapter 7 illustrates how these techniques may be used to help redesign internal processes within library services. Chapter 8 compares two case studies of business process modelling for process improvement. The framework used to compare the studies considers how far each study examined job fit, job satisfaction and the viewpoints of the stakeholders.

Chapter 9 examines the design of online semi-structured documents, such as academic articles, and how to design interfaces that help users to evaluate quickly the information in those semi-structured documents. Design for this type of document triage requires combining research in information behaviour and human–computer interaction. The chapter covers aspects of the information architecture required, how designers can accommodate the likely ways that users may assess information quality, and the tools that can improve information seekers' experience. Chapter 9 presents some evidence-based guidelines for interfaces, but Chapter 10, in contrast, provides examples of work in progress from practice. Three Jisc resource discovery projects are discussed, all different, but each emphasises user experience, or information behaviour (or both). The case studies cover the use of Flickr to promote a photograph collection at Queen's University Belfast; Middlesex University's Museum of Domestic Design and Architecture's use of the balanced value impact model to help analyse the possible purposes of the collection for various stakeholders, and how to choose appropriate social media; and how a better content management system has been built at the Museum of English Rural Life and Special Collections at the University of Reading, to try to meet the challenge of how to work with and for different audiences, and their different reasons for using the website. Chapter 11 takes the idea of the audience deeper, and discusses design for a community, a global community of practice for those with shared interests, in this case for the University-Community Partnership for Social Action Research (UCP-SARnet), an organisation based at Arizona State University. The longitudinal design and evaluation of UCP-SARnet combined a human factors approach and cognitive work analysis with the design principles for supporting a community of practice.

Much of information behaviour research has been interested in getting information to the user, but the rise of social media has emphasised the importance of co-creation of information and knowledge. Chapter 12 discusses the design and development of an online patient support group for renal patients, where co-creation of information was vital. The chapter covers the identification of information needs for this group, how users might engage with the website, an evaluation of the website that demonstrated levels of engagement, and how activity theory contributed to an understanding of the way the information might lead to better patient outcomes. Chapter 13 continues the health theme for these final chapters by examining the research evidence on design of systems for clinical data capture and how these might integrate with electronic health records. Chapter 13 also revisits the idea of document architecture but this time for clinical document architecture and information exchange. Chapter 14 examines aspects of systematic review production and providing easy access to that evidence for clinicians. The chapter describes how to provide easy access to the evidence within clinical workflows, methods for searching for the evidence, management of the systematic review process, and the tools and techniques, such as text mining, that may help to streamline the process of producing a systematic review.

Returning to Shneiderman's plea for combining science, engineering and design, how do we rate on providing a holistic view of information architecture?

First, on the science side, we cover methods for taxonomy testing in Chapter 3. We have an understanding of the operation of large organisational websites in Chapter 4, the use of a theoretical framework for comparing approaches to business process modelling in Chapter 8, and Chapter 9 presents guidelines based on the evidence from human–computer interaction research. Chapter 11 looks at how human factors can be combined with principles of communities of practice. Chapter 12 discusses some of the research on human information behaviour and use of social media that helped in design of the website. Chapter 13 examines 'what works' in design of systems for clinical data capture, and Chapter 14 is concerned with production of the evidence.

Second, on the engineering side and use of innovative technologies, we mention some software tools to help in taxonomy testing (Chapter 3), chapters 6 and 7 discuss the use of Riva and some software tools for business process modelling. The case studies described in Chapter 10 examine different social media tools and techniques for design and evaluation of websites. Chapters 13 and 14 make extensive reference to technologies, such as the design of information systems for electronic clinical data capture, and tools to assist systematic reviewing teams.

Third, on the design aspect of information architecture and the need for fresh thinking to create useful and effective solutions, Chapter 9 presents a framework for thinking about designing interfaces for document triage - fresh thinking about a solution to a problem that most of us simply tolerate. Business process analysis and business process modelling (chapters 5–8) are ways of enquiry that should help people rethink ways of working, workflows, how the organisational processes fit together, whether some processes could be outsourced, whether some activities and roles can be eliminated, and whether some roles should be enhanced. Chapters 13 and 14 emphasise how workflows for some time-intensive activities in health care research can be improved.

Some of the chapters, as you may have noted, fall into more than one category of Shneiderman's framework. That was our aim, when trying to provide our holistic view of information architecture. We have covered content management and taxonomy development, information behaviour research, theoretical and methodological approaches appropriate for design and evaluation of particular types of websites, and the idea of process architecture and process modelling to support improved workflows and how people can effectively manage information in an organisation. There is much more that can be written on some of these topics and techniques, and we have tried to give pointers to other research, and some other background.

References

Goes, P. (2013) Commonalities across IS Silos and Intradisciplinary Information Systems Research, *MIS Quarterly*, **37** (2), iii–vii.

Shneiderman, B. (2016) *The New ABCs of Research: achieving breakthrough through collaborations*, Oxford University Press.

Susskind, R. and Susskind, D. (2015) *The Future of the Professions: how technology will transform the work of human experts*, Oxford University Press.

CHAPTER 2

Approaches to information architecture

Faten Hamad

COMMENTARY: CHRISTINE URQUHART

Chapter 2 introduces the main concerns of information architecture, the design and organisation of websites to support finding, sharing and understanding information across many channels. I was interested in reading the first sections of Chapter 2 on the use of the words ecology and ecosystems by some prominent information architects (Rosenfeld, Morville and Arango, 2015) to describe what information architecture is about. In biological terms ecology means the pattern of relations between organisms and their environment. Such relations are often complex and intricate. We can speculate that the choice of the terms ecosystems and ecology was intended to convey the message that we need to balance many factors in information architecture – the aesthetic design, the feel of the site, the functions supported, the organisation of information and knowledge, and the need to work across different ecosystems or media. An information architecture may be successful as it has happened to find a pattern of relations that works for most users, across their smartphones and their laptops. Other information architects have examined similar themes but have used the word context (Hinton, 2009). Hinton argues that the word context really means the mental map that we have layered on top of our sensory experience, and that information architecture concerns the design of contextual experience using hyperlinks. The web gives new ways of shaping our contextual experience. Get it right and we can share information and knowledge with many more like-minded people, although there may be downsides to the personalisation bubbles that can be created. But, worse for the individual is the possible widespread publication on the web of embarrassing information that was assumed to be forgotten. Those hyperlinks have changed our contextual experience in ways that we are still trying to accommodate.

Hinton (2015) develops the meaning of contextual experience for information architecture further. It would be convenient to assume that we could all define a goal for our information searching at the outset, or that a particular type of goal would require a particular set of information-seeking activities or information behaviour. But often we have to realise that information needs are not pre-ordained at the outset of a search, but that the process of information searching, and our perception of information need, is shaped as we go along. Hinton argues that context is not a given, that context and contextual experience are shaped by action. Chapter 2 stresses the importance of pervasive information architecture where the users need to be viewed as information intermediaries, and that static information provision and use has become a more dynamic and fluid situation. Hinton probably would argue that context always has been dynamic but that it has been convenient to separate out the components for design reasons.

This separation of components is apparent when examining how library and information science departments have approached the teaching of information architecture. Typically, 'information behaviour' is taught in a different module from 'knowledge organisation'. Theories and models of information behaviour are divorced from what we are actually doing when searching – learning, creating meaning for ourselves, and organising our knowledge and experience. Information architecture requires some creative integration of what is learnt in different modules on a typical information science programme. Not easy, perhaps, and as architects we need to understand how the components of buildings work before putting them together as a pleasing space for use. Chapter 3, for example, examines the testing of taxonomies, the knowledge organisation. Chapter 4 examines how web information architecture is practised within large organisations. Chapters 5–8 deal with the analysis of business processes. Information architects need to be aware of how the websites – and the web itself – are used, but they are not often concerned with the organisation of the physical world around the users. Organisations are however organised groups of people working for a particular purpose. Processes get the online order to you, and working out who does what and when is important. Organisations also need to understand how their processes fit together. Chapter 9 combines information-seeking and user experience research for the design of semi-structured online documents. Chapter 10 focuses on the use of social media in the design and evaluation of websites for resource discovery. Chapter 11 discusses how community of practice principles and cognitive work analysis can be used to design a social action partnership website – explaining another approach to thinking about work needs in website design. Chapter 12 uses activity theory to evaluate the design of a website to support patients with chronic kidney disease – here the emphasis was on encouraging patients to share experience and learn from each other, and the users were very much actors. Chapters 13 and 14 consider aspects of workflow for healthcare – from electronic data capture for clinical research and clinical document architecture (another example of online semi-structured documents) to thinking about ways to streamline the production of systematic reviews and getting evidence to clinicians. The authors of the chapters could not be expected to demonstrate how all the components of information architecture work together, but we have tried to present research that focuses on the thinking and doing of information architecture work, and how to analyse the processes that occur when people do their work – using the web and other information systems, and consulting colleagues.

Returning to the theme of ecology, it seems that information architects are not the only people who are thinking on biological themes. Chapter 2 outlines some of the developments around social tagging and folksonomies. Weller (2010, 318) discusses the methods of organising and structuring tags in folksonomy-based systems as 'tag gardening'. There are various 'gardening' activities for enriching folksonomies. Weeding involves the careful elimination of bad tags, and tags with spelling mistakes or with formatting problems. Seeding requires supplementing and complementing the common tag clouds with new terms from infrequently used or recently added tags to help with retrieval, narrowing down search results and ensuring that the folksonomy is fully expressive. Landscape architecture is about the major tidying of the vocabulary problem of folksonomies, to provide labels for the homonyms, to make flower beds for the synonyms to show the relationships among them, and perhaps some pathways to show the hierarchies. Fertilising involves the enrichment of folksonomies with existing knowledge organisation schemes such as thesauri or ontologies, to ensure that the good tags flourish and the flower beds look attractive. The gardening can be done at the individual level, but more often a community is involved. There may be a chief professional tag gardener working with volunteers. Weller (2010) carries on the theme to ontology gardening where the activities are weeding and seeding, fertilising and harvesting (extracting from external resources to enhance the ontology). As Chapter 2 stresses, information architecture is all about the users, creating and developing information spaces that serve needs effectively, and allow knowledge to develop. Or, as Ranganathan's fifth law of library science observed, the library is a growing organism.

References

Hinton, A. (2009) The Machineries of Context, *Journal of Information Architecture*, **1** (1),
http://journalofia.org/volume1/issue1/04-hinton/jofia-0101-04-hinton.pdf.

Hinton, A. (2015) Narratives and Situations. In Hinton, A., *Understanding Context: environment, language and information architecture*, O'Reilly,
www.uxmatters.com/mt/archives/2015/03/understanding-context-environment-language-and-information-architecture.php.

Rosenfeld, L., Morville, P. and Arango, J. (2015) *Information Architecture: for the web and beyond*, 4th edn, O'Reilly Media Inc.

Weller, K. (2010) *Ontology Engineering in the Era of the Social Semantic Web*, de Gruyter.

2.1   Introduction

Finding and re-locating information is important for users and, obviously, the web is the main gateway for information searching. Finding information quickly is important, especially when people feel that they are suffering from information overload. As searching for information is a frustrating process in poorly organised websites, it is crucial to understand the underlying information architecture of a website and how humans interact effectively, or not, with these websites. We need a better understanding of how human information practices develop and evolve, and how systems should handle information practice for the best user-system interaction experience. Information architecture is still a relatively new concept that still does not have a well established theoretical base that governs the design and structure of websites, although aspects of user experience have been well studied. Generally, information architecture is understood to consist of several elements. Morville and Rosenfeld (2007) list these as navigation systems, labelling systems, organisation systems, indexing, searching methods and metaphors. The later edition (Rosenfeld, Morville and Arango, 2015) suggests that the basic concepts are information (distinguished from data or knowledge), structuring (appropriate level of granularity), organising (categories) and labelling (what to call the categories and the navigational elements that lead users to the categories), finding information (browsing, searching and asking) and content management and the aesthetic aspects – the art of good information architecture. Users and developers of websites have their own perspectives on how people using websites could or should seek information, or deal with the organisation of information contained on a website, just as building architects draw on their own professional expertise and feel for satisfactory aesthetics. And just as some buildings strike some people as more pleasing and easier to use than others, the same goes for websites. It may be impossible to design a website that satisfies and pleases every possible user to the same level, but the aim should be to reach a happy compromise between website owners, designers and users, within the resources available.

The chapter provides the background to information architecture, and Chapter 3 provides more details about techniques for taxonomy testing for organising and labelling. Chapter 4 discusses the practice of information architecture in large organisations and Chapter 9 describes an evidence-based framework for the architecture with semi-structured documents. Chapter 10 covers methods for ensuring visitors find a website, Chapter 11 discusses website evaluation and Chapter 13 includes a section on clinical document architecture.

Chapter 2 is organised as follows. Section 2.2 provides an overview of what information architecture means. Section 2.3 discusses information organisation as it is considered to be fundamental for information organisation and retrieval. Section 2.4 discusses labelling as a representation scheme in the information space and Section 2.5 discusses users' information needs and information-seeking behaviour. Section 2.6 covers social media and section 2.7 looks at interfaces, visualisation and interaction.

2.2   What is meant by information architecture?

The key is to create a structured shared information environment that is functional for users. There are, as already noted, several interpretations for information architecture, for instance Dillon (2002) defines information architecture as a process of design, implementation and evaluation, emphasising acceptability to the stakeholders. The Information Architecture Institute (2017) describes information architecture as a practice that requires decisions about arranging the parts in an understandable way. Rosenfeld, Morville and Arango (2015, 24) interpret information architecture as follows:

> 1) the structural design of shared information environments; 2) the synthesis of organisation, labelling, search, and navigation systems within digital, physical, and cross-channel eco-systems; 3) the art and science of shaping information products and experiences to support usability, findability, and understanding; and 4) an emerging discipline and community of practice focused on bringing principles of design and architecture to the digital landscape.

This definition is similar to the definition used in earlier versions of their book on information architecture (e.g. Morville and Rosenfeld (2007) but the later book published in 2015 recognises that information interactions will take place not just on a website but also on smartphone apps and other channels that do not use a traditional web browser. Information architecture is moving beyond being only a web application; it covers mobile applications as well. Similarly, Resmini and Rosati (2012, 33) define information architecture as 'a professional practice and field of studies focused on solving the basic problems of accessing, and using, the vast amounts of information available today'.

Most commentators agree that information architecture focuses on organising, structuring and labelling content in an effective and sustainable way to support navigation, findability and usability of websites – and looking to the future, other channels. This requires, in other words, a good understanding of how users are likely to access information, and what information they are interested to find on the website. It also needs a good understanding of how to label and organise the information and resources. We need therefore to understand the users' content and context and their dependencies. Morville and Rosenfeld (2007) refer to this as information ecology to address the complex dependencies that exist within the information space, between users, content and context. Users interact in different ways with the content within a context, which is influenced by several factors (Figure 2.1).

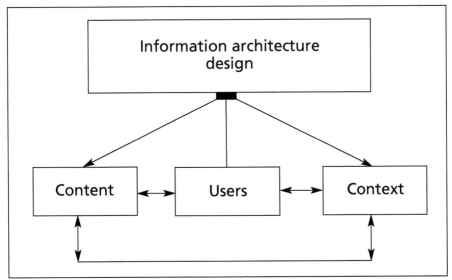

Figure 2.1 *Elements of information architecture* (adapted from Morville and Rosenfeld, 2007, 13, with permission from O'Reilly Media, Inc.)

Here content includes the documents, applications, services, schema and metadata that make up a website. Content includes the communication tool on the website; with it we are able to send a message to users and convey the meaning of the website. We may think of content in terms of ownership, website format, structure, metadata, volume and dynamism (rate of change of content). Context encompasses many concepts to reflect the organisational context of the organisations owning the website. Context covers the organisation goals and strategies, staff, processes and procedures, physical and technology infrastructure, budget and culture, all of which differ from one organisation to another. And finally users, the last element of information architecture, are really the basic element to consider when designing the information system. They have different preferences and behaviour, they have different information needs, different background experience and information seeking behaviour (Rosenfeld, Morville and Arango, 2015).

In other words, for design and implementation we need to understand the business goals behind the website and the resources available in order to set system specifications, design and implementation. We need to be aware of the nature of content and its volume in addition to the expected growth and evolution of content. We also need to understand the needs and information-seeking behaviour of users. The whole user experience should be fully understood and incorporated into the design. It is important, as information architecture is not only about labels, taxonomies or menus, or the design and organisation of content. We have to think about the multiple ways in which users can experience the website, for example.

Information architecture is therefore a very complex concept that involves many aspects that are neither visible nor tangible for users, such as the organisational culture, or the reasoning behind the organisation and labelling. Information architecture and user information interaction are closely related concepts as information systems are set out to enrich users' experience while interacting with the system (Resmini and Rosati, 2011). According to Toms (2002, 856), information interaction 'is a complex process that integrates aspects of the user, the content, and the system that delivers the content to the user'. In this definition, the system is the infrastructure context in which the system is designed and built on. Figure 2.2 shows how users interact with information on a system.

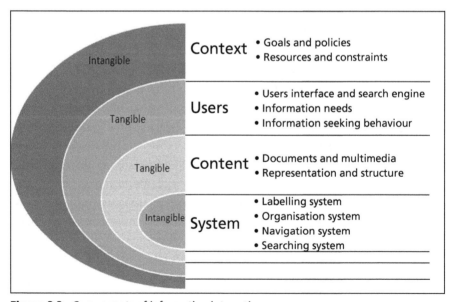

Figure 2.2 *Components of information interaction*

Figure 2.2 shows that users and decision makers are not aware of what is going on underneath the surface. All that they see of the information system is the interface they use. Toms (2002) defines 'system' as containing many of the components of information architecture listed by Rosenfeld, Morville and Arango (2015). When thinking about information-seeking behaviour it is important to know for instance that an effective searching experience requires more than a good search engine or interface, as a carefully integrated system of interdependent parts is required. We must help users to appreciate the invisible through a well planned and structured information system, otherwise the idea of architecture supporting knowledge networks will not succeed.

User experience is changing, as they become producers as well as consumers of information. Information architecture is set to help improve the design of successful user experiences in cross-channel (desktops, laptops, mobile devices, retail stores etc.) environments and therefore information architecture became pervasive information architecture, which is about the arrangement and organisation of the information structure that exists primarily in the mind of the user as a conceptual model (Resmini and Rosati, 2011).

According to Resmini and Rosati (2011) pervasive information architecture has seven manifestos:

- Information architectures become ecosystems – different media and different contexts correlate to each other and the 'whole' should be designed as part of one single, seamless user experience.
- Users become intermediaries. Users are now active contributing participants in the ecosystem, as they produce new content or interact with existing content by ways of linking, commentary or critique.
- Static becomes dynamic. As users become active information intermediaries, content changes from being static and complete to become open, incomplete and dynamic. Content is perpetually open to further refinement and manipulation.
- Dynamic becomes hybrid. Previously there might have been different and distinct domains (physical, digital) and different types of entities – data, physical items, people and different media. If there is now no clear boundary between producers and consumers, between different media and genres, then the user experience spans different environments.
- Horizontal prevails over vertical. The traditional top-down hierarchies

became difficult to maintain and support because of user involvement in this new architecture.

- Product design becomes experience design. User experience becomes the key for design across the entire system components of content, product or service. For example, when we book a flight ticket, some people want not only to find the appropriate price, but also to investigate hotels, car hire and any special assistance required. And then we may visit the web again for rating, updating and socialising with other people about part or all of the experience involved in the trip.
- Experiences become cross-media experiences. The whole experience comes from multiple channels, for instance with a bank account you can use the online banking service to monitor your payments and make a money transfer. You may also need to visit your local bank branch for other transactions, but the whole system should work seamlessly.

Clearly, the web is moving beyond multichannel working towards cross-channel working. Contents and services have more than one medium or channel to accommodate them. In reality, users may move from one channel to another to complete one task, as they might get interrupted at one point, which prevents them from completing their task, or they might move from the digital channel to the physical channel – booking the flight ticket online, and checking in at a desk or check-in booth at the airport. For instance, if we visit an Apple retail store and Apple website we can sense the reflection of the real physical organisation and categorisation of Apple products on the structure and organisation of their website. Moreover, we might explore Apple products in the store and then buy one online using a mobile phone and have it shipped to our address, or vice versa; or might shop online using the website and then collect our purchase from an Apple store. This is a typical cross-channel experience.

Search experience is changing rapidly. Tate and Russell-Rose (2012) propose a framework for describing the differing range of information needs for mobile users, with search motives categorised as being casual (semi-directed, more for pleasure), to look up (known-item searching), to learn (iterative with some degree of interpretation required) and to investigate (longer term exploration requiring higher-level thinking and synthesis). In a matrix these are set against search type, which describes the genre of information required: informational (about a topic), geographic, personal information management and trans-actional.

2.3   Information organisation

Organisation of content is important to provide users with the ability to understand, explain and control things. Information architecture aims to help retrieve information that best matches users' requirements. Therefore, information organisation and/or representations are considered to be fundamental. In reality, organisation should reflect both social and organisational principles – which is why it is difficult as users in different social and organisational situations have different expectations – they use the same word to mean different things, and categories of importance to them may not be those important to others. Information architecture organises information by classification and cataloguing the contents, and then provides labels for these contents. The classification scheme influences the design of a website's information architecture for organising, searching and browsing the website (where things are in relation to each other). However, in the larger picture, organisation is also related to navigation, labelling, and indexing (how we move about the site and choose where to go).

Knowledge organisation systems are based on classification and have two major components for information architecture: organisation scheme and the organisation structure. The organisation scheme for information architecture might be described as a way of sorting the content that makes sense to users; there might be alphabetical ordering when listing department staff, chronological ordering by release date when giving departmental news, or geographical ordering by location for weather forecasts. Knowledge organisation is more importantly based on concepts – the abstract thoughts about or references to objects in the world, usually expressed with words, but also associated with symbols. Often there is more than one word that refers to the concept (these are synonyms).

Concepts can have different levels of specificity or abstraction (e.g. furniture is more abstract than chair, and chair is more abstract than recliner). An information architect must examine the way different concepts are related to each other within the domain of interest, and logically group similar content items into categories or subject groups. Although this is useful, it is challenging to do, as concepts, categories or objects and their labels are social constructs – and can change (think of the effects of political correctness). Different groups of users may approach the architecture with different needs – the specialist may be more interested in the detailed, more specific level (different types of chairs) as opposed to the generalist (who merely wants to distinguish chairs from sofas). The most commonly used organisation structure is the hierarchical classification or taxonomy (usually a simpler form of classification). The hierarchy classification uses levels of specificity – a raspberry is a type of berry fruit, and a berry is a type of fruit (top level). However, when thinking of taxonomies we should think of inclusivity and exclusivity, and the possibility that the item may belong to more than one category. This is known as cross-listing or polyhierarchy. Strictly speaking, a tomato is a berry, but most people would categorise a tomato as a type of vegetable. Information architects need to think about the breadth and depth of their classification and taxonomy. Breadth is usually defined as the number of options in the website, depth is the number of levels within the website.

Faceted classification is another approach for organising website sites, and is widely used in different applications such as shopping sites. A facet is a component or a particular characteristic of a complex object. A faceted classification scheme is one 'that identifies subjects by their component parts and requires fitting together the appropriate parts in order to provide a class mark of work' (Chan and Salaba, 2015, 746).

Faceted classification focuses on using multiple categories to organise contents rather than one single hierarchical structure. For example, a customer may be interested in shirts, in blue (choosing from colour facet choices), for casual wear (from function facet) and in size large (from size facet). By selecting those choices (blue, for casual wear, size large) the customer should have displayed to them all the relevant shirts of interest. In an information science example (Figure 2.3 opposite), users can choose the facets that are provided on the left side bar of the Web of Science website to refine their search based on facets such as example subject field, document type and author(s). In other words, facets provide guided entry points to a set of items of interest to the user.

2.4   Labelling

The labelling system is a representation scheme. It assigns label contents to represent a larger chunk of information in the information space. For example, 'Contact Us' is a label that represents a chunk of content, often including a contact name, an address, and telephone, fax and e-mail information (Morville and Rosenfeld, 2007). Labelling is important to convey meaning and communicate a message. See, for example, the website labels in figures 2.4 and 2.5. Labels can be textual such as hyperlinks, headings, navigation options

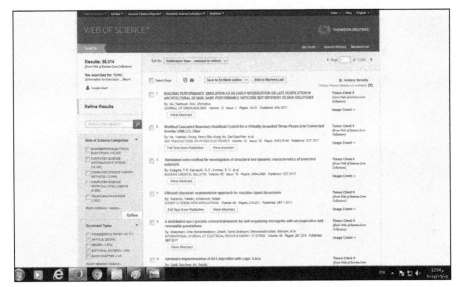

Figure 2.3 *Faceted classification on the Web of Science website* (data included herein are derived and reprinted from the Web of Science® © 2017 Clarivate Analytics, Philadelphia, PA, USA. All rights reserved)

menus and index terms (figures 2.4 and 2.5 on the next page). Iconographic labels are also used – icon or graphic to represent content. Iconographic labelling is more complex than textual labelling. Icons or graphics have more expressive power than words but also can easily be misunderstood. With words, a similar problem can occur if vocabularies used for textual labels are organisational jargon, specialised terms used by the employees but not by external users (Zimmermann, 2005). Common sense and previous experience are important when labelling information space contents. Controlled vocabularies also can be used as a comprehensive and consistent system for some of the content within one label, but users should be familiar with the terms provided in the controlled vocabularies to navigate the information space. Natural language lets users express their needs through their own experience to navigate the information space. Controlled vocabulary revolves around standards and uniformity, while a natural language approach provides users with more flexibility (Chowdhury, 2004). All these labelling sources are measures ensuring accurate representation and consistency.

Recently, a free structured approach for labelling has been advised and used, by allowing users to draw on their own labels to categorise and cluster information. This approach is often referred to as social tagging or

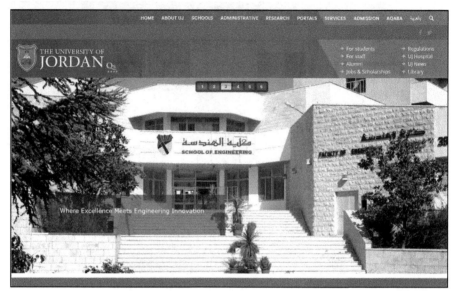

Figure 2.4 *The labelling scheme on the University of Jordan website*

Figure 2.5 *The labelling scheme and taxonomy on the University of Jordan website*

classification and became associated mainly with web resources, e.g. Delicious, as a collaborative tagging system for web bookmarks. Tagging has become a handy way for users to recall information sources for later use as well as to communicate interesting nuggets of information to others (Hammond et al.,

2005). Social tagging or classification allows users to store, organise, manage and retrieve data they intend to share with others with their own freely chosen metadata to describe their information. It does not follow the traditional hierarchical structure of a controlled vocabulary (broader and narrower terms), and being produced by different users the classification scheme reflects personal categories. However, the main problem with it might be a problem in differentiating between general categories, which may exaggerate the system's fuzziness depending on individuals' interpretations of the tags, and such differences may raise conflicts between different parties (Hammond et al., 2005; Golder and Huberman, 2006; Huang and Chuang, 2009).

The interest in natural language versus controlled vocabulary indexing (or combination of controlled plus natural language additions) focused on the technical efficiency and effectiveness of system performance, weighing up the costs (associated with human input) and benefits (representations that might fit the user query better). More recently the interest in social tagging has increased, pointing to the potential this new approach offers, despite the complexity and ambiguity it may offer.

The navigation system is the mechanism to explore the website. It is a guide to help users to understand where they are and where they can go. The navigation system is the context and flexibility of the website. Sitemaps, indexes and guides are the typical ways to provide users with a good navigation experience; websites might use more than one navigation system. For instance, sitemaps provide a visual view of website organisation, while indexes are an alphabetical list of website contents from A to Z.

2.5   Information needs and information-seeking behaviour

Users aim to find information quickly and easily. One important factor to keep in mind is that different people have different information needs and different search practices. For instance, some users know exactly what they are looking for and where to look for it. This is called known-item searching. Others do not know what exactly they are looking for nor where to look for information. They might not know what search terms to use to describe their information needs. They iteratively browse the website and explore its services. A well designed system will leave users with a good experience for searching for items. Such a system should provide users with two searching modes - known-item searching and browsing – to satisfy different people's information needs.

In addition, information-seeking behaviour varies, depending on personality, the characteristics of the information system being used, users' educational levels and background, how experienced they are in using different search methods, and more importantly the type of environment the user is in. Consequently, full understanding of the system, user profiles and their needs is essential for information systems. All this can be achieved by investigating each major environment (organisation, institution or setting in which users are engaged), the major user groups and the main characteristics of individual users (Chowdhury, 2004).

There are various methods architects can use to capture information needs and information-seeking behaviour. The most popular are search analytics and contextual inquiry. In the search analytics method, the architect reviews the most common search queries on the website through users' log files, which are stored on the system. These reflect users' search experience: what they commonly seek, the search query and terms, metadata and navigation behaviour. Unlike search analytics, contextual inquiry makes it possible to observe users interacting with information in their 'natural' settings, and allows information architects to inquire about the reasons why they seek information in a particular way. Other techniques, such as task analysis, surveys and focus groups, can be used. Information architects might combine multiple analysis methods to explore as much as possible of users' needs and information-seeking behaviour. Understanding what users' actual interests are helps information architects to determine and prioritise which architectural components to apply.

Another notion is related to and strongly affects users' needs and information-seeking behaviour. This is relevance judgement and criteria, and much research has tried to address and discuss relevancy (judgement and criteria) in more depth, but up to now there have been no stable and definitive criteria of how to define the relevancy. Most research has concluded that relevancy has certain dynamic characteristics that reflect the human nature of thinking, as the user's cognitive state grows and evolves during the search (Vakkari and Hakala, 2000). Hence the search becomes more focused, but the topicality factor, perhaps, remains the crucial criterion for relevancy.

Apparently, users' experience and cognitive state affect searching, and retrieval of what they really need. For instance, Schaik and Ling (2012, 26) stated that 'within the framework of the person-artefact-task model, cognitive and experiential factors, together, do indeed influence task outcomes in web navigation'. Within the navigation system, Schaik and Ling stressed the point that when website complexity increases, the number of links on the website increases and the error rate in navigating the website increases. In other words, the more links on a page the higher the error rate.

The concept of meeting users' needs has remained a constant undercurrent in much information retrieval research. Ideally, search engines need to capture and observe users' needs and information-seeking behaviour to develop their mechanisms but, as with much human behaviour, information-seeking behaviour is neither predictable nor regular. Kim (2009) affirmed that information-seeking behaviour is correlated with the task being performed by the user and is influenced by it, owing to the wide variation in tasks and activities (professional activities, research activities, personal activities, etc.) being carried out by users. Information-seeking behaviour is complex to define unless we are able to understand the context in which the task is taking place and the nature of information needs as well. Consequently, information systems structure and design might be developed to satisfy users' needs more successfully (Case, 2007; Kim, 2009). It is clear that the user interface, and more importantly the website map and structure, affects the seeking and navigation experience and accordingly human–computer interaction receives much attention in order to maintain search system performance (Gwizdka, 2009).

In line with this comes the decision about whether to integrate dynamic content on the website. Researchers have examined how the nature of dynamic content influences whether or not a user views it. The results confirmed that unless users intentionally triggered an update, for instance by mouse click, they will not be interested in viewing its contents. Mouse hovering appeared to be effective only where the update was something users were really interested in. Research evidence like this helps information architects make decisions about the visual interface, and the degree to which to integrate dynamic contents in the website (Jay, Brown and Harper, 2013).

2.6　Social searching and social tagging – social media effects

This section considers how use of social media, and the ways in which non-expert users can attach tags or keywords to online content (social tagging) and work collaboratively, has changed how searching works. Information architects should take such searching and tagging into account (see also Chapter 10 on resource discovery).

Furnas et al. (2006) believe that social tagging can associate users – a community of users, tag writers and system designers – with documents as the way they tag reflects their cognitive state and perception of document contents when assigning a descriptive tag. This will open the opportunity for information, thoughts and experience to be exchanged between users (Hammond et al., 2005; Chi and Mytkowicz, 2008). Morville and Rosenfeld (2007) think that social tagging could transform user behaviour and tagging patterns into new organisation and navigation systems.

In line with this, and with the growth of social networking tools and the wealth of information available on the web, social searching and social tagging (user-generated contents) can be the approach to help the process of information finding. Many researchers recommend incorporating social tagging into the information space. For instance, Lee, Kim and Kim (2012) proposed a social inverted index – an extended inverted index for social-tagging-based information retrieval. The social inverted index maintains a separate user-generated sub-list for each resource in a resource posting list to contain each user's features as weights. Lee et al.'s findings indicated that social inverted indexing performs better in informational retrieval tasks than a normal inverted index. In line with this, Zhang et al. (2014) found that an index that is enriched with user-generated data improves the retrieval effectiveness, and tags are the best-performed social feature on re-ranking. In social book searching in the discussion forums of LibraryThing, for example, customer reviews, ratings and social comments can help site editors get a sense of how readers are responding to a book, and use this to choose which books to promote. Customer reviews, ratings and social comments help other users to search for books they are interested in.

In this context, the information architect's role is to provide the structure for users to incorporate their experience and improve social practices. Wikis, social networks and bookmark-tagging platforms have architecture, predetermined contexts and functionality.

2.7 Interfaces, visualisation and interaction

Website developers should think of users as consumers of the website contents. Obviously, large websites have a huge volume of information to serve a large number of people. For example, knowing exactly what to put on the home page is important, and requires good understanding of the user community and the website goals. An information architect needs to know where to locate existing information as well as new information when it becomes available, and to understand and convey the big picture of a website. It may be necessary to have a team of information architects who have a full understanding of both external and internal users' needs of the website.

User interfaces serve as the bridge that connects users to the information source. They provide an environment for users to search and browse the information resource, and display the search results. The interface is an important part of the information system as it is the visible part of the system that the user interacts with, and therefore it is important to design an interface that is efficient and easy to understand and manipulate. Moreover, visual representation can communicate more meanings and explanation than the usual methods do (Chowdhury, 2004; Baeza-Yatez and Robeiro-Neto, 2011).

Visualisation is a new trend in information systems, exploring how users interact with systems, and helping to make sense out of a large volume of data depending on specific patterns. For example, visualisation may evolve around the idea of displaying results with a connectivity feature from a broader set of documents (domain A) to another narrower set of documents (domain B). Moreover, it has the capability of reconstructing a query based on the content of the document(s) being previously retrieved, offering more flexibility in search and retrieval strategy (Alhenshiri, Shepherd and Watters, 2010).

2.8   Conclusions

The key to finding information on the web quickly is the web's underlying information architecture. 'Information architecture' is a new concept, which does not have a well established theoretical base, so the choices to be made in the design and structure of websites have not fully developed yet. A good information architecture consists of several elements or concepts: information (distinguished from data or knowledge), structure (appropriate level of granularity), organisation (categories) and labels (what to call the categories and the navigational elements that lead users to the categories), finding information (browsing, searching or asking) and content management (Rosenfeld, Morville and Arango, 2015). Information architecture focuses on organising, structuring and labelling content in an effective and sustainable way to support navigation, findability and usability of websites. This requires good understanding of how users are likely to access information, and what information they are interested to find on the website. It also needs a good understanding of how to label and organise the information and resources.

Organisation of information (content) is important so users are able to understand, explain, control and retrieve things on websites. Users in different social and organisational situations have different expectations and practices and therefore organisation should reflect both social and organisational principles. Information architecture organises information by classifying website contents and then assigning the appropriate labels for the contents. Faceted classification is another approach for organising websites, where information (website contents) is described by particular characteristics and parts of a complex object (Chan and Salaba, 2015). There are multiple categories in this classification scheme to organise contents, which help users to find the information they seek. Labels help people understand website site contents and structure so they can navigate the website effectively. Providing controlled vocabulary and natural language is the standard approach for labelling information space contents. More recently, a free structure approach (social tagging or classification) has been used for labelling, where users are free to assign their own metadata to describe their information – with the Facebook # symbol – for tagging the contents they share. However, this might increase complexity and ambiguity of the information space.

All this depends on users' information needs and information-seeking behaviour. Everyone is different in their information needs and practices for finding, using and sharing information. There are users with basic experience of searching for information and using the information space, and professionals with extensive experience and expertise in this. Neither type of user can accomplish their tasks without well defined information architecture, which can respond effectively to different needs and practices. Search analytics and contextual inquiry are the two methods to capture users' characteristics to learn the most common search queries and navigation behaviour on the website, looking at user's log files (regular users) and observing users' interactions with the system (professional users). In other words, an information architect needs to gather information about both externally and internally expressed user needs to design a well defined information space.

Consequently, information systems structure and design might be developed to satisfy users' needs more successfully (Case, 2007; Kim, 2009). It is clear that the user interface (which connects users to the information source), and more importantly the website map and structure, affects and is affected by seeking and navigation experience and accordingly human–computer interaction receives much attention in order to maintain search system performance (Gwizdka, 2009). Information visualisation helps users to make sense of a large volume of information and to reconstruct a query based on the content of the document(s) being previously retrieved, offering more flexibility in search and retrieval strategy (Alhenshiri, Shepherd and Watters, 2010).

This chapter introduces the main principles and some of the recent trends in information architecture. Readers should also check conference proceedings such as EuroIA (www.euroia.org), the IA Summit (www.iasummit.org/) and user experience events. Other useful books include Russell-Rose and Tate (2012), Hinton (2014) and Morville (2014); the website of the Information Architecture Institute (www.iainstitute.org/what-is-ia) provides details of others.

References

Alhenshiri, A., Shepherd, M. and Watters, C. (2010) Improving Web Search for Information Gathering: visualization in effect. In *Proceedings of the Fourth Workshop of Human-Computer Interaction and Information Retrieval, HCIR 2010,: 22 August 2010, New Brunswick, USA.*

Baeza-Yatez, R. and Robeiro-Neto, B. (2011) *Modern Information Retrieval*, Addison Wesley Longman.

Case, D. O. (2007) *Looking for Information: a survey of research on information seeking, needs, and behavior*, 2nd edn, Elsevier, http://books.google.co.uk.

Chan, L. M. and Salaba, A. (2015) *Cataloging and Classification: an introduction*, Rowman & Littlefield.

Chi, E. H. and Mytkowicz, T. (2008) Understanding the Efficiency of Social Tagging Systems Using Information Theory. In *Proceedings of the Nineteenth ACM Conference on Hypertext and Hypermedia, 19-21 June 2008, Pittsburgh, PA, USA*, ACM.

Chowdhury, G. G. (2004) *Introduction to Modern Information Retrieval*, 2nd edn, Facet Publishing.

Dillon, A. (2002) Information Architecture in JASIST: just where did we come from?, *Journal of the American Society for Information Science and Technology*, **53** (10), 821-3.

Furnas, G. W., Fake, C., von Ahn, L., Schachter, J., Golder, S., Fox, K., Davis,

M., Marlow, C. and Naaman, M. (2006) Why Do Tagging Systems Work? In *CHI '06 Extended Abstracts on Human Factors in Computing Systems, 22-27 April 2006, Montréal, Québec, Canada*, ACM.

Golder, S. and Huberman, B. A. (2006) Usage Patterns of Collaborative Tagging Systems, *Journal of Information Science*, **32** (2), 198–208.

Gwizdka, J. (2009) Assessing Cognitive Load on Web Search Tasks, *The Ergonomics Open Journal*, **2** (1), 114–23.

Hammond, T., Hannay, T., Lund, B. and Scott, J. (2005) Social Bookmarking Tools: a general review, *D-Lib Magazine*, **11** (4), www.dlib.org/dlib/april05/hammond/04hammond.html.

Hinton, A. (2014) *Understanding Context: environment, language and information architecture*, O'Reilly Media Inc.

Huang, A. W. C. and Chuang, T. R. (2009) Social Tagging, Online Communication, and Peircean Semiotics: a conceptual framework, *Journal of Information Science*, **35** (3), 340–57.

Jay, C., Brown, A. and Harper, S. (2013) Predicting Whether Users View Dynamic Content on the World Wide Web, *ACM Transactions on Computer-Human Interaction*, **20** (2), 9.

Kim, J. (2009) Describing and Predicting Information-Seeking Behavior on the Web, *Journal of the American Society and Information Science Technology*, **60** (4), 679–93.

Lee, K. P., Kim, H. G. and Kim, H. J. (2012) A Social Inverted Index for Social-Tagging-Based Information Retrieval, *Journal of Information Science*, **38** (4), 313–32, doi:10.1177/0165551512438357.

Morville, P. (2014) *Intertwingled: information changes everything*, Semantic Studios.

Morville, P. and Rosenfeld, L. (2007) *Information Architecture for the World Wide Web*, O'Reilly Media, Inc.

Resmini, A. and Rosati, L. (2011) *Pervasive Information Architecture: designing cross-channel user experiences*, Elsevier.

Resmini, A. and Rosati, L. (2012) A Brief History of Information Architecture, *Journal of Information Architecture*, **3** (2), http://journalofia.org/volume3/issue2/03-resmini/.

Rosenfeld, L., Morville, P. and Arango, J. (2015) *Information Architecture: for the Web and beyond*, 4th edn, O'Reilly Media Inc.

Russell-Rose, T. and Tate, T. (2012) *Designing the Search Experience: the information architecture of discovery*, Morgan Kaufmann.

Schaik, P. V. and Ling, J. (2012) An Experimental Analysis of Experiential and Cognitive Variables in Web Navigation, *Human-Computer Interaction*, **27** (3), 199–234.

Tate, T. and Russell-Rose, T. (2012) The Information Needs of Mobile Searchers: A framework. In *Proceedings of the ECIR 2012 Workshop on Searching4Fun*.

The Information Architecture Institute (2017) What is Information Architecture?, www.iainstitute.org/what-is-ia.

Toms, E. G. (2002) Information Interaction: providing a framework for information architecture, *Journal of the American Society for Information Science and Technology*, **53** (10), 855–62.

Vakkari, P. and Hakala, N. (2000) Changes in Relevance Criteria and Problem Stages in Task Performance, *Journal of Documentation*, **56** (5), 540–62.

Zhang, B. W., Yin, X. C., Cui, X. P., Qu, J., Geng, B., Zhou, F. and Hao, H. W. (2014) USTB at INEX2014: Social Book Search Track, http://ceur-ws.org/Vol-1180/CLEF2014wn-Inex-ZhangEt2014.pdf.

Zimmermann, T. (2005) Information Architecture, http://wwwmayr.in.tum.de/konferenzen/Jass05/courses/6/Papers/03.pdf.

CHAPTER 3

Taxonomy testing for information architecture

Christine Urquhart

COMMENTARY: FATEN HAMAD

In this chapter Christine Urquhart considers several methods used for taxonomy testing. She starts by discussing taxonomy development, asserting that the term taxonomy is closely related to classification schemes although, strictly speaking, in information science taxonomies mean the subject domain and how labels in that domain are sorted hierarchically (Blackburn, Smallwood and Earley, 2014). Classification schemes on the other hand are the base for knowledge organisation to place an object in the most appropriate place or class; they are based on taxonomies (also discussed in Chapter 2, 'Approaches to information architecture'). In other words, taxonomies generally concern the labels for naming contents in a classification scheme in a standardised manner. The author asserts that social, cultural and political differences have a strong effect on the choice of classification and taxonomies; what might be an appropriate taxonomy in one culture might not be appropriate in another one.

Other considerations include the extent of users' experience, whether they are indexers or end users. For instance, Section 2.5 demonstrated that a person's information-seeking behaviour and their experience and characteristics affect their navigation and use of information space (Schaik and Ling, 2012). Another problem addressed in this chapter is whether the terms are hierarchical or used by association. The most common organisational structure is hierarchical or taxonomical classification. Information architects examine the way different concepts are related to each other within the domain of interest, and group similar content items logically into categories or subject groups. The author emphasises that the hierarchy and associations involved should be tested as well as the taxonomy.

This chapter discusses card sorting methods as useful ways to test taxonomy to ensure usability and accessibility; these often focus on hierarchy testing. The main ones are variations of open and closed card sorting. Case studies (of two academic websites and one database) demonstrate some problems that are associated with website navigation and design; the focus of discussion is the taxonomy testing strategy that authors of each case study employed in their evaluation.

Although the author emphasises that card sorting methods are the main ways to test taxonomy, the case studies present some other techniques: usability tests, personas, conducting user journeys, and sometimes talking directly to users about their information-seeking experience and behaviour. Other testing and evaluation techniques include reviews of web analytics and organising standards, and subject matter expert interviews (Soranzo and Cooksey, 2015). The case studies demonstrate the problems of labelling. For instance, one of them describes a user's lack of understanding of library terminology; another shows that users lack awareness of the label 'subject guide'.

The chapter stresses that users' experience is a major influence on website taxonomies and the overall information architecture.

References

Blackburn, B., Smallwood, R. and Earley, S. (2014) Information Organization and Classification: taxonomies and metadata. In Smallwood, R. F., *Information Governance: concepts, strategies and best practices*, Wiley, 355–84.

Schaik, P. V. and Ling, J. (2012) An Experimental Analysis of Experiential and Cognitive Variables in Web Navigation, *Human–Computer Interaction*, **27** (3), 199–234.

Soranzo, A. and Cooksey, D. (2015) Testing Taxonomies: beyond card sorting, *Bulletin of the Association for Information Science and Technology*, **41** (3), 34–9.

3.1   Introduction

This chapter discusses taxonomy testing, with emphasis on website design and evaluation for library and information services. One of the major sources of advice on website and information product evaluation is the US government service usability.gov (www.usability.gov), on usability testing. This offers advice on the basic principles of designing websites to provide a good user experience and project managing the design process. It has guidelines that indicate the strength of the evidence for various recommendations as well as the recommendation and list of resources used to devise the recommendation. For example, when searching the guidelines database in September 2016, Section 7 (navigation) included Recommendation 7.3 suggesting the use of a clickable list of contents for long pages. The recommendation's importance rating was 4 out of 5, and the strength of evidence rating was 3 out of 5. The website explains that the strength of evidence rating was obtained from a panel of eight domain expert reviewers, who constructed a set of criteria for judging the strength of the evidence for each guideline. This is a rating judgement from experts, rather than research evidence, as understood in health and social sciences. Another source of information is Boxes and Arrows (www.boxesandarrows.com), a site aimed at the information architecture and user experience community. It encourages contributions from people writing about examples of successes and failures.

This chapter is limited in size so only a few features are explored, as a background to the case studies discussed. For more details about taxonomy testing consult usability.gov (www.usability.gov) and Boxes and Arrows (www.boxesandarrows.com). This chapter reflects on common problems for designers of websites and web-based services for library and information services, and compares some advantages and disadvantages of particular methods and tools. It follows on from Chapter 2, on the principles of information architecture. Chapter 10 (sections 10.6–10.8) also discusses categorisation and pathways for information searching.

Section 3.2 outlines the main features of taxonomy development, Section 3.3 looks at methods of taxonomy testing, and sections 3.4, 3.5 and 3.6 examine some published case studies of taxonomy testing, with conclusions in Section 3.7.

3.2   Taxonomy development

Before discussing testing of taxonomies, we need to outline the main features of taxonomies, vocabularies, thesauri and classification schemes, how these are developed, and their relation to taxonomy testing and information architecture.

Classification is the arrangement of terms, usually hierarchical, with the common relations between the terms as sub-types or super-types. The term taxonomy is often used interchangeably with classification scheme, but taxonomies generally concern one subject domain and have clear organising principles for sorting the levels of the hierarchy. Classification schemes (e.g. Dewey Decimal; www.oclc.org/en/dewey.html) are usually more general organisations of knowledge, traditionally used to find the most appropriate slot to place something. Unfortunately, what seems appropriate in some cultures and settings may seem very inappropriate in others, as Bowker and Star (1999) discuss for the International Classification of Diseases, and other classification schemes. Scientific classifications and taxonomies may seem easier to develop and manage but scientific knowledge develops, ordering principles are questioned, and social and political differences present themselves even in what seems an objective setting. Aristotelian classifications work on mutually exclusive categories – at any level the object either has a property or does not have a property. Other theories of classification stress that classification is much fuzzier than we think, and Rosch's prototype theory (Rosch and Lloyd, 1978) suggests that individuals develop an idea of what the best example of a bird is, or a chair, or another class of objects. With new things, we decide whether it is reasonable to call something a bird, or chair, by invoking our examples and testing out the comparison. Even though small children often confuse cat and dog (for example) as they are learning to talk, it is amazing how quickly they classify things of importance in their setting – classification is a very human activity. Unfortunately, therefore, testing of taxonomies is complicated by the different emphases people put on different properties. Bowker and Star (1999, 66) point out the political, religious and ethical debates over what counts as legal or illegal abortion. The linguist Lakoff (1987, 92–102) famously pointed out that in the Dyirbal language aboriginal Australians had a category for 'women, fire and dangerous things'. He proposed that our cognition depends on metaphor, defined as a mapping of conceptual structures from one domain on to another. Some metaphors – and therefore categories – may be specific to particular cultures, others may be more general human metaphors. Different life experiences lead to different reactions to a classification presented to users, and the types of associations between terms may be different. It is not surprising that terms in knowledge representations (whether classification, thesaurus or taxonomy) that are somehow 'related', and which are not equivalent or in a hierarchical relationship, can be associated in many different ways.

For knowledge organisation representations that have to be read by computer – ontologies – ontology designers have therefore to specify which associations are relevant to them. When rating knowledge organisation systems by complexity, the ontology is at the top, followed by the thesaurus, which specifies a hierarchy of terms and, importantly, the related terms (although the type of relationship may not be specified) (Weller, 2010, 115-240). Those testing taxonomies need to check not only that the hierarchies of terms make sense to users, but whether some of the associations work – do the mechanisms to support browsing help?

Sometimes the hierarchy is not simple, which makes it difficult to construct the relational database that supports searching. One class of objects may have different parent classes (polyhierarchy, or multiple inheritance). For example, in MeSH, the US National Library of Medicine's thesaurus of medical subject headings (www.nlm.nih.gov/mesh/), telemedicine may be regarded as a type of medicine, a type of telecommunications, or a type of healthcare delivery. In a pure faceted classification, the facets represent the fundamental categories of interest to a domain. Online shopping sites, for example, allow one to search 'all dresses', or carry out a narrower search for dresses in a particular size, or by brand, type of dress, colour, or a combination of facets – blue 'day dresses', costing not more than a particular amount. Shopping sites have to assess whether their choice of facets suits the factors that shoppers are likely to use to discriminate between items.

In taxonomy testing the range of aspects to be tested usually involves considering the hierarchy of terms (does this accord with users' ideas, and will it work for specialists as well as general users?), the terminology itself (is this appropriate and meaningful for users?) and whether the associations work (can users browse successfully, navigate up, down and across?).

Another problem for some taxonomy testing is that for some databases people (professional indexers) have analysed documents and added subject terms from a taxonomy or thesaurus. The aim of such indexing is to provide more tags to the document or item, to help users find as many relevant items as possible, and hopefully reduce the number of irrelevant items retrieved. Sadly, human indexers are unreliable (Frické, 2012, 234), even when using controlled vocabulary. Computers do better in many circumstances, as they are likely to be better at extraction. On the other hand, for tasks that require understanding, such as summing up what we have read in more abstract terms, such as a 'hunted man' type of adventure story, humans should do better.

3.3   Methods for taxonomy testing

The main methods for taxonomy testing include variants on sorting cards, labelled with the terms relevant to the domain. In the open card sort, participants sort and label categories themselves. Often researchers ask participants to explain why they have sorted the cards in a particular way. Once each participant has done a sort, the researchers have to develop a cluster analysis type of dendrogram to illustrate common groupings across participants. In a comparison of methods, Jim Ross (2011) suggests that this method allows appreciation of the mental models used, alternative groups, and some of the links. However, it is time-consuming to analyse such groups, particularly when at least 30 participants may be required to come to an understanding of a common accepted grouping. There are web tools to help, but while these are useful to the researcher in documenting the grouping, the participants probably prefer working with cards on a table, to see everything at once, and to come to a conclusion unfettered by dealing with a web tool. A compromise is to use a smaller number of personal sessions, working at a table, and then record the reasons for decisions made. This may be combined with online card sorting with a larger number of participants.

An alternative is the modified Delphi card sorting, when the first participant does an open card sort, as defined in the previous paragraph. The next participant starts with the organisation of cards the previous person has left, and may start afresh, or modify the organisation of categories. The sessions continue until there is a stable organisation and participants are no longer making major changes. This method requires fewer participants, it is neater to operate, and there is time for participants to think aloud about their reasons for changing or not changing the card organisation. The downside is that there can be a starting anchoring problem, as where and how you start affects future moves, and the related problem of groupthink, that people get swayed by one viewpoint. Soranzo and Cooksey (2015) overcome these problems by seeding the deck initially to avoid the outlier and anchoring problems. They recommend labelling the cards, printing them to distinguish them from cards added by participants. Recording need not require expensive equipment - a smartphone or digital camera may be sufficient. It is important to interview participants before they start, explain the exercise, then let them work, and observe them carefully. In probing the reasons for their choices, the watchword is 'dialogue', as participants should feel that their views are important. Soranzo and Cooksey (2015) suggest that up to ten sessions may be necessary to assess whether the same issues are emerging.

If the categories can be preset, at least provisionally, then participants can do closed card sorting which merely requires them to sort what they think should go into the various categories. Online tools can be used for this. It is easy to see whether the preset categories are going to work, and whether participants agree about the meaning for each category label. However, it is difficult to go beyond a near top-level view, and if there is major disagreement it is necessary to go back to open card sorting. In reverse card sorting, the researchers show participants the first level of a taxonomy and present a series of findability tasks, asking where they would start searching to find each item.

Donna Spencer (2003) developed card-based classification evaluation. This is a simple way of testing whether the levels of the hierarchy work for participants, going beyond reverse card sorting, and presenting participants with realistic tasks for usability testing, rather than asking where they would expect to find an item. Participants are given the question to answer, and are then presented with the cards with level 1 hierarchy labels. Once this is selected, the cards below that level in the hierarchy are presented and participants are asked where they would go next – to carry on with the hierarchy, or perhaps to go back.

Testing with low fidelity prototypes of the interface allows researchers to check that participants are not confused by the taxonomy or the navigation choices. Online testing tools are available, and may help to save time with the analysis. Treejack (https://www.optimalworkshop.com/) is one of several tools available from Optimal Workshop to evaluate the schema, in a type of closed card sort approach, or card-based classification. The documentation of problems may be useful to provide evidence for the organisation that has requested the testing. Graph visualisations (Paul, 2014) provide graphs that show connections between concepts in a way that differs from the usual histogram–matrix methods.

Finally, how should the division of labour work between those undertaking taxonomy testing and those looking at the general aspects of user experience and accessibility requirements? Hert, Carlson and Wessel (2013) suggest that both teams should integrate their work as much as possible. Experience with evaluation of the problems on the Social Care Online website (www.scie-socialcareonline.org.uk) and subsequent evaluation of the improved database website backs this up (Dunn and Urquhart, 2011, 2014). In both cases, the taxonomy was evaluated alongside accessibility, and the taxonomy evaluation allowed a more detailed understanding of some of the usability problems identified in the accessibility evaluation.

3.4   Case study – website redesign at the University of Illinois

Lewis and Hepburn (2010) based their methodology on recommendations from the literature. A survey had indicated that users had problems navigating around the library website, compounded by the problems they had with the terminology. This suggested that an open card sort approach was required. The sample was chosen from 50 volunteers, mostly graduate students, and efforts were made to ensure that the sample was representative. Out of the scheduled 18 tests, 15 participants eventually completed the card sort. The test presented a participant with 93 cards labelled with existing or potential future content for the library website, based on existing links and suggestions from the user survey. Participants also had blank index cards, pens and post-it notes. The instructions asked participants to sort the cards into categories, as many or as few as they liked, talking aloud through the process to explain their reasoning, and then to label each pile with a post-it note. The blank index cards could be used to indicate anything that was missing, or to create a duplicate if a card seemed to belong to two categories. Participants were also asked to have a discard pile for anything that seemed useless to them, and also to have a pile (Other or General) for things that they thought should be there, but which could not be placed easily.

The researchers allowed the participants to create hierarchies, if they wished – and some did, which made for a more difficult analysis. Eventually, after considering some other approaches, the evaluation team asked for advice from a class on statistical evaluation that required real-life datasets for student projects. Students used factor analysis, which accommodated the nested categories and duplicate cards. The first calculation was the similarity of pairing of each two cards (how many times do the cards appear together compared with the number of times they appear at all) (Jaccard's coefficient of community). The Jaccard scores were entered into a 93 x 93 matrix. Factor analysis was then performed on this covariance matrix to calculate factor loadings, essentially assessing which cards seemed to group together (showing what the main categories might include). This was not a magic solution to reveal the truth, however, as the researchers had to review the reasons that the participants presented for their arrangements, and why some cards were discarded. A common problem was misunderstanding library terminology; researchers found that participants were sorting not only by format, but also by proposed processes and tasks associated with some of the labels. Some participants found some redundancy with the labels. The researchers were able to use the independent student analysis alongside their own scan of the data as a check that they had identified the main trends.

3.5   Case study – Hunter College Libraries, New York

Becker and Yannotta (2013) discuss the two-year website redesign process for Hunter College Libraries. They stress the importance of iterative design, and development of a mechanism to incorporate new tools and technologies, so that the information architecture is sustainable.

The redesign process involved a formal usability test of the existing site, followed by drafts of the redesigned site, and tests with users over an 18-month period. The design team aimed to eliminate library jargon, and to ensure that as far as possible users should reach the high-level information they needed from the library website within three clicks. Their review of the literature led them to choose iterative testing for the usability study. They were guided by recommendations for using a think aloud protocol, asking participants to explain their thought processes as they attempt the requested tasks. After piloting the questions, and developing a new website prototype, ethical approval was obtained. Recruitment was by convenience sample and, as students were the only applicants, the focus of the study became usability for students. The researchers conducted four rounds of tests, with five student participants per round. The two researchers switched questioner and observer role after each round of testing. The usability test consisted of 15 questions around tasks; in the first round participants studied the old website, and in the next three rounds they studied the new draft website. After conducting the tests, the participants were asked some general questions about their searching habits and their overall opinion of the website. Initially the tests were recorded using Camtasia software but the researchers found that observing and taking notes was sufficient. The participants were allowed as long as they liked to answer questions, but could skip them if they could not answer them.

The findings demonstrated that the users found the newly designed website, built using a content management system, easier to use than the old website, and participants generally were more successful with the questions on the new site. The results confirmed the difficulty of guiding students to use databases to find articles, and the lack of awareness of what the label 'subject guides' meant.

3.6   Case study – evaluation of Social Care Online

In 2013 the Social Care Institute for Excellence redesigned its database Social Care Online, informed by reviews and evaluations that included work by SaraDunn Associates (Dunn and Urquhart, 2011) on the browsing and search functionality. A later review of the redesigned site (Dunn and Urquhart, 2014) used similar methods to those used in the 2011 evaluation.

ISO criteria (ISO/TR 16982:2002) were used to assess the quality of online information services:

- Effectiveness – is the user able to achieve their aims?
- Efficiency – does the user achieve their aims easily?
- Satisfaction – does the user find the system pleasant to use?

Secondary criteria that provided the specific focus for the review were:

- Relevance – does the user consider the results to be relevant to their information need?
- Comprehensiveness – does the user consider the results to be providing full coverage?

Four personas were used for the 2011 and 2014 reviews, developed for the 2011 review based on real members of the social care workforce and their genuine information needs. The personas were 'Rebecca', 'Alan', 'Emma' and 'Zita'.

3.6.1 'Rebecca'

I am a forensic social worker and an approved mental health professional. I am a local authority employee but I work in an NHS [National Health Service] mental health trust doing inpatient forensic work. So, I provide social work services for people with a mental health problem who have been through court or have an offending history.

3.6.1.1 Scenario

I supervise a social work student. My student is about to undertake some family work with a service user, and we discussed various theoretical approaches and tools. One of these was genograms. I need to undertake some research into this.

3.6.1.2 Research task

To find out how best to use genograms therapeutically in a mental health context.

3.6.2 'Alan'

I am a frontline care co-ordinator working in a mental health and learning disabilities NHS Foundation Trust. I am a qualified social worker and I work in the learning disabilities team.

3.6.2.1 Scenario

I was asked to take part in interviewing possible social work students at my local university for the September intake. During the interviews, a number of students discussed personalisation. I wanted to find out more on personalisation and its implementation in my area of work. I currently work for the NHS, which sometimes uses different theoretical frameworks from social care.

3.6.2.2 Research task

To find out about personalisation and its implementation in NHS learning disabilities services.

3.6.3 'Emma'

I am a social worker and manager in the voluntary sector. I work in a small team with two other safeguarding officers. Our responsibility overall is to ensure that the organisation is safe for all the people who use our services, mainly children and adults with cerebral palsy.

3.6.3.1 Scenario

In my role as safeguarding officer I was asked to provide a briefing session on institutional abuse to a group of staff at one of our services.

3.6.3.2 Research task

What definitions are there for institutional abuse?

3.6.4 'Zita'

I am senior support worker and team leader in a national voluntary sector organisation that supports people with epilepsy. I am studying a course on epilepsy at my local university.

3.6.4.1 Scenario

I have an assignment on user involvement coming up for my course.

3.6.4.2 Research task

Some background research on the involvement of people with epilepsy in health and social care services.

3.6.5 Discussion of persona use

In 2014 the interface of Social Care Online offered standard and advanced search options. Various likely paths for user journeys employing standard and advanced search options were explored and documented. The researchers conducted some additional supplementary user journeys to further investigate issues revealed. Another team had investigated general usability and accessibility issues and the problems they encountered were mostly demonstrated again in the user journeys.

Using the personas helped to identify some of the possible refinements that could be made to the redesigned system. The 2011 evaluation had identified major problems with the taxonomy or thesaurus used. Social care is inevitably a difficult subject area as some new terms may be coined for political and social reasons but their relationship with the older subject terms may be unclear. There might also be differences between North American and UK English usage. In the 2013 redesign, the taxonomy was effectively hidden from users. There was a predictive text function, intended to help users, but the evaluation found a few problems with the way this operated. It was not clear whether the predictive text was using the taxonomy in the background or titles (or both). Sometimes adding a term to a search line produced vastly more results, which is not what would be expected of a Google type search. For busy professionals, the filter options are important for efficient searching, and should allow such users quickly to find some recent research, reviews or material that relates only to their national or regional area. In addition, it is important for some members of the social care workforce to find material that is available free of charge. The 2014 evaluation was careful to examine how the filter options were described and how they operated, in both the standard search and advanced search. Other important functions of Social Care Online, such as saving searches and exporting search results, were also evaluated.

Evaluators used the personas and user journeys to identify many desirable refinements, and to check that the redesigned taxonomy or thesaurus was working well. The user journey searching could be performed at researchers' convenience, and allowed them to follow up particular problems they identified, to check the conditions that produced the effect, and whether the problem could be avoided. The disadvantage is that researchers may themselves be expert searchers, and unconsciously avoid some routes that novice searchers might use.

3.6.6 'Louise'

The main alternative to using personas and possible user journeys is to sit with an information seeker and have a talk-aloud session, or ask them to log a recent search. For the evaluation, the expert user 'Louise' presented their problem as follows.

I am a research and information officer in the Knowledge Management Team of a county council. We are located within one directorate, and provide a dedicated service to adult social care and local services (including libraries and archives). We regularly conduct searches for social care information on a wide range of topics. This might be to inform individual casework or to provide literature searches for projects, service development and so on.

3.6.6.1   Scenario

The search was requested by the project manager working on the re-commissioning of Night Services (generic domiciliary care). It was intended to use the information to develop the specification for services.

3.6.6.2   Research task

To find examples of user views on night services (not limited to the UK) – including anything referenced in national guidance, good practice and evaluation results from other local areas in the UK.

During the search, the user wanted to eliminate items that dealt with particular subjects such as homelessness. Trying to search on generic domiciliary care had produced too many items for the user, and it seemed that the search was simply providing items on domiciliary care – not items on generic domiciliary care (night services). Night services as a search phrase only produced older material (in the first set of search page results), which indicated to the user that they should try another approach.

Another part of the evaluation was to compare the final outputs of one of the user journeys (simple search) with a similar search on two other databases or search engines (Google Scholar and NHS Evidence). The results indicated that Social Care Online outperformed the others, which provided confirmation that the indexing – and taxonomy – were generally working well.

Other findings indicated that the problems were often not so much the taxonomy as some of the labels used on the searching pages, the operation of the filters (including the subject terms filter), the way the search strings were allowed to operate in advanced searching, and the way phrase searches operated in standard search.

3.7 Conclusions

The chapter has considered some of the methods used for taxonomy testing and described some case studies of website (and database) evaluation. Unsurprisingly, perhaps, for a topic that is concerned with problems in vocabulary usage and relationships among different terms, there is some confusion over the terms vocabularies, taxonomies, thesauri and classification schemes. As the chapter has discussed, different people will think about the same general topic in different ways, and place different emphases on the topic and related topics (producing different topic maps and perhaps different hierarchies for themselves). Knowledge representations that have to be read by computer (ontologies) need to have associations specified.

Testing taxonomies often involves testing the hierarchy of terms, normally through a card sorting method. Open card sorting does not place any restriction on the participants, and the aim is to have a generally acceptable arrangement that suits most people. Closed card sorting, where the categories are already preset, allows researchers to check where they might expect to find items. Using realistic tasks allows researchers to check whether participants can operate the hierarchy successfully.

The case studies (of two academic websites and one database) demonstrate the problems of labelling (professional versus lay meanings), and the variety of testing methods that may be used. Generally, it is not just the taxonomy that needs to be tested, but the likely paths through and around the taxonomy (to broader, narrower or related terms). That requires some emphasis on replicating realistic search tasks, particularly those that help users to find what they need quickly.

References

Becker, D. A. and Yannotta, L. (2013) Modeling a Library Website Redesign Process: developing a user-centered website through usability testing, *Information Technology and Libraries*, **32** (1), 6.

Bowker, G. and Star, S. L. (1999) *Sorting Things Out: classification and its consequences*, MIT Press.

Dunn, S. and Urquhart, C. (2011) *Social Care Online: supplementary expert review*, SaraDunn Associates report to Social Care Institute for Excellence, unpublished.

Dunn, S. and Urquhart, C. (2014) *Social Care Online: supplementary expert review*, SaraDunn Associates report to Social Care Institute for Excellence, unpublished.

Frické, M. (2012) *Logic and the Organization of Information*, Springer.

Hert, C. A., Carlson, G. and Wessel, B. (2013) Building User Experiences: synchronizing user experience design and the supporting metadata and taxonomy infrastructure, *Bulletin of the American Society for Information Science and Technology*, **39** (2), 26–9.

ISO/TR 16982:2002, *Ergonomics of human-system interaction - Usability methods supporting human-centred design*, International Organization for Standardization, https://www.iso.org/standard/31176.html.

Lakoff, G. (1987) *Women, Fire and Dangerous Things: what categories reveal about the mind*, University of Chicago Press.

Lewis, K. M. and Hepburn, P. (2010) Open Card Sorting and Factor Analysis, *The Electronic Library*, **28** (3), 401–16.

Paul, C. L. (2014) Analysing Card Sorting Data Using Graph Visualization, *Journal of Usability Studies*, **9** (3), 87–104.

Rosch, E. and Lloyd, B. (eds) (1978) *Cognition and Categorization*, L. Erlbaum Associates.

Ross, J. (2011) Comparing User Research Methods for Information Architecture, www.uxmatters.com/mt/archives/2011/06/comparing-user-research-methods-for-information-architecture.php.

Soranzo, A. and Cooksey, D. (2015) Testing Taxonomies: beyond card sorting, *Bulletin of the Association for Information Science and Technology*, **41** (3), 34–9.

Spencer, D. (2003) Card-based Classification Evaluation, http://boxesandarrows.com/card-based-classification-evaluation/.

Weller, K. (2010) *Knowledge Representation in the Social Semantic Web*, De Gruyter Saur.

CHAPTER 4

The enterprise website and its information structures

Sally Burford

COMMENTARY: CHRISTINE URQUHART

Sally Burford's grounded theory of practising web information architecture is a contrast to the project phases advocated by many information architecture consultants. There are echoes here of earlier information systems research that demonstrated that design and implementation was a messy process, not something neat where packages of activities followed each other in a logical and orderly sequence. Rosenfeld, Morville and Arango (2015, 356) describe an information architecture strategy as organising and structuring an information environment to provide direction and scope, before moving into the design and implementation phase. However, they acknowledge that, in practice, the business strategy is likely to co-evolve with the information architecture (358).

One question that interested me when reading Sally Burford's research was whether there were aspects of the four foundational constructs (owning information architecture, negotiating information architecture, enacting information architecture, knowing information architecture) that were missing from some of the classic advice on information architecture. Table 4.1 illustrates the components Burford identified, set against comments other information architecture consultants or researchers made. As far as possible, I have used library and information service case studies, and references to other chapters in the book.

Table 4.1 *Comparison of Burford's construct on the grounded theory of practising web information architecture and other information architecture advice or research*

Burford construct	Other related information architecture advice or research
Owning information architecture • Governing • New work • Resourcing • Legitimising and locating • Managing	Sharpe and Vacek (2010) – staff intranet design – required acceptance for change of staff working practice. Black (2011) discusses problems of a large site with a large number of content providers.
Negotiating information architecture • Following the business • Compromising • Conflict • Collaboration • Working with marketing • Gaining acceptance	Land (2013) on content migration notes that an inventory needs to identify what must be removed, but also what can be salvaged. Sharpe and Vacek (2010) conclude that building consensus, with a representational taskforce for research and design, was important to success of the staff intranet. Corrall and Roberts (2012) and Roberts (2013, 248) discuss different views of library 'collection' that might better serve users in social enterprise (collection-as-process, collection-as-access, rather than collection-as-thing). Chapter 3 describes methods of taxonomy testing that involve negotiation.
Enacting information architecture • Meeting restrictions • Opportunism • Who does information architecture? • Project or process • Neglected components • Using technology • Business readiness	Sharpe and Vacek (2010), noting need for informal staff communication channels in the research for new site design. For a new content management system, Black (2011) wanted separation of content and presentation, with intuitive web-based content editing. Land (2013) discusses the roles and responsibilities of content strategists and information architects. Rocha and Sá (2014) suggest how to help order development priorities, examining potential benefits, impact, probability of success and demand.
Knowing information architecture • Abstract knowledge • Locating expertise • Mindlessness • Organisational learning • Learning on the job	Cox and Emmott (2007) found that university web management in the UK varied, with web teams usually located within external relations or IT services. Cox (2008) found that a listserv supporting web management in UK universities provided a network of practice, not a close-knit community of practice.

I have not done a comprehensive search to find examples, but it is likely that the areas identified by Burford, and which may be overlooked (or perhaps dealt with implicitly), concern governance, making the most of opportunities (and acting fast), and trying to ensure that organisational learning about information architecture takes place across the organisation.

If, as Burford indicates, practising information architecture often comes with fuzzy responsibilities, the need to connect with many different aspects of the organisation (marketing, customer services), and is an emerging practice, then how can those involved make the communication easier? Chapter 7 discusses how the process architecture may be obtained, and stresses the importance for libraries of relating to the main functions of the organisation. Elmendorf, Hinton and Hoff (2015) look at other modelling techniques that help the information architecture team and the organisation understand what the problem space includes, before moving on to resolving how to meet the needs. Seeing the problems visually as a conceptual model helps everyone involved to appreciate what the priorities really are.

In some settings, a structured approach is more appropriate, and there are different methodologies to consider. Rocha and Sá (2014) compare several, such as the business systems planning methodology, the adapted business systems planning methodology, Zachman's framework, the federal enterprise architecture framework, and the enterprise architecture planning methodology. These methodologies all represent a structured approach to practising information architecture – usually a linear stepwise process. For the project in a local public administration organisation, they chose the adapted business systems planning methodology as it suited the context. There are six steps:

- preliminary activities
- study preparation
- study beginning
- information system characterisation
- construction of alternative scenarios for prospective information system
- negotiation, implementation and control of solutions.

It was important for their work for Rocha and Sá (2014) to identify which data was created and used in each process in the municipality – producing a process or data class matrix.

Often the need for a better information architecture for users requires a complete rethink of what libraries should do. Chapter 5 considers some of the approaches that may be used to derive a process architecture, though evidence from users and potential users may overturn accepted ideas about a library's responsibilities. Roberts (2013) describes doctoral research on views of 'collection' set against the needs of users in social enterprise, noting the discrepancies between library staff and social enterprise user perspectives. Collection-as-thing encourages thinking about the boundaries of the collection, and how it could be divided into subsets. Collection-as-access, on the other hand, encourages thinking about links, locating various access points, and collection-as-process is helpful to planning user self-archiving, and automation of metadata generation and preservation. Thinking about collection from different perspectives should encourage libraries to spot opportunities for new services.

In conclusion, Burford's research reminds us that for many organisations, information architecture requires agility, responsiveness and integrated but holistic thinking – and that more people are involved in information architecture than we might think at first.

References

Black, E. P. (2011) Selecting a Web Content Management System for an Academic Library Website, *Information Technology and Libraries*, **30** (4), 185–9.

Corrall, S. and Roberts, A. (2012) Information Resource Development and 'Collection' in the Digital Age: conceptual frameworks and new definitions for the network world, *Libraries in the Digital Age (LIDA) Proceedings*, **12**, http://d-scholarship.pitt.edu/25171/1/Corrall_%26_Roberts_(2012).pdf.

Cox, A. M. (2008) An Exploration of Concepts of Community Through a Case Study of UK University Web Production, *Journal of Information Science*, **34** (3), 327–45.

Cox, A. and Emmott, S. (2007) A Survey of UK University Web Management: staffing, systems and issues, *Campus-Wide Information Systems*, **24** (5), 308–30.

Elmendorf, J., Hinton, A. and Hoff, K. (2015) Practical Modeling: making the invisible visible, *Bulletin of the American Society for Information Science and Technology*, **41** (5), 20–5.

Land, P. (2013) Migrations: not just for developers anymore, *Bulletin of the American Society for Information Science and Technology*, **40** (1), 42–4.

Roberts, A. (2013) Conceptualising the Library Collection for the Digital World: a case study of social enterprise, PhD thesis, University of Sheffield.

Rocha, Á. and Sá, F. (2014) Planning the Information Architecture in a Local Public Administration Organization, *Information Development*, **30** (3), 223–34.

Rosenfeld, L., Morville, P. and Arango, J. (2015) *Information Architecture: for the Web and beyond*, 4th edn, O'Reilly Media Inc.

Sharpe, P. A. and Vacek, R. E. (2010) Intranet 2.0 from a Project Management Perspective, *Journal of Web Librarianship*, **4** (2/3), 239–49.

4.1   Introduction

All sectors of society – from government and private enterprise to education and community – look to the web for information delivery and consumption, and an organisation's website has become an important business platform. To support the design of website information a number of scholars (Morville and Rosenfeld, 2006; Wodtke and Govella, 2009) have proposed structured processes in an attempt to represent best practice. Burford (2011a), however, challenged the appropriateness of structured methods for information architecture by studying the practice in the environs of large organisations and found the metaphor of complex adaptive systems to be a useful theoretical lens for practice in that context. In 2014, Burford proposed a grounded theory of web information architecture in large organisations, which is revisited in this chapter. Her theory acknowledges and accommodates documented best practice for information architecture yet absorbs them into a complex milieu of social activity.

The internet technologies of social media created a second wave of innovation and opportunity for the enterprise and demanded the engagement and attention of all contemporary organisations. Made popular in individualistic and open use on the internet, Web 2.0 tools or social media offer significant potential to organisations in pursuit of informational and communicative goals. Audience contribution and conversation are now a desirable addition to the information delivered by large organisations to the website's audience.

McAfee (2009, 1) claimed valuable opportunities for organisations in the relocation of these technologies from the open web to corporate web space and used the term Enterprise 2.0 to describe the internal hosting and use of social media technologies. Thus the tools of social media, such as Twitter, Facebook and Instagram, are frequently woven into the information structures of enterprise websites. The paradigm of interaction and engagement adds an additional layer of complexity to web information architecture.

Resmini and Rosati (2011) highlighted the emergence of cross-channel contexts for information and communication. A website is now seen as one of multiple digital and printed artefacts that make up an information ecology that serves the enterprise and its clients. Multiple and mobile channels of web, tablet devices, smart phones, print and physical spaces all play a role in an organisation's repertoire of information and engagement. Accordingly, a pervasive information layer that binds all channels in an architecture of meaning is desirable (Resmini and Rosati, 2011).

The information architecture of the enterprise website thus becomes a crucial business activity and it is an imperative of the 21st century to achieve optimal information structures. Burford (2014) presented an integrated theoretical framework of the practice of web information architecture in large organisations. This chapter revisits this grounded theory of the situated practice of web information architecture in large organisations, offering a more nuanced description and expanding on the theory's nature and use. The implications of this grounded research outcome for web managers and information architects are discussed to conclude the chapter.

This chapter complements the case studies discussed in Chapter 3, where the composition of the web team for redesign of library websites is mentioned, alongside testing and evaluation methods. Chapters 6 and 7 explain that a process analysis would probably have revealed some of the fluidity of roles and responsibilities for web information architecture in large organisations.

Section 4.2 presents a grounded theory of the situated practice of web information architecture in large organizations, and Section 4.3 then examines the implications of the research evidence for those involved in aspects of information architecture. Section 4.4 draws conclusions.

4.2   A grounded theory of the situated practice of web information architecture in large organisations

Burford's (2014) theory of the situated practice of web information architecture in large organisations is presented diagrammatically in Figure 4.1. It was constructed using a constructivist grounded theory methodology, which involved an intense and detailed examination of data collected from those who practise information architecture in large organisations. The transcribed data was scrutinised using NVivo as an analysing tool, and incidents and details of the data were coded into preliminary conceptualisations or open codes (Charmaz, 2006, 57). With those constructs in place, a second phase of analysis took place; focused coding examined the most significant and frequently used open codes seeking higher levels of abstraction. These higher-level constructs were iteratively tested across the large data set to establish that they would 'categorise the data incisively and completely' (Charmaz, 2006, 57). The purpose of open coding is to fracture the data and the purpose of focused coding is to draw a coherent picture from the pieces (Charmaz, 2006, 57-60). In a third stage of analysis, the interrelatedness of the emergent conceptualisations gave rise to an integrating core construct.

The resultant theoretical framework, Figure 4.1, has a central emphasis on practising web information architecture and four supporting constructs that

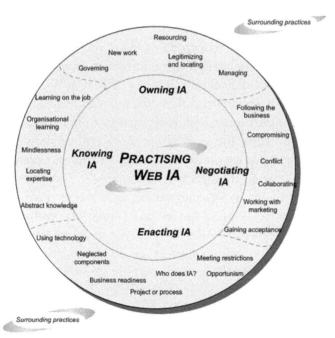

Figure 4.1 *Burford's grounded theory of the situated practice of web information architecture in large organisations* (based on Burford, S. (2014) A Grounded Theory of the Practice of Web Information Architecture in Large Organisations, *Journal of the American Society of Information Science and Technology,* **65** (10), 2017–2034)

provide significant abstractions of practice. Owning, negotiating, enacting and knowing web information architecture all present a perspective and draw attention to the more specific conceptual outcomes of the research. Each of these four foundational constructs assembles a particular focus and a set of related activities. The connectedness of web information architecture to surrounding practices is acknowledged in Burford's (2014) constructed theory of practice.

This grounded theory is not strongly delimited; with practising web information architecture at the centre, the four foundational constructs of owning, negotiating, enacting and knowing occupy a 'space' in the framework allowing fluent interplay between them. Owning, negotiating, enacting and knowing can be called into use as a theoretical account of practice is required. Use of this theoretical framework provides an opportunity to examine the situated practice of web information architecture as a whole. It attends to the social, intellectual and material aspects of the practice of web information architecture in large organisations. Practising web information architecture is a unifying and integrating construct.

The fluid theoretical framework allows multiple viewpoints for understanding the phenomenon of web information architecture. A focus on any one of the four foundational constructs is enabled, as is attention to those specific concepts that are housed within each foundational construct. Equally a theoretical account of an entire situated practice of information architecture is made possible. Thus intricate and multifaceted understandings and illuminations of practice are possible, revealing a richer interpretation of the complex practice of web information architecture.

This grounded theory of web information architecture yields and morphs to reveal ongoing tensions, absences and shifts in practice. The four foundational constructs can overlap or overlay each other. Alternatively, they can pull firmly apart creating tension or accommodating weakness. In organisations that acknowledge and resource expertise in information architecture for the website, knowing web information architecture is strong and optimal information structures should result. However, an equal strength in the ability of powerful stakeholders to dictate content and its position on the organisation's homepage will compete with expertise and optimal outcomes. Negotiating web information architecture has a simultaneous dominating presence. Burford's (2014) framework provides a lens should these two foundational constructs compete. The practising of web information architecture always takes place in a specific context, each organisation being different from the next. The theory also captures the tensions and imbalances in the everyday practice of web information architecture and becomes a valuable tool for understanding a specific environment. Burford's (2014) theoretical framework accommodates each specific context and unique practice of information architecture.

4.2.1   The four foundational constructs

4.2.1.1   Owning web information architecture

Owning web information architecture occurs when an organisation takes responsibility for web information architecture and it is a pre-condition for its effective practice. Owning web information architecture is enclosed in a broader owning of the web. When organisations 'own' their websites, they provide adequate management, governance, co-ordination and resources to achieve the goals that they have implicitly or explicitly made known in their use of the enterprise web. Rhetoric is followed by attention actions and resources. Attention is paid to the website's information and navigational structures. Owning web information architecture includes allowing time, resources and expertise for web information architecture. Owning web information architecture is about setting up structures and environments in which web information architecture can prosper and pragmatic outcomes are required. New roles, authorities, expertise, resources and policies are put in place to achieve an online environment that informs its audience effectively. Ensuring the work of web information architecture is enabled within and across established boundaries requires the co-operative participation of the entire organisation.

4.2.1.2   Negotiating web information architecture

Negotiating web information architecture is the human exchange in the space between best practice for web information architecture and meeting the needs, desires and demands of diverse stakeholders in the web delivery of information. A website must quickly reflect changes in business activity and this need for responsivity brings conversation and sometimes controversy. Timeframes, urgency and information structures themselves all give rise to debate in a large organisational context. Diverse and sometimes competing business demands bring bargaining and conceding to the practice of web information architecture. As a result, the information structures are not always optimal; rather, they are the result of compromise. Negotiating web information architecture has connotations of unresolved dialogue and tension. Significant interest in web information structures exists across an organisation. Stakeholders bring myriad perceptions and motivations to the purpose of the enterprise web and the value of web information architecture. This provides an ongoing conversation that is fraught with opposing and competing claims, especially on the high-level pages of a website. Over time, a professional web information architect earns a place of credibility and acceptance in these conversations.

4.2.1.3   Enacting web information architecture

Enacting web information architecture is the human endeavour that creates an organisation's website no matter what the surrounding circumstances. It addresses the existence of information on an enterprise website, but not the effectiveness of its structure. A website is a digital imperative for a large organisation; hence, the work of web information architecture will be done. Enacting web information architecture is about doing the best that is possible at the time. Enacting web information architecture considers the practitioners of web information architecture. Diverse and un-named actors within an organisation participate, so uniformity of approach is not ensured. Such is the connective nature of hypertext that every practice outcome constitutes the whole website. Enacting web information architecture signals improvisation in order to achieve. Acting to reconcile a mismatch between information that is included in a design but not made available by the business is an example of enactment.

4.2.1.4   Knowing web information architecture

Knowing web information architecture, composed of abstract knowledge and knowledge in activity, is an essential, integral and fluid construct in Burford's (2014) grounded theory. It is applied to individuals and the organisation itself as it comes to understand the practice and its needs. Knowing web information architecture involves learning from instruction and from doing, and the subsequent and ongoing transformations of the way the practice is carried out.

Various facets of teaching are embedded in the organisational knowing of web information architecture. Intentional mentoring, coaching and collaborative work all contribute to individual and organisational knowledge in the practice of web information architecture. More instructive vehicles, such as training courses and conferences, make a contribution. Expertise in the construction of online information spaces and being aware of when that expertise is needed are facets of knowing web information architecture. Locating and using that expertise within or external to an organisation is part of the organisational knowing. When the knowing of web information architecture is weak at the organisational level, a mindlessness of the practice exists. A lack of organisational knowing impacts on decision making and adversely affects the website's information structures.

4.2.2   The properties of practising web information architecture

While each instance of practising web information architecture is unique, the construct itself is rich with specific characteristics or 'properties' (Glaser and Strauss, 1967, 36). Charmaz (2006, 103) sees these properties as further 'elaborations' of a concept. From these properties or aspects of practising web information architecture, more is gleaned about the practice in general terms and at higher levels of abstraction. Three properties of practising web information architecture were identified: the practice takes on a variable shape or form within an organisation; the maturity of the practice of web information architecture varies across organisations, yet demonstrates an overall youthfulness; and the use of the web itself in the practice.

4.2.2.1   The shape of practice

With contextual influences, constraints and realities, the work of web information architecture arranges itself within an organisation in an evolving manner. It continually finds its place. At one extreme the practice of web information architecture is a thin layer, spread loosely across an organisation. At the other extreme, it is pulled tightly to the organisation's centre. When practising web information architecture has a strong central aspect to its shape, it is frequently manifested in a central web team. At other times a significant core of responsibility and leadership for web information architecture is difficult to discern. The outreaches of practising web information architecture include occasional stakeholders and peripheral practitioners, and influencing political figures and transient consultants. Hybrids of these two extremes are more likely to occur.

As a practice, web information architecture operates with great variability at its fringes where people create web information structures, as they must. Many people at the periphery of the practice come and go, attending to the information structures on the website of a devolved business unit and then moving on, perhaps handing the work to another. There are few restrictions as to who may step into the fringes of this practice.

Within an organisation the practice does not reveal a characteristic or defining location and may lodge in semi-permanence in information management or marketing divisions. It is not consistently housed in any one place and is likely to be moved to a more suitable location.

Practising web information architecture involves connecting and interrelating with many other practices. It occurs alongside marketing and information management practices and is deeply connected to the practice of web visual and aesthetic design. Practising web information architecture has dependencies on the practices that surround the infrastructure and technological systems that create a backbone for the information structures. Web information architecture is affected by these other work activities and, in its turn, has an impact on them. The edges of the practice are fluid and inclusive.

4.2.2.2 An emerging practice

Practising web information architecture is a set of activities imbued with learning and self-formation. The availability of expertise in web information architecture, for example, is revealed as a continuum across the studied cases. While a progression of maturity in web information architecture is noted, the practising of web information architecture in large organisations presents as a fledgling practice. The practising of web information architecture is finding its way and constructing itself. Shared understanding of the way that things are done is being formed (Gherardi, 2009, 356) and there is much learning about web information architecture.

There is great variation in the extent to which the activities of web information architecture in organisational life are acknowledged and understood outside the practice itself. That variation ranges from organisations that create roles titled 'web information architect' to places where the words 'information architecture' are little understood. Gherardi (2009, 356) talks about a practice stabilising and becoming institutionalised and legitimised, 'even when its institutionalization is contested or challenged'. This study established that the organisational understanding of the practice of web information architecture was still in the making. The practising of web information architecture has not yet come to a comfortable position or status within an organisation. Among senior executives and others in the organisation, the activity of web information architecture is not acknowledged as a known and stable practice with a well formed identity. Practising web information architecture is still in the process of building a consistent and recognisable role in work environments.

As web information architecture establishes its boundaries and identity other practices influence its emergence. Well meaning practitioners from other disciplines advise the practice of web information architecture with prior perceptions. This input is part of the maturing of web information architecture. Practitioners of web information architecture themselves come to it from other established practices with previous ways of knowing. They are building a new practice and developing new shared understandings within an organisational context. Part of establishing the practice of web information architecture is letting go of the traditions of previous practices.

4.2.2.3 Using the web

Web information architecture is considered both practice and its outcome (Morville and Rosenfeld 2006, 4). The web gives impetus and reason for the practice and houses the outcomes of the work of web information architecture. It is useful to isolate and look at the material, albeit virtual, components of practising web information architecture, as well as the social. One major object that sits outside human-to-human interaction is a website itself. The web gives back to the people who develop its information structures. It informs them with suggestions, exemplars and possibilities that are shared openly globally. The web presents bold new ideas and innovations, as well as emerging consistencies to the practitioner of web information architecture. It provides a market place for comparison and learning in which practitioners immerse themselves.

At times, practising web information architecture is supported and communicated by the design documents of blueprints, wireframes, taxonomies and content inventories that are presented prior to the construction of an information design on the web. At other times, practitioners shun these design artefacts and use the web itself to prototype, display and to communicate design outcomes. The web proves to be a palatable medium for the presentation of information design in greater fidelity to interested stakeholders.

The materiality of the web offers a place in which decisions, consistencies and norms can be technically enacted, bypassing committees, policy and high-level decisions. Practising web information architecture is supported by the web's material authority as it enforces the placement of sub-components of an information architecture by enactment rather than governance. With the wise use of web technologies, those practising web information architecture rapidly create and modify structures that immediately become an organisation's de facto standard.

The demands of different spaces or components on a website dictate to the practising of web information architecture. Many global aspects of an organisational website require consistency and cohesiveness. Someone must tend to the overarching components, such as search and sitemaps, and assemble them cohesively across a web presence. Yet local information structures require a contextually focused and responsive approach. Attention to the specifics and volatilities of information structures on organisational sub-sites demands an inward focus, detailed attention and a unique and localised approach to practising web information architecture.

The large organisational website, as a site of intense engagement for practitioners of web information architecture, is not a simple object. It is not bounded and can grow, limitlessly, through the extensions of hypertext. Any sense of attainment is a momentary phase before changes in the web are required. A large website is complex and always inducing scrutiny, inquiry and evaluation. Its complexity and incompleteness continually evoke the active engagement of practitioners of web information architecture.

4.3   Implications for practitioners and organisations

A grounded theory approach to research promises a theoretical outcome that resonates with practitioners (Glaser, 1978, 142). New knowledge about the situated practice of web information architecture benefits its practitioners and those who carry management responsibility. This section makes suggestions to managers and practitioners that are of practical benefit. The constructed understandings and conceptualisations about web information architecture, created by the research, are offered back to enterprises to enrich and advance practice. The insights and outcomes gained from this research are presented first as key points and then discussed in more detail.

4.3.1   Web information architecture is social and responsive

Key points:

- The practice of web information architecture must allow an agile response to an organisational need for almost real-time delivery of information on the web.
- Negotiation and compromise of optimal information structures are everyday facets of this intensively inclusive information practice.

Web information architecture is best embraced as a negotiation with business stakeholders who have strong interests in the timely delivery of information to web audiences. This draws the work of web information architecture very close to the business of the organisation. Other information practices are characterised by information professionals who take an authoritative lead and consult the business. But this is not a suitable balance for the practice of web information architecture where the business stakeholder is intrinsic to the work in an ongoing interaction – consultation is too remote. The demand for immediate and agile responses to information structures that inform the organisation's clients creates the need for this close liaison. Responsive and integrative work with the owners of information for the web is essential to the practice of web information architecture.

The work of web information architecture requires an agile and adaptive stance. In its intricate connection to the information that it houses, information design must match the volatility of web content. Waiting during times of uncertainty, making expedient design decisions to enable an agile response, and being opportunistic in choosing the time for information architecture improvement that suits the business stakeholder are all effective strategies in the practice of web information architecture in organisational life. The complexity of the environment requires an ongoing and appropriate adaptive response.

Compromise is another key characteristic of the practice of web information architecture. There are occasions when timelines, politics and power win out over optimal information design. Information on public-facing websites is allied to an organisation's political stance in the world, and web information architecture is affected by the worldliness of the information that it houses. Similarly, internal organisational politics has its impact on information architecture. Restrictive timelines for web information structures or lack of content to fill those structures contribute to compromised assemblages of information on the web. The practice of web information architecture does not always reach the ideals of its expert practitioners.

An exception to the social and negotiable nature of web information architecture should be noted. There is an expectation and a need for cohesion and consistency across an enterprise website that allows ease of navigation to its audience. The responsibility and authority for the global utility navigation and page layout is best located in a central web team who can expertly enact their work without broad consultation.

The social nature of the practice of web information architecture comes into play with the information and its arrangement. It makes good sense to expect negotiation, compromise and close liaison with business stakeholders in the practice of web information architecture. Attending to the social complexity of web information architecture leads to more valuable outcomes.

4.3.2   The dilemma of best practice

Key points:

- A project approach to web information architecture that promises a stable end state will not succeed – web information structures are not likely to last.
- Structured, predefined solution methodologies are not suitable for the ongoing social practice of web information architecture.
- Fixed term consultants contribute to the take-up of structured methodologies and fixed information design outcomes.
- The practice of web information architecture is carried out by experts and novices alike in large organisations. It escapes the confines of the information specialist and should be supported accordingly.

The dynamic and complex nature of web information architecture as an information practice has ramifications for the use of design methods. Design methods introduce sequence, control and discipline (Morrogh, 2002, 110). The lack of stability and predictability in the structure of web information and the activities and demands that achieve them do not lend themselves to sequence and order. A sequenced, structured methodology does not meet the needs of the ongoing practice of web information architecture. While defining a solution approach or a methodology is the dominant discourse in information organisation, this research attests to the fact that web information architecture is a fluid and emergent environment and one that defies linear and rational solutions.

A project with a durable end state is not applicable to the activity of web information architecture in large organisations. Web information structures are provisional and as soon as a 'project' concludes, changes to its outcomes should be expected. Responsive and frequent changes to the structures are required. Web information structures are not buried beneath an interface built for human interaction – they lie on the surface and become the interface and are the means of traversing the website. Thus organic and agile change to web information structures is highly desirable and should be catered for by the practitioners of web information architecture.

Expert information architects who are employed as contractors or consultants compound the project approach. Employed for fixed periods of time within an organisation that is redeveloping its web information structures as a project, consultants are expected to deliver a design product documenting the web information architecture at the conclusion of their work. The fixed term nature of the work of consultants contributes to the demand for an outcome or product.

Yet heuristics and known ways are the toolkit of experts, whether or not they are made explicit. While web information architecture does not fit an ideology of control or regularity, the accumulated abstracted knowledge of this practice is valuable and has a role to play. It is best envisaged as a part of the practice that can be considered, modified to fit the context and adopted as required. Accumulated and propositional knowledge of web information architecture is a component of its practice rather than a blueprint for it.

The complexity of the practice of web information architecture should be acknowledged and de-coupled from the rationalist disposition and traditions of information organisation. In this paradigm of information organisation orderly images of information architecture, conducted as project with defined end state using structured methodology in the custody of information professionals, are no longer useful.

4.3.3   Managing web information architecture

Key points:

- The practice of web information architecture is young and thus requires attention in organisations. Senior managers are mindless of the practice and prone to make detrimental decisions.
- Web information architecture is knowledge work, and while its outcomes are enmeshed in visual design and aspects of technology, it benefits from being acknowledged as an epistemic practice.
- Overarching management of web information architecture must embody the traditional aspects of resourcing and apportioning responsibility, and understand that complexity cannot be managed by rationality alone. Noticing the patterns of how an organisation is practising web information architecture and acting to foster or disrupt those patterns is a necessary capability of management.

Web information architecture requires greater attention in organisational life. It is a new practice that is still in its formation and not widely understood. The identity of the practice of web information architecture is not well established within organisations. Those with overarching responsibilities for the delivery of information on the web need to focus their attention and increase their knowledge of web information architecture. An executive mindlessness of the practice of web information architecture and its resultant detrimental decision making must be overcome in large organisations for successful use of the web for information delivery.

Information infrastructures are representational and intangible, and are not in the forefront of the mind of those who regularly use them. When working well, their lack of visibility is compounded by a seamless experience of use – they do not draw attention. Information structures in general and on the web become more visible when they are ineffective and contentious and block access to information.

A flow-on of highly usable, invisible information architectures on the web, is that the work required to construct them is also invisible. Optimal web information design occurs as if by magic. Invisibility of the work and its outcome hampers the conversations with higher-level managers and requests for resources, staffing and supportive governance and organisational structures are difficult to achieve.

Many practices of information organisation are separate from the general populace of an organisation. Some information infrastructures are made 'standard' before they arrive at an organisation, and others are buried deep within the layers of an information system. Expertise can be isolated in libraries and at the desk of business analysts. In contrast, web information architecture is practised by the everyday peripheral practitioner with little expertise in structuring information. The work of web information architecture is widely distributed and the situated practice takes place in many locales across an organisation.

Thus web information architecture is conducted by the masses as well as the experts – an organisational website is a collage of these extremes and all points in between them. This research points to the reality that many people across an organisation are undertaking web information architecture and some are doing so reluctantly. It disrupts the tradition of information organisation as the closed domain of the specialist information professional. The practice of web information architecture is obliged to acknowledge and make room for peripheral practitioners with little identity, expertise or commitment to organising web information. When organisations call on staff whose key responsibilities and abilities lie elsewhere to structure information on websites, that call should be accompanied by awareness and supportive underpinnings.

As engagement in the practice of web information architecture is undertaken by many and diverse contributors, organisations are required to adopt new ways and thinking about organising information as they approach the online environment. The new approach must cut across organisational structures and facilitate people working collaboratively and temporarily in structuring web information. The nature of the web and the ongoing change in the way that organisations are using the web call for a new way of using expertise in information organisation practices. Expertise in web information architecture cannot be remote or distant from the many practitioners. If the practice of web information architecture is considered as participatory, frequently taken up by the non-expert, yet strongly influenced by expertise and knowledge, then web information architecture must be recognised as an intensively inclusive practice (Burford, 2011b) and fostered within organisations to function in that way.

Web information architecture draws together organisational information and tacit knowledge, and repurposes them for consumption by a web audience. While it has close dependencies on the practices of visual design and marketing for its outcomes, web information architecture is inarguably knowledge work and should be supported as such. A clearer perception and explicit acknowledgement of the work of information architecture as knowledge work is needed to hasten the developing maturity and identity of the practice.

This research has established that web information architecture is a complex practice. Information structures are always provisional and are highly volatile. A large number of people of varying backgrounds are involved in owning, negotiating, enacting and knowing web information architecture in large organisations. A complex, epistemic practice has management implications. Balancing the management requirements of the practice of web information architecture in organisational life is a delicate act. Traditional management functions of resourcing, providing expertise and governance are required in increasing amounts to support the work of web information architecture. Acceptance of the responsibility for the information structures of enterprise websites is demanded by the practice for its legitimate place in organisational life.

At the same time the complex and emergent nature of the practice of web information architecture is better supported by a style of management that allows the practice to flourish by noticing and influencing its patterns. Rather than predetermined strategies and specified approaches, there is need for those responsible for facilitating the work of information architecture in organisations to observe in some detail the patterns of interactivity and process that have developed, possibly without intention or reflection. Then the practice of web information architecture can be managed by disrupting or promoting those patterns (Snowden, 2002).

4.4 Conclusions

Burford's (2014) theoretical framework encompasses the owning, negotiating, enacting and knowing of web information architecture as major constructs, which are integrated by a central construct of practising web information architecture. The grounded theory is fluid and accommodates multiple instances of practice. It is, however, possible to deduce a common set of properties of the practice of information architecture. This chapter concludes by interpreting the significance of this grounded theory for practitioners and managers of information architecture in large organisational settings.

References

Burford, S. (2011a) Complexity and the Practice of Web Information Architecture, *Journal of the American Society of Information Science and Technology*, **62** (10), 2024-37.

Burford, S. (2011b) Web Information Architecture – a very inclusive practice, *Journal of Information Architecture*, **3** (1), http://journalofia.org/volume3/issue1/03-burford/.

Burford, S. (2014) A Grounded Theory of the Practice of Web Information Architecture in Large Organisations, *Journal of the American Society of Information Science and Technology*, **65** (10), 2017-34.

Charmaz, K. (2006) *Constructing Grounded Theory*, Sage.

Gherardi, S. (2009) Knowing and Learning in Practice-based Studies: an introduction, *The Learning Organization*, **16** (5), 352-9.

Glaser, B. (1978) *Theoretical Sensitivity*, The Sociology Press.

Glaser, B. and Strauss, A. (1967) *The Discovery of Grounded Theory*, Aldine.

McAfee, A. (2009) *Enterprise 2.0: new collaborative tools for your organization's toughest challenges*, Harvard Business Press.

Morrogh, E. (2002) *Information Architecture: an emerging 21st century profession*, Prentice Hall.

Morville, P. and Rosenfeld, L. (2006) *Information Architecture for the World Wide Web*, 3rd edn, O'Reilly.

Resmini, A. and Rosati, L. (2011) *Pervasive Information Architecture: designing cross-channel user experiences*, Morgan Kaufmann.

Snowden, D. (2002) Complex Acts of Knowing: paradox and descriptive self-awareness, *Journal of Knowledge Management*, **6** (2), 100-11.

Wodtke, C. and Govella, A. (2009) *Information Architecture: blueprints for the web*, 2nd edn, New Riders.

CHAPTER 5

Analysing activities, roles and processes

Christine Urquhart and Dina Tbaishat

5.1   Introduction

This chapter introduces some of the terminology used in chapters 6, 7 and 8 on process modelling. Chapter 7 explains how to apply a particular business process modelling technique called Riva, but other approaches can be taken and the current chapter starts with an overview of what is meant by 'use cases' and how use case descriptions help when trying to analyse activities. This is followed by a brief explanation of object-oriented analysis and unified modelling language (UML). This is extremely brief, but we need to put some aspects of systems analysis and modelling into place against some library work that may be familiar to most readers. We cannot do much more here than indicate that there is work going on, for example, on the Functional Requirements for Bibliographic Records (FRBR) to map FRBR to other schemes that use an object-oriented approach. Despite efforts to implement a more systematic and unified approach, using UML, business systems analysis methods continue to diverge in ways that sometimes make conversations between library staff and the IT developers more difficult. It is very easy to get bogged down in the detail of mapping from one modelling method to another, and forget the big picture of how the processes actually fit together. The chapter concludes with an overview of the Riva methodology for deriving the process architecture for an organisation (or library service within an organisation).

Chapter 4 emphasised that the practice of information architecture may be fluid, and that roles and responsibilities may be diffuse. It is therefore important to be able to check the big picture of what is going on, and to identify the important processes and how they relate to the business of the organisation.

Section 5.2 discusses what the term use case means and how use cases are used in information systems modelling. Section 5.3 explains basic process concepts, Section 5.4 explains how to derive a process architecture, and there are conclusions in Section 5.5.

5.2   Modelling the functions of an information system – use cases

Digitisation has changed many of the activities undertaken by libraries by introducing new functions, changing roles and relationships among different staff roles. Jisc work on digitisation and documents often refers to use cases, for example the use cases of the Copac Collection Management (CCM) Tools Project (https://ccm.copac.jisc.ac.uk/use-cases/). The presentation of these use cases varies but by taking one example from the CCM Tools Project, it is possible to identify what a use case is, and explain what it signifies. Later, some more examples are given to help understand where use cases come from in the world of systems analysis and modelling, and how they can be developed beyond the descriptions given in the Jisc CCM Tools example. You might want to start by thinking about the functions offered (places where you click) when planning a journey or buying tickets online. Use cases describe the interaction between the users of the system and the high-level functions within the system. For a travel situation the use cases are likely to include these functions: 'plan a single journey', 'buy ticket', 'add another journey', 'pay for ticket' and 'change ticket'.

The title of the Jisc CCM Tools Project example is use case 1: identifying last copies among titles considered for withdrawal. Next comes a brief description of the background (context) that explains the reasons for this use case. When academic libraries are under pressure for space, there should be a programme of stock editing, with selective withdrawal of items from teaching or research collections. However, if every academic library slavishly did this, there is a danger that some titles would be lost, or that titles unknowingly become very rare. The library may therefore wish to retain the item, or offer it to another library for permanent retention. There should therefore be a

function with collection management for 'identifying last copies'.
In the Jisc CCM Tools Project example, under procedure, the steps are:

- Step 1. Using its library management system, the library establishes a list of candidates for withdrawal based on various criteria such as recent usage statistics, relevance to current teaching and research interests within the institution, etc.
- Step 2. Once a final list has been agreed, a file is exported from the library management system, listing the record number of each title, and this is submitted to the CCM tool in batch mode. The record number is used by the tool to identify each title within the Copac database and hence the number of copies of that title held by other institutions. If any institution has recorded a reservation status for their copy (e.g. 'permanent retention'), then this too can be identified.
- Step 3. A file is output by Copac containing, for each title, the same record number that was submitted, the number of copies held nationally, plus any data regarding preservation status.

Looking at these steps, we can identify some actors in this use case. Someone, or some group, let's say the Collection Development Team, has established criteria for withdrawal. Someone (possibly within the Collection Development Team) uses the library management system (another actor) to obtain a list of candidates for withdrawal. The next system interaction we can identify is with the Copac CCM tool (another actor).

The next two steps in the example are:

- Step 4. The Library loads this file into its library management system, matching on record number and updating the original catalogue record with the additional information supplied by Copac.
- Step 5. The list of candidate titles can then be manipulated using this additional information in order to generate a definitive list of items for withdrawal. Typically, the file would be sorted by the number of copies held nationally and any title with fewer than five other holding institutions would either be retained or offered to other research libraries with an interest in that subject area.

The important thing to notice in Step 5 is the word 'typically'. This implies that there may be alternative steps involved, depending on the institution. Sometimes there might be a process that extends the use case (see the use case diagram in Figure 5.1) for offering a rare title to another research library for conservation and retention.

Use cases describe the interaction between the users of a system and the high-level functions within the system. Use cases are concerned with what happens, not how it happens. In this example, the description of the actor has deliberately been left general as different libraries may have different names for the role of the actor (collection development, deputy librarian etc.), which is the user involved in the interaction. There are no details given about how the library management system is used, as this is not the purpose of this use case. It is a top-level, general description of the interaction between library staff (and we have added conservation staff as well to the use case diagram in Figure 5.1, their library management system and the Copac tool – in this example there may be two related systems operating).

For a training manual for a new member of staff, a library might want a more detailed (extended) use case description that specified in more detail who

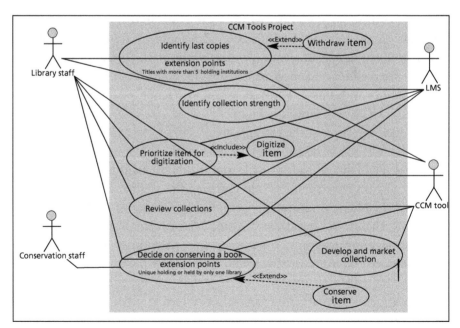

Figure 5.1 *A use case diagram for a Copac Collection Management Tools Project* (based on © 2013 Amy Devenney and Graham Stone, used under a Creative Commons Attribution license: http://creativecommons.org/licenses/by/3.0/)

did what, and how. An extended use case description normally includes the goal (what the use case is about, the context as detailed above), scope of the system under discussion (which would refer to the library management system and use of the CCM Copac tool in batch mode), whether the use case is invoked at a single sitting (which probably does not happen here with the use of the tool in batch mode), the primary actor (the library role responsible for this) and the stakeholder (the vested interest in the system – here likely to be a local library consortium as well as the British Library). Other parts of the extended use case description set out preconditions (what must be true before the use case runs, and here that would cover the agreed criteria for withdrawal, and a library management system that can work with those criteria). The trigger or event that invoked the use case is the need for weeding. Success guarantees, what must be true after the use case runs, is the definitive list for withdrawal, with information provided on the number of items held nationally. The 'happy day' scenario is the main success scenario, and an extension use case describes what can happen differently.

If you have many use cases you may need to devise a numbering scheme that helps you find related use cases easily. Sometimes, one use case can incorporate another use case. An example is the use case 'digitise item' in Figure 5.1. Several other use cases (not all illustrated here) could include the use case for 'digitise item'.

The terminology varies among various textbooks and website guides on developing use cases, but the principles are much the same. For example, instead of 'procedure' and steps, the term used may be 'basic flow'.

Here, in the CCM example various use cases are listed, all to do with different functions where CCM tools can help library staff deal with collection management. The use cases are:

- identifying last copies among titles considered for withdrawal
- identifying collection strengths
- deciding whether to conserve a book
- reviewing a collection at the shelves
- prioritising a collection or item for digitisation
- subject searching – collection development and marketing.

We have had to abbreviate the titles of the use cases to make Figure 5.1 easier to read.

Within the rectangular box are all the use cases dealing with collection management using CCM tools. Each use case is shown as an ellipse. We have just put in two actors (library staff and conservation staff) as explained by this project's scenario, along with the two systems indicated (library management system and CCM tool), since actors in the use case diagram can be human or system. However, for a particular institution you might have several actor roles, depending on the way responsibilities are allocated. A use case diagram is a useful and neat summary of the functionality of the system, from the user perspective.

Note that the use case diagram is developed according to the scenario suggested by the CCM use case description, with main success scenarios and possible extensions (as in Step 5, noted above) - where there is a condition that involves a different procedure. Typically, one set of interactions may occur (main success scenario) but sometimes an alternative, discrete set of steps occurs (extension use case).

Use case diagrams along with their descriptions are one of the modelling techniques used for a particular type of business systems analysis called UML, which is the common notation for object-oriented analysis. And object-oriented analysis is associated with the common Java programming language, but you can carry out basic object-oriented analysis, and develop some of the diagrams without having to do the programming. Systems development can be very tedious, and years ago developers did not have tools that made communication with the users of a system very easy. Object-oriented techniques use a way of thinking that is much closer to the way we naturally classify and categorise things (or 'objects') in the real world. For librarians used to broader and narrower terms, object-oriented analysis should come very naturally.

For more details about object-oriented analysis, please consult one of the textbooks (e.g. Bennett, McRobb and Farmer, 2010). The textbooks will also explain what an 'object' is, in the full definition required by object-oriented analysis and design, and some of the reasons that object-oriented analysis provides patterns for reusing objects in different areas, in a way different from classic entity–relationship models. Think about libraries and lending books, and compare that with car hire agencies. There are similar patterns (loan or hire period, customer or borrower details) as well as some differences. The theory is that the similar patterns could be transferred from one situation to another, and perhaps other object classes developed to deal additionally with insurance (for example, for the car hire scenario). The thinking has been done for the main classes, and we can simply add another object class if necessary. The objects are acting like cells, and an object class is simply a representation of a type of object. It is the blueprint that describes the details of an object. A class is the blueprint from which the individual objects are created. Class is composed of three things: a name, attributes and operations. The important thing to remember is that what the attributes are and what the object can do are wrapped up within the object class. There are possible relationships among object classes, but we can make changes to what an object class does, or has in the way of attributes, without affecting everything else. This is not true of entity-relationship models.

In librarianship, FRBR (Tillett and Orlando, 2003) is a conceptual entity-relationship model. Figure 5.2 shows how the Group 1 entities (work, expression, manifestation, item) operate.

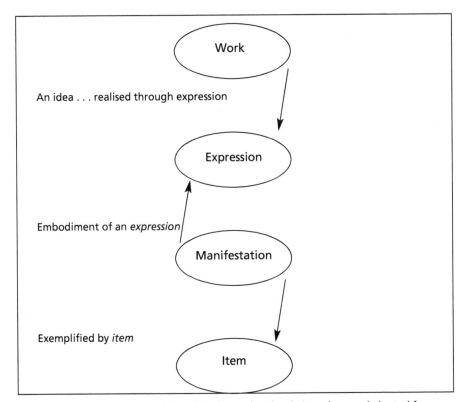

Figure 5.2 *FRBR Group 1 entities of intellectual and artistic endeavour* (adapted from Tillett and Orlando, 2003)

The *work* is a distinct intellectual creation. Shakespeare's play *Hamlet* is a distinct intellectual creation. There may be different *expressions* of *Hamlet*, such as an abridged version for schools to use, or a translation into another language. The *manifestation* of an *expression* (e.g. abridged version for schools) refers to the set of copies published by a particular publisher in print form and an e-book version of the print book would be a different *manifestation*. The fourth entity is the *item*, often a particular physical copy, for example one I might have sitting on my bookshelf.

Object-oriented analysis looks at this in a completely different way. The object is defined as a thing of interest to the system, and contains a collection of related procedures (called methods) and data with attributes. The object is like a cell as messages can be sent to the object to change the variables inside the object, but the inside of the cell is protected from the outside. Changes can be made to the methods inside the cell (the object) without affecting the rest of the system. Importantly, we can have super-classes, and sub-classes in object-oriented modelling, which are how we classify naturally. Furniture is a super-class, table might be a class. We might have a class vehicle with sub-classes including bus, car and bicycle. In object-oriented analysis, the principle of inheritance means that the sub-class inherits the methods and variables of the class above, and may have additional methods and variables of its own. This is important to remember.

For an object-oriented view of the main ideas in FRBR, we would have the top level (super-class) and probably have *work*. Hamlet becomes an instance of the top-level class. *Expression* may be viewed as a sub-class of *work* and *manifestation* as a sub-class of *expression*, although the naming of those classes might need to change. From my perspective, FRBR could have been developed as an object-oriented scheme from the outset quite successfully, as it seems to be fitted for that, and might have been more intuitive for many librarians to use – broader and narrow terms are familiar to librarians. To give an example of how inheritance of methods and variables works, it may be easier to think bottom-up about methods and variables for each level of class. If we do this, we can think of that school version of *Hamlet*, the copy held in library Y, and published in year XXXX (an instance of the object class *manifestation*). What do we need to know about this particular copy? Libraries need to know about loan status, the publisher, the date of publication, and probably want to specify the condition of an individual copy. For the higher classes, such as *expression*, we may not need or want to know all those properties, we might simply be searching for the existence of translations of *Hamlet*, or particular editions or imprints.

As other cultural heritage modelling has used object-oriented methods, in order to provide interoperability there is now an object-oriented model for FRBR, and considerable efforts put into mapping across various models. Documents about the mapping (even simple guides, e.g. Le Boeuf, 2015) can be very confusing to read, but that principle of inheritance is important to remember. Needless to say, the terminology also varies in some of the mapping documents and the term 'properties' is used instead of attributes. With all these complications, we can only wish that FRBR and CIDOC CRM had started off together. In addition, we also need to remember that for linked data applications we probably need to draw on resource description and access cataloguing guidelines that use the FRBR conceptual model. Surprisingly, there have been few published attempts to check with readers whether the FRBR model is intuitive, but one study (Pisanki and Žumer, 2012) suggests it may work for most users.

5.3   Basic process concepts

UML is not just concerned with object classes and use cases. It also has notation for activity diagrams that can be used to specify the logic of procedurally complex operations. In their simplest form these are very similar to flowcharts that illustrate the sequence of activities and the decision points. UML therefore has some possibilities for modelling aspects of processes. Normally activity diagrams are used to help design a system, so that the developer and the user can agree on what happens – and when. Theoretically it is possible to use UML notation such as activity diagrams to analyse processes within an organisation, even if the aim is not strictly to develop a system, but simply to check whether the work could be done better.

In practice, process analysis is better done by a distinct business process modelling method, of which there are several to choose from. In chapters 6 and 7, the business process modelling approach developed by Martyn Ould (2005) is discussed. Ould (2005, 4) defines a process as 'a coherent body of organisational activity: activity that goes on in the organisation and that in some sense comes as a unit'. Typically 'comes as a unit' means is 'all focused on a certain outcome.' Ould also defines a role as a responsibility within a process, an actor carries out a role, and a role carries out actions following business rules. A role has props, which it uses to carry out its responsibility. Roles have interactions in order to collaborate. A process has goals and outcomes.

5.4   Modelling how an information service works within an organisation: the process architecture

There are many more details about process modelling in chapters 6 and 7 (in particular), but one important part of Ould's process modelling (Riva) is the derivation of the process architecture. Riva has three main process types: case processes, case management processes and case strategy processes. To explain this, we need to understand Ould's definition of a unit of work. The unit of work for a library help desk would be concerned with handling enquiries. The case process is 'Handle an enquiry', but we also need to look for a case management process that is concerned with managing the continuing flow of enquiries, monitoring and scheduling them. We also need to look for a case strategy process that looks at long-term performance and trends (perhaps the senior management perspective). It is possible that the case management process and case strategy process are not required in the end but they need to be considered initially.

How do we identify those units of work? How is the work of an organisation broken down in a sensible and useful way? Ideally, we need to see the connections between the processes, and start to identify what belongs properly to the organisation (or part of the organisation) and which processes are general solutions. Ould explains how to identify the essential business entities that have a lifetime during which we need to look after them. This identification usually happens during brainstorming with staff and the questions to ask include: What do we make? What do we sell? For a library or information service the more usual questions would be: What services do we offer? What service lines do we have? What things can we simply not get away from (e.g. copyright licensing)? Who are our customers – internal and external? Are there things our customers have or want or do that might be essential business entities for us? What sort of things do we deal with, day in, day out (e.g. loans)? What events in the outside world do we need to respond to (e.g. flooding)? What things do our information systems keep information on? This exercise should generate many candidates for essential business entities.

The next stage is to check whether these are truly entities, and if it makes sense to put 'a' or 'the' in front, then we keep these and bracket the others that do not make sense. For example, 'a loan' works, but 'a disaster management' does not sound quite right. It is important to check whether the essential business entities are truly the work of the organisation (or department) or whether they belong to some other department or possibly an external organisation. It is also important to identify any less visible units of work; Ould (2005, 178) suggests putting 'change to' in front of each to see if this creates another unit of work. For example, for an educational institution 'change to student record' might remind us whether we need to have a unit of work for checking how to transfer students into a programme through accreditation of prior experiential learning, or when transferring students from a degree scheme elsewhere into a new university system. In addition, putting 'collection of' in front of the essential business entity may indicate we need to have another unit of work.

The final list of units of work should have lists for those things (entities) that have a lifetime during which we must look after them (essential units of work), those that arise from designed business entities, rather than essential (to the department or organisation) (designed units of work), and those that may be collections of other things or changes to other things. The next stage is to look at the relationships between those units of work. In particular, does one unit of work generate, involve or require another unit of work?

For example, for a library service, a loan (unit of work) generates a reminder (unit of work). A loan also generates a fine (unit of work). A module generates a reading list. And so it continues, trying to arrange what we believe to be our essential units of work into some sort of meaningful pattern of relationships. There may be some units of work that do not fit, but leave these at this point. The next stage is to look carefully at the units of work on our first draft of the process architecture and check whether we have the case process, the case management process and the case strategic process for each unit of work. If not, do we need them?

The next stage is to examine the 'generates' relationship between two units of work, to see how the relationship works (for further details, see Ould, 2005, 154 and 184). For module and reading list, Figure 5.3 on the next page shows the types of relationships to examine. As 'module' generates 'reading list', then 'handle a module' and 'handle a reading list' have a relationship and one module may have many reading lists associated with it (versions for different academic years, draft versions). Ould shows how to convert a service relationship between units of work into processes, and this works but looks formulaic to start with.

'Handle a module' requests the case management process for 'handle a reading list' (in other words, the generation of the modules for the new academic year requests the start of a process to manage the flow of reading list production). And the case management process for 'handle a reading list' negotiates with 'handle a module'. Or, putting this very simply in human terms, a deputy librarian checks the diary and asks the subject librarians to start amending the reading lists for the new academic year. The subject librarians then attempt to negotiate with their module co-ordinators. In Riva terminology, the case management process for 'handle a reading list' starts, then monitors, intervenes and stops the case process 'handle a reading list'. The case process 'handle a reading list' delivers to the case process 'handle a module', and reports to its case management process for 'handle a reading list'. Again, putting this in human terms, the subject librarian's amended reading list is finally ready for association with the module, and the deputy librarian can check off that that module's reading list is ready, and whether the other reading lists are ready. Having both the case process and case management process for 'handle a reading list' may seem complicated, certainly, but any member of library staff who has to extract reading lists from academic members of staff will recognise the negotiation required, the monitoring (how many reading lists are available by a certain date), and deciding – often by a more senior member of staff – when the process of producing reading lists is deemed complete.

There are several rounds to producing a process architecture, and the final version will look a lot neater and simpler than the first-round diagram. There is a lot of work in producing the detail of the actual process and the

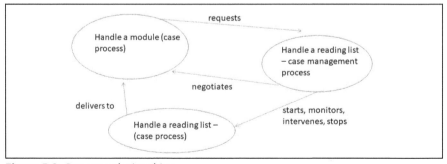

Figure 5.3 *Process relationships*

interactions between roles (see Chapter 7). It is worth the effort for library and information services to examine the relationships between their processes, and from the process architecture to ask whether some units of work can be outsourced (paying fines directly to a finance department, for example), or whether some relationships can be made more efficient, and as effective, by eliminating a case management process.

5.5   Conclusions

Modelling systems, activities and processes is not, as some might hope, a matter of putting a few diagrams and arrows on a whiteboard and inviting comments from staff. It requires time to prepare, for staff to learn enough about the basics of the methods being used to enable useful discussion. It is not surprising that some examples discussed in the chapter involved digitisation activities as these posed many challenges to library and information services – where did the activities fit into the organisational processes, what new roles and relationships with other roles were required? Chapter 6 provides an overview of the history of operational research and process modelling in libraries, and Chapter 7 discusses how to carry out process modelling in a way that allows library staff to query possible improvements to processes. Chapter 8 contrasts two published studies that used process modelling or mapping approaches.

References

Bennett, S., McRobb, S. and Farmer, R. (2010) *Object-Oriented Systems Analysis and Design Using UML*, 4th edn, McGraw-Hill.

Le Boeuf, P. (2015) A Basic Introduction to FRBR and PRESS, IFLA, http://library.ifla.org/1150/1/207-leboeuf-en.pdf.

Ould, M. A. (2005) *Business Process Management: a rigorous approach*, British Computer Society.

Pisanski, J. and Žumer, M. (2012) User Verification of the FRBR Conceptual Model, *Journal of Documentation*, **68** (4), 582–92, doi:10.1108/00220411211239129.

Tillett, B. B. and Orlando, A. L. A. (2003) FRBR (Functional Requirements for Bibliographic Records), *Technicalities*, **23** (5), 1.

CHAPTER 6

Libraries and the organisation of library processes – a history of operational research, and the use of process modelling

Dina Tbaishat

COMMENTARY: CHRISTINE URQUHART

Chapter 6 examines the history of operations research within libraries, and some of the more recent changes to academic libraries, the new roles required for staff, and the challenges to provide services that meet needs, within budgetary constraints. The chapter concludes with an overview of some examples of the use of business process modelling techniques. Strategic planning is mentioned frequently in the library literature but mostly in aspirational terms – urging staff (presumably) onwards for the greater good of the library and its users. It is more common to read about the challenges of new roles – but what happens to the old roles? Pritchard (2013) points out that libraries need a strategic approach to training that goes beyond individual development needs, but looks at organisational needs at several levels. She suggests that libraries identify which skills and competencies are required by all staff, which are required somewhere, and which could be obtained from external resources. Some skills will be required to advance strategic library goals, others for operational purposes. Ideally such attention to skills and role redevelopment should link to the institutional goals.

Chapter 5 discussed how a process architecture could be developed that might help libraries assess their fit within an organisation, but it is unclear from the literature how many libraries do more than pay lip service to the principles of serving the mission of the organisation. Franklin (2012), for example, suggests that academic libraries should shift from divisions of activities based on traditional library functions to structures that reflect organisational goals (undergraduate education, research, outreach etc.). This might be bewildering to many staff if there was total upheaval, and a likely mid-road compromise might be some relabelling, but the same functions would continue as before. As Chapter 5 emphasises, business process analysis requires commitment and time to succeed. The suspicion that most library staff do not feel they have the time or the energy for anything other than tinkering at the edges might be confirmed by the survey of library mission statements compared with institutional mission statements, where a discourse analysis found very weak links between the sets of statements (Wadas, 2017). On the other hand, in practice, when library staff are confronted with users with needs, they may well get on with the job as best they can at the operational level.

In addition, libraries are increasingly aware of the need to demonstrate their value and impact to their stakeholders – their users and parent institutions. Cmor (2016) notes that a full library impact assessment can be a time-consuming operation but that it is possible to communicate news about the effectiveness of library activities, sustainably, by using a simple infographic that requires details about the objectives of the service, event, resource or tool under examination, what was offered to the users, and the impact of the service, event, resource or tool. There are similar examples of visualisation tools and techniques mentioned in Chapter 14, for presenting the research evidence to clinicians (and patients). In Cmor's university library (Nanyang Technological University, Singapore) professional development sessions are also sustainably managed, but they are aimed at deep learning rather than a purely skills-based approach.

Chapter 6 provides an opportunity to reflect on what has been achieved in the past, and the approaches taken to analyse what libraries do, and what they should do. Whether we talk about managing change, strategic planning, re-engineering, or changing roles and responsibilities, Chapter 6 helps to assess the background, and provides some directions on priorities for the future for analysing and planning what libraries should do.

References

Cmor, D. (2016) Strategies for Sustainable Services in Academic Libraries,

Library Management, **37** (6/7) 298–307, https://doi.org/10.1108/LM-05-2016.

Franklin, B. (2012) Surviving to Thriving: advancing the institutional mission, *Journal of Library Administration*, **52** (1), 94–107, doi:10.1080/01930826.2012.630244.

Pritchard, S. M. (2013) Leave No Jobs or Staff Members Unturned, *Portal: Libraries and the Academy*, **13** (1), 1–3.

Wadas, L. R. (2017) Mission Statements in Academic Libraries: a discourse analysis, *Library Management*, **38** (2), 108–16.

6.1   Introduction

In 1931 Ranganathan (1963) – one of the founding fathers of library science – proposed five laws that may still be applied in essence to library operations today. The fifth law, that the library is 'a growing organism', emphasises the need to plan and design for the future. Academic libraries serve diverse users, and can be considered as systems of integrated activities around resources (Akeroyd, 2001) and business processes that collaborate to achieve organisational goals.

Academic libraries contribute to the role academic institutions play in directing the cultural, political, social, scientific and technological development of a nation (Chaturvedi, 1994). Changes in the way of working within libraries and information services in the UK were stressed by the Follett report (Corrall, 1995). Much of the literature on academic library development during the years 1999-2006 stressed the need for academic librarians to re-orient their outcomes and to persuade existing staff, for example in merged library and computing services, that change was necessary and inevitable. Academic libraries have been encouraged to complete the migration from print to electronic collections, to reposition and focus on curation rather than collection (Lewis, 2007). The role of 'the librarian' has changed, professional role boundaries are less clear (Wilson and Halpin, 2006), and organisational models and culture of working have changed (Reid and Foster, 2000).

DePew applied modelling to acquisitions decision making in 1975, claiming that some modelling of routine activities had occurred, but few studies looked at modelling intellectual processes for making decisions in libraries. Some of these documents may still lie as flowcharts in library staff desks for individual processes but very little in the literature examines how and why certain processes and functions are conducted in academic libraries. In addition there are few hints of systematic models demonstrating how the academic library and information service processes relate to the mission and work of the institution. This chapter examines the history of operations and business process analysis in academic libraries.

Section 6.2 outlines the history of the main changes in academic libraries; Section 6.3 describes some of the performance improvement and quality management initiatives. Section 6.4 examines approaches to business process modelling and how these techniques have been used in libraries, and Section 6.5 draws conclusions.

6.2   Organisation and change: academic library response

6.2.1   Changes in libraries

Academic libraries have been dominated by books, following the increase in book publishing during the 19th century (Johnson, 1970). By the middle of the 20th century, several other changes were affecting academic libraries. First, following the release of documents from wartime, coupled with an increase in scientific research, the traditional systems of bibliographic control, suited to books, were no longer suitable for the increase in articles in journals and scientific reports (Rau, 2007). Academic, national and research libraries had to collaborate on policies and standards. A minimum standard for academic library provision was developed with the establishment of the Standing Conference of National and University Libraries (SCONUL) in 1950 (Brophy, 2000). In 1994 SCONUL merged with the Council of Polytechnic Librarians (COPOL), and many of the British polytechnics were reconstituted as universities around that time. In 2001 SCONUL changed its name to the Society of College, National and University Libraries, to include colleges of higher education (often teacher training colleges in origin) into its membership. SCONUL collects statistics from academic libraries and shares and develops good practice among its members. In North America the Association of Research Libraries (ARL) represents most of the research intensive universities in the USA and Canada, and is partnered with other organisations including the Scholarly Publishing and Academic Resources Coalition (SPARC) and the Coalition for Networked Information.

In the late 1970s a few approaches to examining library activities were developed. Lancaster and Cleverdon (1977) predicted, and developed methods to assess the outcomes of library use, and they explained what users did with the information they obtained. In the 1990s there was an increase in the UK student population and there was also an increase in higher education courses in universities and further education colleges (reflected by changes in the composition of SCONUL).

After 2000, the pace of change in collection development and integration of digital collections increased, but the increase in number of journals and subscription costs did not keep pace with library budgets, requiring libraries to focus on core purposes (Rathe and Blankenship, 2005), and ensure resources, particularly the newer electronic information services, were used effectively by students (Hepworth, 2000; Owusu-Ansah, 2001; Urquhart et al., 2003; Rowley and Urquhart, 2007; Urquhart and Rowley, 2007; Streatfield and Markless, 2008).

Information literacy was discussed in a briefing paper prepared by the SCONUL Advisory Committee on Information Literacy (1999). The SCONUL e-learning taskforce final report was issued in 2005, and recommended work on case studies, new staff roles and skills, for example. To help achieve improvement, an information literacy model based on seven sets of skills was proposed in 1999, and was later revised in 2011. These skills were developed from a basic competence in library and information technology skills. The term information literacy is used very broadly, covering concepts such as digital literacy, information handling, information skills, data curation and data management (Bent and Stubbings, 2011a, b).

More recently, SCONUL explored the change over the coming decade, particularly how the internet of things will affect libraries and how blended learning can affect libraries' operations (SCONUL, 2015). The internet of things connects products and enables better interaction. Ng (2015) discussed the transformation caused by the internet of things; everything can hold data, everything can be a source of information. Blended learning on the other hand has allowed access for everyone, learning on the go, and connecting with a community. However, the same challenges remain: staff adaptability, user digital capabilities and quality of service.

Changes in collection development were necessary (Kulp and Rupp-Serrano, 2005) but changes in library culture, from a resources and collection-led attitude to a services-led culture, were often harder to achieve at the library service desk than many managers realised (Davies, Kirkpatrick and Oliver, 1992). Mismatches were common, and gaps occurred between the strategies stated and the actual way staff at the frontline managed their work (espoused culture versus reality of practice). Atkinson (2003) identified some factors related to all higher education libraries and information services that would help with managing change; one factor was the extent to which individual library staff were able to deal effectively with change issues.

At the policy level, important developments for academic libraries were the establishment of the Joint Funding Council's Libraries Review Group in 1992, with subsequent publication of its report (the Follett report) in December 1993 (Joint Funding Council's Libraries Review Group, 1993; Corrall, 1995). As well as confirming the need to focus on information and access, the report called for changed attitudes, changes in the functions and ways of working of library and information services in universities. The Joint Information Systems Committee of the Funding Councils funded many electronic library initiatives under the e-Lib programme (Law, 1997), and Jisc continues to fund a range of development work for information services in higher and further education.

Debates about use of library space started with major evaluations of space use (Houlihan, 2005). Perhaps a return to basic principles is required. Ranganathan (1963) discussed the main parts of the library that are capable of growing: the books, the staff and the readers. He referred to them as the trinity. Therefore, Ranganathan's study of space management offers a baseline perspective for developing later studies of space as a resource. Focusing on space alone can lead to erroneous conclusions.

The annual national student satisfaction survey has been a big lever for universities and libraries in the UK. It started in 2005 and is still running across all publicly funded higher education institutions in England, Wales, Northern Ireland and some participating institutions in Scotland. The survey takes many aspects of student life into consideration such as organisation and management, learning resources and overall satisfaction (National Student Survey, 2016).

Corrall (2012) discusses how the library environment became, and is becoming, more complex. A review (Hurst, 2017) of the main changes to university libraries in the UK during the period 2011-2015 notes the impact of the introduction of student fees on the relationship between universities and students. Collections were still important but the focus changed to providing access and support to students and staff. This, together with cost pressures from the economic crisis, has resulted in universities in the UK and elsewhere restructuring their services. Ways of working are changing, and convergence with other library services, and collaboration, internal and external, is more common. Such streamlining, and consequent redesign of library processes, is not a comfortable experience for many staff (see Chapter 8 for discussion of how different libraries have approached this, Chapter 7 explains how to carry out a process analysis). Chapter 5 emphasised the need to look at the way the library processes mapped to the business of the organisation and this may help staff to appreciate that the streamlining is undertaken not simply in the interests of greater efficiency, although that is often the main driver. Joint procurement helps libraries to achieve value for money (e.g. Jisc Collections in the UK), and other collaborations include work on e-theses and cataloguing (Ayris, 2012).

The changes in the scope of academic library activities have included a greater emphasis on demonstrating value for money (Urquhart, 2017), perhaps using data analytics in more creative ways not just to show that library usage correlates to a student's degree outcome, but to identify students that need more support – again suggesting that library collaboration with other student support services is desirable.

Use of electronic resources continues to accelerate, although use of e-books has been more difficult for technical reasons. Library staff may co-operate with faculty on provision of learning resources on learning management or virtual learning environments, and may provide more personalised support for students on information literacy, within the online environment. Staff involved with information literacy are probably more concerned with ensuring that they add value to students' interactions with resources. Since 2011, more articles have referred to embedding librarians' activities (reference enquiries, information literacy support) in learning management or virtual learning environments (e.g. Tumbleson, 2016).

There have been huge changes in journal publishing since 2011. Increased costs of electronic resources for libraries have led to rationalisation of collections (Section 5.2, use case example) alongside increased collaboration. Horava and Levine-Clark (2016) review the trends, which include demand driven acquisition, big deals, rationalisation of print collections, stewarding local digital collections and demonstrating value. The collections budget is being used to fund operations other than content (memberships, MARC records for example). Open access models (several) have emerged, and some research funding bodies demand that publicly funded research outputs are made freely available. The role of acquisitions has therefore changed, as in some universities the library holds the money for funding open access publication (Hampson, 2014). In line with the emphasis on user needs first, patron driven acquisition or demand driven acquisition models of service have been developed. Chadwell and Sutton (2014) suggest that the repository model of publishing articles may shift from a focus on offering access to articles published in journals to publishing original content through the institutional repository. If so, then new roles and responsibilities for library staff will emerge, with changes to the liaison role, development of the digital publishing librarian, the alt-metric expert (to assess impact of repository content) and data management. There is a need to develop best practice in workflows around open access management; one approach is to use social media to share experience among libraries (Emery and Stone, 2014).

There are changing views around resource discovery (see Chapter 10) – instead of expecting users to go to library resource discovery systems first, libraries increasingly use social media and other platforms, to then direct them to the library resources. A survey (Boateng and Liu, 2014) of Web 2.0 applications in major US academic libraries found that Facebook and Twitter were the most popular and all libraries used social networking services. Wikis were less used, but blogs were popular.

Open access to resource outputs has been accompanied more recently by the open data movement. This is a new area of responsibility for academic library service staff, working with staff and research students to manage research data and outputs (Cox and Pinfield, 2014). Health sciences library staff are developing different information service models to support researchers, which are applicable to other disciplines (Cain at el., 2016). A survey (Si et al., 2015) of the top world university libraries indicated that around half offered research data services of various types (introductions, data curation and storage, data management guidelines, data management reference and resource recommendations, with around a quarter offering data management training). Many university libraries were at the planning stage, as Tenopir et al. (2014) confirmed.

A later survey of the European situation (Tenopir et al., 2017) showed similar interest in research data services, and associated planning and collaboration activities. Kruse and Thestrup (2014) describe the work to develop an IT infrastructure and research data management policies in Denmark. In the UK, Jisc has funded open access good practice pathfinder projects, to demonstrate how open access can support research (Awre, Stainthorp and Stone, 2016). Data governance and data literacy are becoming required expertise for librarians supporting researchers (Koltay, 2016). Embedded services and re-engineered roles for data management librarians in different disciplines are likely to emerge (Lyon, 2016). Roles and responsibilities are unclear for faculty and research staff; university infrastructures (e.g. repository and research support) may be sufficient but faculty are unaware that libraries could help with research data management (Diekema, Wesolek and Walters, 2014). An information-gathering study with early career researchers shows that processes and activities to support this group may need careful planning, rather than simplistic assumptions that support can be mapped to the research lifecycle (Mattern et al., 2015).

A survey of practice in Australia, New Zealand, Canada, Germany, the Netherlands and the UK (Cox et al., 2017) showed that responsibility for setting research data management policies varied. In the Netherlands and the UK, library services or research support services were equally likely to take the lead, in Australia the research support services were more likely to lead. Levels of collaboration varied as well – across countries and within countries – as did expectations of restructuring of library services. To reach a higher level of maturity in research data management service provision, more attention to technical aspects of stewardship is necessary.

6.2.2   The librarian's role

As Section 6.2.1 has noted, roles in academic libraries have changed over the last 20–30 years (e.g. Bryan, 1976). Roles should be well defined and understood, at least by those working within one organisation. Although the role of 'the librarian' has changed, professional role boundaries are less clear (Wilson and Halpin, 2006), and this may be the result of changes in organisational models and cultures of working (Reid and Foster, 2000) in academic libraries – initially with convergence of IT or information services and library services, either directly or indirectly.

Some general policy statements have been made on the general role of academic librarians. For example, in 1988, the Canadian Association of College and University Libraries released a statement that defines the university librarian's role independent of faculty status. Veaner (1990, 64) emphasised that statement, part of which says: 'College and university librarians play an integral role in the educational process of their institutions by their contributions to the pursuit, dissemination and structuring of knowledge and understanding. . . . Librarians' responsibilities are diverse and may include development and evaluation of library resources collections.' Pinfield (2001) notes that subject librarians in the UK were adding new roles that required more emphasis on liaison with users, involvement in the learning environment, selection of e-resources, working with technical staff and advocacy of the collections, and Parsons (2010) discusses problems of the academic liaison librarian and the collaboration with faculty. Since 2011, the challenge of research data management and development of research data services has added another layer of uncertainty around professional roles and responsibilities within the institution (Section 6.2.1). The survey work by Cox et al. (2017) and especially research by Lyon (2016) show that the scope of particular roles and responsibilities for particular processes may be very unclear. The current situation is similar to the 'organic' situation described by Burns and Stalker (1961) in their study of the management of innovation in organisations. In contrast to mechanistic (bureaucratic) systems, organic systems are not hierarchical, but they are stratified according to expertise. Job roles are not self-contained in organic systems and require continuous participation with others, and awareness of how the role and associated activities fit into the mission of the organisation.

Huvila (2006) defines a work role as a set of activities within work; a role acts as a viewpoint situated within work, just as 'work' is situated within a human life world, given that the latter is in a broader scope. According to Huvila (2008), an individual may perform more than one work role and may share work roles with others, so someone's roles are not exclusive. On the other hand, and from a more technical but simpler perspective, Ould (2005) indicates that a role is a responsibility, as it carries out actions that follow business rules. Chapter 7 explains how to model role interactions, and although such analyses may seem to depend on a mechanistic view of roles, in practice they are not mechanistic. In fact, they may help to illuminate some of the less visible, but necessary, collaborations of responsibilities to enable a process to function effectively.

6.3   Improvements in libraries and quality assurance

Evaluation and management principles developed for the commercial sector have been perceived to apply to libraries for at least the last 20 years: 'Performance measurements in library and information services has since kept pace with the range of methodologies used in the profit, and not-for-profit sectors' (Cullen, 1998).

Within the UK, SCONUL (2016) represents the views and interests of academic librarians to government, regulators and other stakeholders, and SCONUL helps academic libraries collaborate to share knowledge and best practice. One of SCONUL's main activities is the collection of activity statistics, which helps develop performance indicators and allows university libraries to benchmark their performance against other similar libraries.

Many academic libraries have experimented with using the Balanced Scorecard model – created by Harvard business professors Kaplan and Norton in 1993 (Balanced Scorecard Institute, 2011) – as a conceptual framework to translate the organisation's vision into a set of performance indicators distributed among four perspectives:

- financial (emphasising cost efficiency)
- customer (reflecting overall customer service and satisfaction)
- internal business processes at which organisation must excel to meet expected performance
- learning and growth (quality of information systems quality, employees' abilities).

According to Norton and Daum (1999), the Balanced Scorecard is a performance management methodology that uses performance measurement information to assess current programs or policies to meet organisational goals. In academic libraries, the emphasis on producing a balanced overall assessment of the library is similar (Ceynowa, 2000). 'You can't manage what you can't measure' was the message of a statement made by the ARL, which in 2009 invited interested libraries to participate in a pilot project in an attempt to develop library scorecards following the Balanced Scorecard approach to build up metrics that are directly tied to the libraries' strategic goals. The collaborating institutions were Johns Hopkins University, McMaster University, University of Virginia and University of Washington, with external consultant Ascendant Strategy Management Group. In spite of differences, in all individual libraries there seem to be key processes that are consistently important, according to Kyrillidou (2010): setting strategic objectives directly tied to the organisation's mission; visualising them into a strategy map; and communicating the map, objectives and metrics.

Cribb and Hogan (2003) discussed issues and strategies in implementing the Balanced Scorecard in a small private university library, such as challenges in selecting an appropriate performance measure for the four perspectives of the model; Calhoun (2004) argues that considerable thought and time are needed to develop a scorecard. There has been less emphasis in scorecard work on really rethinking what the library does, but one example is a paper by Town (2011) on the transcendent value of the academic library. Urquhart and Tbaishat (2016) review the use of scorecards (macro-frameworks) and micro-frameworks for library assessment, and discuss how to use data analytics to help question the value of some services.

6.4   Business process modelling

Opdahl and Sindre (1995) argue that it is necessary to model not only the automatable information processing activities, but also material and human activities occurring around the computerised information system. Such human activities involve modelling of roles, actors, organisational units and the relationship between them all.

Business process modelling helps understand processes and supports process improvement. Business process re-engineering or improvement is quite new, however, and there has been a change in terminology since the early 1990s. The original perspective on business processes was to use information technology to achieve efficiency, or to use methods to improve operative manufacturing processes (Tinnilä, 1995). Many articles have emerged in the literature since then, supporting the concept of process management and improvement, using different terms such as business process redesign, business restructuring and business process re-engineering (Zairi and Sinclair, 1995).

There are various methods for modelling business processes. Each method employs a set of notations that represent business processes from different perspectives. Simple flow charts are still used. Data flow diagrams are another example of modelling methods.

Similarly, the Business Process Management Initiative working group released Business Process Modeling Notation designed for describing processes in business process diagrams. In addition, there is the Integration DEFinition (IDEF) family, which covers a large area from function modelling to information, knowledge acquisition, simulation, object-oriented analysis and design. Odeh et al. (2003) demonstrated the differences and similarities between role activity diagrams and Unified Modelling Language (UML), and the paper showed that it is possible to translate from role activity diagrams to UML, but it will still rely on the translator's ability to maintain the equivalence between the two.

Little work appears to have been done and published on modelling library processes. The role activity diagram has been used as a modelling tool to represent some library-related processes, for example, the process of checking out a book in a library (Liu, Alderson and Qureshi, 1999). In 2003, McKnight and Livingston applied the model to the learning services at Deakin University, which is the major academic support unit for the university. The whole aim is to improve students' learning outcomes. Other modelling methods have been used within academic libraries to model and improve processes. McKnight and Austin (2008) used the Customer Value Discovery model at Nottingham Trent University's library. This model has been used in Australia since 1994 and in the UK since 2002. The model has been constantly refined since it was released to maximise its efficiency. It is used to discover all success factors and irritants through group feedback in a meeting.

There has been an emphasis on outcomes rather than internal processes when measuring the performance of academic libraries. Library performance was frequently assessed in terms of quality expectations. The performance assessment framework that includes a criterion for internal processes has been used much less. A rare example, Kettunen (2007), uses the 'internal processes' to assess the effectiveness of co-operation activities in a university library consortium in Finland. Town (2004) suggests that measures in the process perspective area need to be based on a full understanding of the processes involved in delivering e-services.

Process analysis is not very dominant in academic libraries. Most attention has been placed on analysis of e-resource usage, and the analysis of electronic journal usage statistics, for example, can be time-consuming and the task is more complex than it might appear (Conyers and Dalton, 2007). However, it is important to mention that although recent evidence shows that there is an apparent lack of interest in process analysis within academic libraries (Lakos, 2007), the absence of discussion of processes in academic libraries from the peer-reviewed journals and literature does not mean that there are no concerns or work done in that field, as there may be some internal unpublished reports, such as Stanford University's approach to business process redesign (Stanford University, 2005). The systematic approaches to examining library operations appear to explore the human roles and responsibilities in far more depth than earlier operations research. Lewis (2001) examined the role of the electronic resource librarian and used some workflows to explain the suggested model for the academic libraries strategy suggested. Similarly, Ehrlich and Cash (1999) investigated the work of information intermediaries and how their support tools were used in their work.

Guise (2005) suggests a systematic approach that academic libraries can use to analyse their reference and instruction programming. Kennedy (2005) investigated how digitisation affected workload, staffing and outsourcing in resource preservation. In addition, McKiernan and Ohler (2006) discuss some of the changes to traditional technical services, and they refer to workflows but do not discuss or chart them. Similarly, Schwartzkopf (2007) reports a presentation by Amanda Yesilbas on changes to the workflow for e-journal check-in, but no detail of the process is provided, only an outline. Capture of organisational learning and knowledge sharing requirements are proposed by Daneshgar and Parirokh (2007). In summary, the work may have been carried out, but few in-depth examples reach the peer-reviewed literature and therefore learning from the experience of others is limited.

6.5   Conclusions

It would be tempting to hope that 'Business Process Modelling comes to the rescue' (Havey, 2005) and that identification of task, role and knowledge artefacts will identify and enable collaboration among staff. However, the comparison of models by Lin et al. shows that gaps have existed in previous methods (Lin, Yang and Pai, 2002) and that it is difficult to find a business process modelling method that works for all circumstances. The review of the changes in organisational processes in academic libraries over the past 30 years demonstrates how many changes there have been in the roles and responsibilities of librarians in academic libraries. In recent years, more people are asking for a complete rethink of the way the library operates, how the library collaborates with academic departments and support services, and how the library should position itself, within the organisation, and externally with other organisations and their libraries. Views differ, unsurprisingly, but there is a need for better ways of understanding how roles interact, and what the business processes, rather than library functions and services, should be. Chapter 5 (Section 5.4) explained how a process architecture could be developed. Chapter 7 deals with the analysis of roles and responsibilities and how roles interact, using role activity diagrams (part of the Riva method proposed by Ould, 2005).

References

Akeroyd, J. (2001) The Future of Academic Libraries, *Aslib Proceedings*, **53** (3), 79-84.

Atkinson, J. (2003) Managing Change and Embedding Innovation in Academic Libraries and Information Services, *New Review of Academic Librarianship*, **9** (1), 25-41.

Awre, C., Stainthorp, P. and Stone, G. (2016) Supporting Open Access through Collaboration, *Collaborative Librarianship*, **8** (2), 99-110.

Ayris, P. (2012) Developing European Library Services in Changing Times, *Liber Quarterly: the Journal of European Research Libraries*, **12** (3/4), 331-46.

Balanced Scorecard Institute (2011) *Balanced Scorecard Basics*, www.balancedscorecard.org/BSCResources/AbouttheBalancedScorecard/ tabid/55/Default.aspx.

Bent, M. and Stubbings, R. (2011a) *The SCONUL Seven Pillars Model of Information Literacy: core model for higher education*, www.sconul.ac.uk/sites/default/files/documents/coremodel.pdf.

Bent, M. and Stubbings, R. (2011b) The SCONUL Seven Pillars Model of Information Literacy: 2011 update, *SCONUL Focus*, **52**, 48.

Boateng, F. and Liu, Y. Q. (2014) Web 2.0 Applications' Usage and Trends in Top US Academic Libraries, *Library Hi-Tech*, **32** (1), 120-38.

Brophy, P. (2000) *The Academic Library*, Library Association.

Bryan, H. (1976) *University Libraries in Britain*, Clive Bingley.

Burns, T. and Stalker, G. M. (1961) *The Management of Innovation*, Tavistock.

Cain, T. J., Cheek, F. M., Kupsco, J., Hartel, L. J. and Getelsman, A. (2016) Health Sciences Libraries Forecasting Information Service Trends for Researchers: models applicable to all academic libraries, *College & Research Libraries*, **77** (5), 595-613.

Calhoun, B. D. (2004) *Using the Balanced Scorecard to Determine Corporate Information Needs*, University College, www.designbydi.com/documents/BalScrCrd.pdf.

Ceynowa, K. (2000) Managing Academic Information Provision with the Balanced Scorecard: a project of the German Research Association,

Performance Measurement and Metrics, **1** (3), 157-64.

Chadwell, F. and Sutton, S. C. (2014) The Future of Open Access and Library Publishing, *New Library World*, **115** (5/6), 225-36.

Chaturvedi, D. (ed.) (1994) *Academic Libraries*, Anmol Publications.

Conyers, A. and Dalton, P. (2007) Electronic Resource Measurement: linking research to practice, *The Library Quarterly*, **77** (4), 463-70.

Corrall, S. (1995) Academic Libraries in the Information Society, *New Library World*, **96** (3), 35-42.

Corrall, S. (2012) The Concept of Collection Development in the Digital World. In Fieldhouse, M. and Marshall, A. (eds.), *Collection Development in the Digital Age*, Facet Publishing.

Cox, A. M. and Pinfield, S. (2014) Research Data Management and Libraries: current activities and future priorities, *Journal of Librarianship and Information Science*, **46** (4), 299-316.

Cox, A. M., Kennan, M. A., Lyon, L. and Pinfield, S. (2017) Developments in Research Data Management in Academic Libraries: towards an understanding of research data service maturity, *Journal of the Association for Information Science and Technology*, doi:10.1002/asi.23781.

Cribb, G. and Hogan, C. (2003) *Balanced Scorecard: linking strategic planning to measurement and communication*, paper presented at the 24th Annual IATUL Conference, Ankara, Turkey, 2-5 June 2003.

Cullen, R. (1998) *Measure for Measure: a post modern critique of performance measurement in libraries and information services*, paper presented at the International Association of Technological University Libraries, Pretoria, South Africa, 1-5 June 1998, www.eric.ed.gov/PDFS/ED434664.pdf.

Daneshgar, F. and Parirokh, M. (2007) A Knowledge Schema for Organizational Learning in Academic Libraries, *Knowledge Management Research and Practice*, **5** (1), 22-33.

Davies, A., Kirkpatrick, I. and Oliver, N. (1992) The Organizational Culture of an Academic Library: implications for library strategy, *British Journal of Academic Librarianship*, **7** (2), 69-89.

DePew, J. N. (1975) An Acquisitions Decision Model for Academic Libraries, *Journal of the American Society for Information Science*, July-August, 237-46.

Diekema, A. R., Wesolek, A. and Walters, C. D. (2014) The NSF/NIH Effect: surveying the effect of data management requirements on faculty, sponsored programs, and institutional repositories, *Journal of Academic Librarianship*, **40** (3), 322-31.

Ehrlich, K. and Cash, D. (1999) The Invisible World of Intermediaries: a cautionary tale, *Computer Supported Cooperative Work*, **8** (1-2), 147-67.

Emery, J. and Stone, G. (2014) The Sound of the Crowd: using social media to develop best practices for open access workflows for academic librarians (OAWAL), *Collaborative Librarianship*, **6** (3), 104-11.

Guise, J. L. (2005) Toward a Template for Systematic Reference and Instruction Programme Analysis, *New Library World*, **106** (1-2), 29-42.

Hampson, C. (2014) The Adoption of Open Access Funds among Canadian Academic Research Libraries, *Partnership: The Canadian Journal of Library & Information Practice & Research*, **9** (2), 1-14.

Havey, M. (2005) *Essential Business Process Modelling*, O'Reilly.

Hepworth, M. (2000) Approaches to Providing Information Literacy Training in Higher Education: challenges for librarians, *New Review of Academic Librarianship*, **6** (1), 21-34.

Horava, T. and Levine-Clark, M. (2016) Current Trends in Collection Development Practices and Policies, *Collection Building*, **35** (4), 97-102.

Houlihan, R. (2005) The Academic Library as Congenial Space: more on the St Mary's experience, *New Library World*, **106** (1-2), 7-15.

Hurst, S. (2017) University Libraries. In Bowman, J. H. (ed.), *British Librarianship and Information Work 2011-2015*, published by the editor, via www.lulu.com.

Huvila, I. (2006) *The Ecology of Information Work - a case study of bridging archaeological work and virtual reality based knowledge organization*, PhD thesis, Åbo Akademi University Press, https://ils.unc.edu/~wildem/ASIST2007/Huvila_dissertation.pdf.

Huvila, I. (2008) Work and Work Roles: a context of tasks, *Journal of Documentation*, **64** (6), 797-815.

Johnson, E. D. (1970) *History of Libraries in the Western World*, Scarecrow.

Joint Funding Council's Libraries Review Group (1993) *The Follett Report*, www.ukoln.ac.uk/services/papers/follett/report/.

Kennedy, M. R. (2005) Reformatting Preservation Departments: the effect of digitization on workload and staff, *College and Research Libraries*, **66** (6), 543-51.

Kettunen, J. (2007) The Strategic Evaluation of Academic Libraries, *Library Hi-Tech*, **25** (3), 409-21.

Koltay, T. (2016) Data Governance, Data Literacy and the Management of Data Quality, *IFLA Journal*, **42** (4), 303-12.

Kruse, F. and Thestrup, J. B. (2014) Research Libraries' New Role in Research Data Management: current trends and visions in Denmark, *Liber Quarterly: the Journal of European Research Libraries*, **23** (4), 310-35.

Kulp, C. and Rupp-Serrano, K. (2005) Organizational Approaches to Electronic Resource Acquisitions: decision-making models in libraries, *Collection Management*, **30** (4), 3-29.

Kyrillidou, M. (2010) The ARL Library Scorecard Pilot: using the Balanced Scorecard in research libraries, *Research Library Issues* (271), 36-40.

Lakos, A. (2007) Evidence-based Library Management: the leadership challenge, *Portal: Libraries and the Academy*, **7** (4), 431-50.

Lancaster, F. W. and Cleverdon, C. W. (1977) *Evaluation and Scientific Management of Libraries and Information Centres*, Vol. 18, Noordhoff.

Law, D. (1997) National Library Initiatives: the UK higher education experience, *Journal of Academic Librarianship*, **23** (2), 127-31.

Lewis, D. W. (2007) A Strategy for Academic Libraries in the First Quarter of the 21st Century, *College & Research Libraries*, **68** (5), 418-34.

Lewis, N. (2001) Redefining Roles: developing an electronic journals collection at the University of East Anglia, *Information Services and Use*, **21** (3-4), 181-7.

Lin, F-R., Yang, M-C. and Pai, Y-H. (2002) A Generic Structure for Business Process Modelling, *Business Process Management Journal*, **8** (1), 19-41.

Liu, K., Alderson, A. and Qureshi, Z. (1999) *Requirements Recovery from Legacy Systems by Analyzing and Modelling Behaviour*, paper presented at the 15th IEEE International Conference on Software Maintenance, Oxford, England, 30 August - 3 September 1999.

Lyon, L. (2016) Librarians in the Lab: toward radically re-engineering data curation services at the research coalface. *New Review of Academic Librarianship*, **22** (4), 391-409.

Mattern, E., Jeng, W., He, D., Lyon, L. and Brenner, A. (2015) Using Participatory Design and Visual Narrative Inquiry to Investigate Researchers' Data Challenges and Recommendations for Library Research Data Services, *Program: electronic library and information systems*, **49** (4), 408-23.

McKiernan, G. and Ohler, L. A. (2006) The Keys to Successful Change Management for Serials, *The Serials Librarian*, **51** (1), 37-72.

McKnight, S. and Austin, K. (2008) *Customer Value Discovery for the Not-for-Profit Sector*, http://irep.ntu.ac.uk/15805/.

McKnight, S. and Livingston, H. (2003) *So What Do Customer Value Propositions and Strategic Planning Have to do with Teaching and Learning?*, paper presented at EDUCAUSE in Australasia 03: Expanding the Learning Community, Meeting the Challenges, Adelaide, Australia, 6–9 May 2003.

National Student Survey (2016) About the NSS, www.thestudentsurvey.com/about.php.

Ng, I. (2015) University and the Internet of Things, blog, University of Warwick, www.wmgshapingthefuture.co.uk/the-university-and-the-iot/.

Norton, D. and Daum, J. H. (1999) *SAP Strategic Enterprise Management: translating strategy into action; the Balanced Scorecard*, brochure, SAP AG, www.juergendaum.com/news/sap_sem_wp_bsc.pdf.

Odeh, M., Beeson, I., Green, S. and Sá, J. (2003) *Modeling Processes Using RAD and UML Activity Diagrams: an Exploratory Study*, paper presented at the 3rd International Arab Conference on Information Technology, ACIT2002, Doha, Qatar, 16–19 December 2003.

Opdahl, A. L. and Sindre, G. (1995) *Representing Real World Processes*, paper presented at the 28th Hawaii International Conference on System Sciences, HICSS'95, Hawaii, IEEE Computer Society.

Ould, M. (2005) *Business Process Management: a rigorous approach*, British Computer Society.

Owusu-Ansah, E. K. (2001) The Academic Library in the Enterprise of Colleges and Universities: toward a new paradigm, *Journal of Academic Librarianship*, **27** (4), 282–94.

Parsons, A. (2010) Academic Liaison Librarianship: curatorial pedagogy or pedagogical curation, *Ariadne*, **65**.

Pinfield, S. (2001) The Changing Role of Subject Librarians in Academic Libraries, *Journal of Librarianship and Information Science*, **33** (1), 32–8.

Ranganathan, S. (1963) *The Five Laws of Library Science*, Asia Publishing House.

Rathe, B. and Blankenship, L. (2005) Recreational Reading Collections in Academic Libraries, *Collection Management*, **30** (2), 73–85.

Rau, E. P. (2007) Managing the Machine in the Stacks: operations research, bibliographic control and library computerization, 1950–2000, *Library History*, **23** (2), 151–68.

Reid, B. J. and Foster, W. (2000) *Achieving Cultural Change in Networked Libraries*, Gower.

Rowley, J. and Urquhart, C. (2007) Understanding Student Information

Behavior in Relation to Electronic Information Services: lessons from longitudinal monitoring and evaluation, part 1, *Journal of the Association for Information Science and Technology*, **58** (8), 1162-74.

Schwartzkopf, B. (2007) Old is New Again: using established workflows to handle electronic resources, *Serials Librarian*, **52** (3-4), 277-80.

SCONUL (2005) *E-learning Taskforce Final Report*, http://milunesco.unaoc.org/e-learning-taskforce-final-report/.

SCONUL (2015) SCONUL Summer Conference 2015 presentations, 6 July 2015, Southampton, www.sconul.ac.uk/news/sconul-summer-conference-2015-presentations.

SCONUL (2016) Guide to SCONUL, https://www.sconul.ac.uk/sites/default/files/documents/ Guide%20to%20SCONUL.pdf.

SCONUL Advisory Committee on Information Literacy (1999) *Information Skills in Higher Education*, www.sconul.ac.uk/sites/default/files/documents/Seven_pillars2.pdf.

Si, L., Xing, W., Zhuang, X., Hua, X. and Zhou, L. (2015) Investigation and Analysis of Research Data Services in University Libraries, *Electronic Library*, **33** (3), 417-49.

Stanford University (2005) Discussion on process changes. In *Stanford University Libraries Redesign Report*, http://web.stanford.edu/dept/SUL/library/prod/depts/ts/about/redesign/ report/sect10.html.

Streatfield, D. and Markless, S. (2008) Evaluating the Impact of Information Literacy in Higher Education: progress and prospects, *Libri*, **58**, 102-9.

Tenopir, C., Sandusky, R. J., Allard, S. and Birch, B. (2014) Research Data Management Services in Academic Research Libraries and Perceptions of Librarians, *Library & Information Science Research*, **36** (2), 84-90.

Tenopir, C., Talja, S., Horstmann, W., Late, E., Hughes, D., Pollock, D., Schmidt, B., Baird, L., Sandusky, R. and Allard, S. (2017) Research Data Services in European Academic Research Libraries, *Liber Quarterly*, **27** (1), 23-44.

Tinnilä, M. (1995) Strategic Perspective to Business Process Redesign, *Business Process Re-engineering and Management Journal*, **1** (1), 44-59.

Town, S. (2004) E-measures: comprehensive waste of time, *VINE: The Journal of Information and Knowledge Management Systems*, **34** (4), 190-5.

Town, S. (2011) Value, Impact, and the Transcendent Library: progress and pressures in performance measurement, *The Library Quarterly*, **81** (1), 111-25.

Tumbleson, B. E. (2016) Collaborating in Research: embedded librarianship in the learning management system, *Reference Librarian*, **57** (3), 224-34.

Urquhart, C. (2017) Principles and Practice in Impact Assessment for Academic Libraries, *Information and Learning Science*, in press.

Urquhart, C. and Rowley, J. (2007) Understanding Student Information Behavior in Relation to Electronic Information Services: lessons from longitudinal monitoring and evaluation, Part 2, *Journal of the Association for Information Science and Technology*, **58** (8), 1188-97.

Urquhart, C. and Tbaishat, D. (2016) Reflections of the Value and Impact of Information Services: part 3, towards an assessment culture, *Performance Management and Metrics*, **17** (1), 29-44.

Urquhart, C., Thomas, R., Lonsdale, R., Spink, S., Yeoman, A., Fenton, R. and Armstrong, C. (2003) Uptake and Use of Electronic Information Services: trends in UK higher education from the JUSTEIS project, *Program*, **37** (3), 168-80.

Veaner, B. A. (1990) *Academic Librarianship in a Transformational Age: program, politics and personnel*, G. K. Hall & Co.

Wilson, K. M. and Halpin, E. (2006) Convergence and Professional Identity in the Academic Library, *Journal of Librarianship and Information Science*, **38** (2), 79-91.

Zairi, M. and Sinclair, D. (1995) Business Process Re-engineering and Process Management: a survey of current practice and future trends in integrated management, *Business Process Re-engineering and Management Journal*, **1** (1), 8-30.

CHAPTER 7

Using Riva process modelling to study book acquisition in academic libraries

Dina Tbaishat

COMMENTARY: CHRISTINE URQUHART

This chapter uses the example of processes involved in book acquisitions to illustrate how Riva process modelling techniques for role activity diagrams are applied. As Chapter 5 demonstrated, there are other ways of looking at what is done in a set of activities that belong together to achieve some purpose. Chapter 5 examines use case descriptions and use case diagrams. Many readers will be familiar with simple flow diagrams where the diamonds indicate decision points. Flowcharts are perfectly effective, but for complicated situations many sheets are required. Many years ago, I remember an assignment received from a distance learning student working in a government department where the flowchart for the decision processes involved in deciding on the amount of money to be awarded to a claimant spread over many pages. The role activity diagramming, in contrast, is much neater and much easier for the analyst and members of staff involved in the roles presented to discuss. The decision points are clearly marked and, quite important, the activities that can take place in parallel are displayed.

The chapter outlines some of the business process modelling work that has taken place in libraries; it seems that there is little in the published literature. Research work suggests that the work is often done, but casually, and the work stored as flowcharts in desk drawers, or possibly attached to procedure manuals.

Perhaps such work is not deemed suitable for publication – just task-based guidelines that only apply, it is assumed, to one library and information service. Perhaps there is a feeling that it should not be possible to decompose professional work, that there is judgement and expertise involved that cannot be expressed in the black and white of an activity diagram or flowchart. The professional librarian's work at the enquiry desk cannot be reduced to the scripts followed by call centre staff. Or can it? While librarians and information professionals do not fall wholly into the professional groups that strictly control the acquisition and application of various kinds of knowledge, as information professionals we are known to vaunt expertise in information literacy, for example, or information retrieval (see Chapter 14, on searching for systematic reviews).

The practice of information architecture (Chapter 4) is a much younger professional practice and the body of required professional knowledge has not been agreed – and is changing rapidly, in any case. Librarians and information professionals have felt the need to demonstrate their value and impact for many years, and budgetary restraints in many libraries have forced a re-evaluation of roles, and what work can be outsourced (such as providing shelf-ready books, for example), as this can often be cheaper than doing the work in-house. Much of the outsourcing may have affected clerical and administrative tasks, and professionals have been busy enhancing the roles, learning new skills and expanding their knowledge and expertise. All professionals may be in for a shock, however, according to Susskind and Susskind (2015). The internet has enabled patients to access far more medical information than ever before, and while there are undoubtedly problems with ensuring that patients use proper evidence, not claims based on dubious data, medical expertise is to some extent available for anyone to use. I hardly need to mention what Google has done for information searching.

Susskind and Susskind (2015, 211) argue that professional work should be decomposed, broken down into its constituent tasks. Once decomposed, the challenge is then to identify the most efficient way of handling such tasks, retaining the quality of the work needed, the level of human interaction required, and how the decomposed tasks could be put together to make a coherent whole. That does not mean that we are constantly looking for ways of outsourcing tasks, or delegating some work to non-professionals, with less work for professionals (and therefore fewer professionals). The roles may change for professionals, who may take on different work (just as some information professionals have become information architects). In case you are still not convinced of the value of decomposing and analysing work tasks, perhaps you need to read page 266 of Susskind and Susskind (2015) where they list possible future roles and include process analysts, and also, incidentally, moderators of communities of practice – relevant to chapters 11 and 12.

References

Susskind, R. and Susskind, D. (2015) *The Future of the Professions: how technology will transform the work of human experts*, Oxford University Press.

7.1   Introduction

This chapter highlights changes in book acquisitions departments that have been taking place in academic libraries, and examines collection development activities. It considers examples of business process modelling in academic libraries, and focuses on modelling the process of electronic and print book acquisition in two UK university libraries using role activity diagram notation, part of the Riva method for business process modelling (Ould, 2005, see also Section 5.4). One university library was known for different ways of organising its activities. The analysis includes a third role activity diagram for the patron driven acquisition process, as a special type of acquisition. The detailed activities involved in the first two role activity diagrams were gathered from the acquisitions department staff in 2008 at both sites where the author conducted research for her PhD degree. The diagrams were shown to the staff for checking and for any necessary amendments. The third role activity diagram, which represents the patron driven acquisition process, was created recently by the author and then passed on to a member of staff in a UK academic library for comments. The role activity diagrams provided are followed by analysis of the diagrams, to reveal some potential problems, and indicate possible ways of improving processes.

As Chapter 6 emphasised, there have been many changes in roles and responsibilities for academic library staff; in this chapter examples show the techniques for role activity diagrams, not as exemplars of how book acquisitions should be operated. Chapter 4 emphasised the fluidity of roles and responsibilities in information architecture practice for large organisational websites, and fluidity is a feature of the roles and responsibilities of academic library staff. Developing a role activity diagram is a learning activity in itself, helping to show staff whether there are any gaps in procedures, necessary or unnecessary collaborations, or bottlenecks that need attention. The role activity diagram complements the process architecture diagram explained in Chapter 5. Both concern modelling processes, one a high-level view (process architecture diagram), the other looking at the detail (role activity diagram).

Section 7.2 introduces some of the changes in acquisitions, and Section 7.3 outlines changes in collection development and management. Section 7.4 discusses business process modelling in academic libraries, with two contrasting examples of book acquisitions, and a third example of an ideal patron driven acquisition process. Section 7.5 discusses how analysis of the role activity diagrams can help pinpoint possible improvements, and Section 7.6 draws conclusions.

7.2   Changes in acquisitions

The acquisitions department in academic libraries is considered one of the most fundamental and important units within the library, as it is mainly responsible for providing the library, and the academic organisation as a whole, with resources such as books and journals. Books and periodicals, in print or in electronic format, are considered a major source of exchanging information. Before 1990, the physical format predominated, but since then academic libraries moved to give priority to access rather than holdings, making resources available electronically. According to Kont (2015), acquisitions departments in academic libraries have been witnessing great changes that require them to make more effort to justify their costs to their parent organisations. Acquisitions departments are under pressure to find ways to change and streamline processes. For example, the 'collection management' team in one of the UK universities featured in this chapter was established in 2004, when the library realised that managing access to electronic resources had become a more complex process than in the past. New roles of staff in academic libraries were required to meet new responsibilities, and changes in the research and educational environment have strengthened the need for qualified library staff with a range of different skills, and required changes in roles.

The change in the nature of work in academic libraries is reflected in the changed position titles for librarians. In a content analysis of advertisements for jobs in some academic libraries in the USA over a 25-year period, Lynch and Smith (2001) noted the later inclusion of 'instruction' in the reference librarian job in the 1990s, and the emergence of combination jobs (which might also be the result of budget concerns). Pinfield (2001) noted that by the end of the 20th century, in the UK there was more emphasis on user liaison, involvement with e-resources and with learning management systems or virtual learning environments. Technical expertise became more important. Academic liaison library work continued to change (Parsons, 2010).

More recent changes, as explained in more detail in Chapter 6 (sections 6.2.1, 6.2.2), include developing possible roles and responsibilities for research data services, making changes in acquisitions (e.g. patron driven acquisition, demand drive acquisition), supporting new roles, and perhaps taking more responsibility for open access publishing instead of a passive role in repository management.

7.3   Collection development and management

'The concept of collection development is central to the professional practice of librarianship, since the whole notion of a library is fundamentally associated with the idea of a collection, to the extent that the words "library" and "collection" are almost synonymous' (Corrall, 2012, 3).

Change continues and academic libraries continue to seek better collection management methods. A recurrent theme has been the need for academic libraries to provide access to more content cost-effectively. Library users have grown to expect instant access to information, and a diverse range of information. The traditional inter-library loan (ILL) (Mortimore, 2005) operated reactively, with users identifying the material they required and making the request, and library staff processing the request, and then sending the item to the user.

Various ways of speeding up the processes of document delivery have been trialled, which include changes to make document delivery more active for the users. Carroll and Brink (2007) introduced the Infotrieve service to supply articles on demand to University of New Hampshire library users. Infotrieve included unlimited access to tables of contents, and allowed users to view article prices as they ordered them; this feature raised the awareness of information cost for users. The implementation of this service at University of New Hampshire library led to a drop in requests for new journals. This raised the challenge of deciding how to determine which service to use for document delivery: ILL or Infotrieve? The authors suggest that the optimal workflow would be to stream all requests to one librarian and allow that person to advise users which channel was most appropriate for the document they required.

Kont (2015) discussed some optimisation methods of the book acquisitions budget, such as co-operative acquisitions and patron driven acquisition, which has been operating in collection management for at least 15 years. Patron driven acquisition is a purchasing model partnering a library with an e-book platform. MARC records for the non-purchased records (or subset of these records) are loaded on to the library catalogue and usage is monitored in real time. Once a threshold level of usage is reached, a purchase or request for purchase is triggered. Sometimes rentals or short-term loans may be allowed. Most patron driven acquisition models vary according to the terms the library agrees with the e-book platform to trigger rental: short-term access or full purchase. These arrangements vary from one e-book supplier to another. In fact, sometimes purchasing on demand is not very efficient as the cost of maintaining the system can be very high and buying a package would be easier for staff and users (Chadwell, 2009).

Money can be an obstacle in times of economic downturn; it is likely that most academic libraries are unable to make separate funding available for patron driven acquisition, and Chadwell (2009) suggests that collection managers should carve out funding for patron driven acquisition from existing budgets to succeed in implementing this user-centred service.

Many collection managers in academic libraries have become aware of the concept of cost per use, which is the total cost of a resource (say a journal) divided by the number of times it is used. It is an indicator that can help collection managers take decisions about sustaining or cancelling resources. In 1997 a survey for Trent University Library was conducted to explore the cost per use for bound and microform serials to identify candidates for cancellation. This type of cost data helps collection development teams and relevant faculty staff decide whether to maintain a serial subscription or use document delivery (Scigliano, 2000).

Library staff are not necessarily always happy with changes happening within libraries. Lewis (2001) comments on user-driven acquisitions that such purchase models, like NetLibrary's patron driven acquisition model, pass the selection task to library users and can be frequently more effective than traditional ways of selection. However, since models such as these threaten to displace the traditional roles of librarians, the author notes there will be resistance to this change. Siddiqui (2003) believes that library staff resist change when they feel threatened by it; they yearn for stability when they face too much change. This certainly creates a challenge for library managers.

Feather (2007) states that electronic resources acquisitions and management is complex as communications in the workflow are numerous and need to be evaluated, hence improved, continuously. The author investigated workflow communications at Ohio State University libraries in order to use these communication methods effectively. The communication network was improved in many ways, for example by reducing the number of staff involved in certain workflow communications or updating online request forms.

A Jisc-funded project where library processes were investigated through modelling and then improved was the Huddersfield, Intota, KB+ Evaluation (HIKE) project, which examined how suitable Intota and KB+ are for the higher education marketplace and recommended improvements for both products, replacing the traditional library management system. To achieve that, detailed understanding of the issues arising from the workflow and processes must be acquired. This would allow further understanding of the new system, what it should embrace and what it must avoid. The project concentrated on acquisitions workflow including patron driven acquisition, which was considered 'fairly new' to the team (Devenney and Stone, 2013, 5). The report presented the existing workflows in Huddersfield, and then produced a number of ideal workflows such as electronic patron driven acquisition. The role activity diagram provided in this chapter to model the patron driven acquisition process is inspired by the HIKE report – an ideal workflow. The report suggests that little input is needed for this process. It stresses the need to remove the task of uploading and removing MARC records to the catalogue as it consumes too much time.

Electronic resources management systems in academic libraries have big deficiencies. In Collins and Grogg's (2011) survey of 66 academic librarians, it was found that workflow and communication management is ranked as the greatest cause of disappointment for library management. Other librarians criticised the management system workflow for its inability to be customised to their local processes. This problem existed in Duke University libraries in the transition from print to electronic resources, and at a time when most academic libraries struggled with the impact on workflows. Therefore, the Electronic Resources Workflow Analysis and Process Improvement Team (ERWAPIT) team was established at the Duke Libraries to set out the requirements and find out where existing workflows were failing, instead of just buying a new management system. This was achieved by documenting and analysing all existing e-resource workflows. The analysis results stressed the need for new products, not just a traditional management system, and Duke Libraries considered Microsoft SharePoint Designer, ImageNow and IBM products. IBM offered two systems that worked hand in hand: Blueworks Live and Business Process Manager. It was found that Blueworks Live and Business Process Manager suited the Duke Libraries the most as it could be configured to various levels of complexity (Dowdy and Raeford, 2014). There is an analysis of the work of the ERWAPIT team in Chapter 8.

7.4   Business process modelling in academic libraries

Business process modelling is the activity of representing organisational processes in an attempt to improve them. Rosemann (2006, 251) describes process modelling in an interesting way:

> Process modelling is an area where artists (heavy right brain utilisation) meet scientists (heavy left brain utilisation), internal knowledge workers meet external knowledge owners and business meets IT. It is not only about the final artefacts (the models), which represent the outcome of these modelling sessions, but it is the process of modelling itself and its impact on subsequent activities and projects, which deserves attention.

According to Lin, Yang and Pai (2002), a business process manager exists to play one of the following main roles: capturing existing organisational processes or evaluating their performance. This chapter explains both roles of business process modelling using role activity diagrams. Many initiatives in the literature considered organisational processes in an attempt to improve them. Davenport (1992) adopted the term process innovation to reflect not only the current design but also the radical change of a process.

Various software tools have emerged to support business process modelling and make it more feasible to define and create business models. Business process modelling has replaced the term workflow, which used to be more dominant (Havey, 2005). The scope of process models has broadened, and been implemented in many organisations. However, business process modelling has not been adopted as a practice in academic libraries; very little is published in the literature on academic library operations that examines how and why certain functions and processes are conducted or how academic libraries identify essential roles and processes. In a history of operations research in academic libraries, Liu, Alderson and Qureshi (1999) investigated the process of checking out a book in Staffordshire University Library; they used more than one method including role activity diagrams to model the process. Khan, Odeh and McClatchey (2006) used role activity diagrams to model the process of scientific publishing for digital libraries. Rau (2007) argues that with the expansion of scientific research after 1945, research libraries started to drown in information, which made skills and knowledge – developed by operations research practitioners – attractive to them. There was a need for more approaches to library operations and for management and control of information. Warwick (2008) used system dynamics – positive and negative feedback loops – as a modelling tool for part of a library system relating to loan and duplication policy: 'System dynamics is a methodology that is oriented towards explanation of system behaviour through an analysis of the feedback structure of the system' (2008, 37). However, it does not explore detailed activities in a process. Finally, the author has published some related work investigating business process modelling – specifically the Riva method – in academic libraries (Tbaishat, 2010, 2016; Urquhart and Tbaishat, 2016). Other work may be found in unpublished internal reports or brief items providing sketches for process redesign (Stanford University, 2005).

Open Access Workflows for Academic Librarians (OAWAL) is one of the newer initiatives that may support use of business process modelling in academic libraries. It discusses multiple business models for open access publishing through 'an openly accessible wiki or blog site for librarians working on the management of Open Access workflow within their given institutions' (Emery and Stone, 2014, 83).

The next section illustrates role activity diagrams for book acquisitions processes in two UK university libraries and introduces one role activity diagram for a patron driven acquisition process, as a special type of acquisitions. The latter is inspired by the ideal workflow suggested in the HIKE report (Devenney and Stone, 2013). As pointed out in the literature, little work considers any modelling such as role activity diagrams within the library environment. Role activity diagrams are part of the Riva method created by Ould (1995); they are concerned with individual processes. It is a visual and analytical method of representing the roles and sequence of activities in processes, as explained in Chapter 6.

7.4.1   Book acquisitions in UK Library A

The role activity diagram shown in Figure 7.1 shows the book acquisitions process in UK Library A. It includes both print and electronic versions of books. The roles participating in this process are:

- department representative: a person representing any of the teaching departments within the university
- acquisitions: responsible for material acquisitions for this UK university library, ordering all materials, whether books, journals or another format
- supplier: the book suppliers that this library deals with, whether online (e.g. Amazon.com) or print
- finance: deals with payments.

The process starts with the academics; they send requests of titles in different formats (e-mail, internal mail, etc.). The acquisitions team dates the request, checks if the title is already in the catalogue and if the details are correct. If there is a catalogue record, it is used, but if none is found they create a new one. Someone in the acquisitions team decides on the supplier – usually the cheapest of their regular suppliers. Figure 7.1 on the opposite page shows the different paths taken at decision points – e.g. if this, then the following activities occur, if that, another set of activities follows.

Another 'if statement' appears on the role activity diagram to check whether the order is an online or print order; if it is online, it is sent directly via the system to the supplier. If it is a print order, authorisation is needed from the assistant director and then the order is posted to the supplier. When books are received (whether only the URL for e-books or the physical books), invoices are created online. The total amount and a code are entered; the code tells the finance team from which budget the money should be taken. Paper invoices used to be coded on a code slip but now are coded with a stamp. A member of staff interviewed from the acquisitions team argued that the slips looked better and the rubber stamp does not necessarily stamp properly. Invoices are then double checked, signed and counted. There is a cut-off point of two years for receiving books.

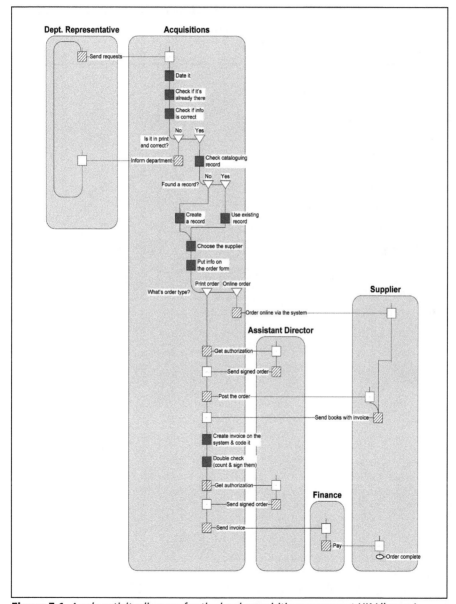

Figure 7.1 *A role activity diagram for the book acquisitions process at UK Library A*

7.4.2   Book acquisitions in UK Library B

The next role activity diagram (Figure 7.2) shows the book acquisitions process in UK Library B. The roles involved in this process are:

- academics: representing any teaching department within the university
- subject specialists: who liaise with academics to help choose the appropriate material for the library

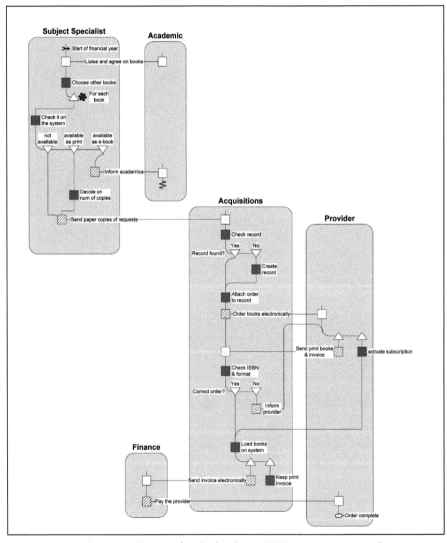

Figure 7.2 *A role activity diagram for the book acquisitions process at UK Library B*

- acquisitions: responsible for book acquisitions in the library
- provider: the book suppliers that the library deals with
- finance: deals with payments.

The process usually starts at the beginning of the financial year, in August, but books can be ordered throughout the year. Academics and subject specialists meet at the start of the financial year to decide what books to order. When a list of books is ready, the subject specialist checks their availability on the system. If the book is available electronically, the academic department is informed. If there are few copies available in print or the requested book is not available at all the subject specialist decides on the number of copies or extra copies needed.

When subject specialists choose books, they take into consideration any requests from students asking for extra copies of core texts. Subject specialist librarians liaise with academics; they take the reading lists and choose other books to order. When they send the paper copies of requests to the member of staff responsible for book ordering in acquisitions they make two things clear in the paper copy of the order: from which budget they wish to deduct the cost and how many copies are needed.

The subject specialists send paper copies of requests to acquisitions staff, who create a record if there is none on the system, and attach the order to the record. Books are then ordered electronically (whether a print or electronic copy). The provider activates the subscription and – at the same time – sends the books with their invoices (or just the invoice and the URL if the book is requested in electronic format). Note the use of concurrent paths in the role activity diagram, the facility of presenting activities performed in parallel (subscription activation with dispatch of books and invoices). The acquisitions team validates the order and loads books on the system. The concurrent paths appear again when acquisitions staff keep the print copy of the invoice and send an electronic one to the finance department staff, who process the payment.

This way the process is complete, but there are a few points associated with this process:

- When ordering books, there are no negotiations with providers; there is usually a fixed 20% discount.
- Secondhand or online orders (like those from Amazon) need credit card use, which any team leader must authorise. If the amount exceeds £10,000 it must be authorised by the assistant director.

- Payments are never processed in advance for books.
- After payment, books go to the classification department (if it is a first copy), or straight for processing if there are other copies on the shelves.
- Although orders (titles of books requested) are received by acquisitions in the form of print copies, orders from providers are processed electronically through Electronic Data Interchange.
- The member of staff in acquisitions who downloads a brief record or creates a new record is different from the person who receives the book and deals with the barcode later at the classification and cataloguing stage.
- The acquisition team in this library uses a simple process chart of their own to show the process of book acquisition; this demonstrates that there is some modelling of library processes – even though it is hidden from view.

7.4.3   The patron driven acquisitions process

Figure 7.3 shows the patron driven acquisition process. The roles and activities involved are inspired from the HIKE report (Devenney and Stone, 2013), where an ideal workflow was suggested for electronic patron driven acquisition.

Figure 7.4 (on page 122) shows the roles involved in the patron driven acquisition process:

- acquisitions: the acquisitions team in the library
- supplier: the book suppliers that the library deals with.

7.5   **Discussion**

Looking at book acquisitions processes in the two selected libraries, it is noticeable that both libraries struggled to integrate electronic resources into their workflow.

As mentioned in chapters 5 and 6, role activity diagrams reveal features and do not solve problems. They act as a searchlight, reveal problems and suggest potential ways of tackling them (Ould, 1995).

Comparing the models of role activity diagrams presented in book acquisition helps to reveal the following three types of improvement possible: flow-wise improvements, improvements by restructuring roles and realigning the organisation. They are listed according to the four different styles of improvements suggested by Ould (2005).

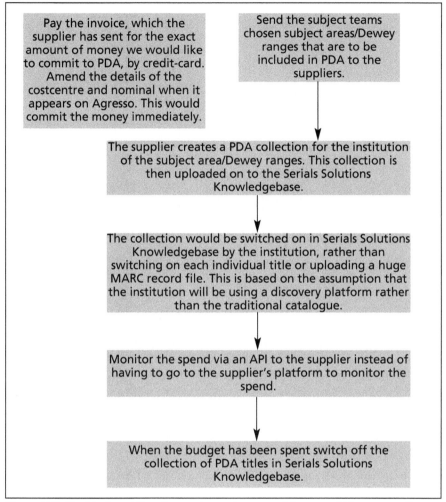

Figure 7.3 *The ideal workflow for an electronic patron driven acquisition process* (from Devenney and Stone, 2013)

7.5.1 Make flow-wise improvements

Does every purchase need to be authorised by the director? Note Figure 7.2, where the role 'director' does not exist. In Figure 7.1 however, it is necessary to get authorisation from the assistant director. This could lead to a bottleneck, which could be relieved if the need for obtaining approval was limited to those purchases above a certain value.

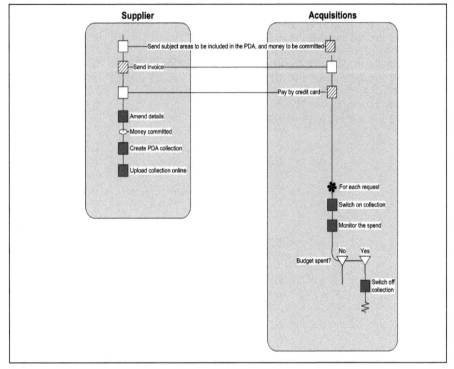

Figure 7.4 *A role activity diagram for the patron driven acquisition process*

7.5.2   Restructure roles

Reduce interactions. Note the paper work in Figure 7.1, where authorisation is needed twice from the library director. Interactions can be reduced between roles to speed up the process. This is an example of restructuring roles and what they do.

Review the work load of the different roles. There is a difference in work load between acquisitions in figures 7.1 and 7.2. The subject specialist in Figure 7.2 shared some activities and responsibilities in common with the role of department representative in Figure 7.1, but the subject specialist in Figure 7.2 seems to do more acquisition work – perhaps this simply reflects where the roles are based. But it is useful to question who is responsible for what, and consider whether some activities might be moved from one role to another. Note that in Figure 7.2, the library seems to have achieved some balance in activities between acquisitions and subject specialists.

7.5.3 Realign the organisation to the process

Add more activities within roles. Figure 7.1 does not show what happens if the ordered book was not correct. An 'if statement' is needed, just as in Figure 7.2. When drafting a role activity diagram, it is sometimes necessary to go back to the library staff and check what they actually do in some circumstances.

After analysing the diagrams extracted for possible process improvements, there are still some factors that affect the quantitative behaviour, or actual amount done, at particular times of the process (Ould, 1995):

- The number of staff carrying out activities affects the efficiency of the overall process. This can be seen in Figure 7.1, where acquisitions has a huge work load with a small number of staff, primarily one person, doing the job.
- Seasonal work is clearly represented in Figure 7.2, where book orders usually start when the financial year does.
- Economic and currency situation: budgeting is a crucial aspect of the book acquisitions process, particularly in times of economic uncertainty and fluctuating exchange rates.

7.6   Conclusions

Chapter 7 discussed the process of book acquisition in two UK academic libraries, to illustrate how role activity diagrams could be developed, and followed up by illustrating a possible patron driven acquisition process. The examples of role activity diagrams for book acquisitions showed how both libraries struggled to integrate electronic resources into their workflows. The role activity diagrams provided were used to visualise the processes and suggest possible process improvements derived from Ould's four process improvement types. The suggested improvements were threefold: flow-wise improvements such as saving time by removing unnecessary authorisation tasks; restructuring roles, for example reducing interactions and moving activities between roles to reduce the work load; and realigning the organisation to the process, such as by adding new activities.

Chapter 8 considers two different approaches to business process modelling in academic libraries, and examines the assumptions made by those involved. The Riva method, with a top-down process activity diagram (discussed in Chapter 5) and bottom-up role activity diagrams is comprehensive, although perhaps best used when complete restructuring is necessary, and the effort required would be worthwhile. Even if roles appear fluid (see Chapter 4, for example) modelling helps staff to ask questions and appreciate how their work fits within the organisation.

References

Carroll, J. and Brink, J. (2007) Changing the Access from Subscription to Article in the Academic Library: using Infotrieve as one of the solutions to the journal problem, *Collection Management*, **31** (3), 3-13.

Chadwell, F. A. (2009) What's Next for Collection Management and Managers? User-centred collection management, *Collection Management*, **34** (2), 69-78.

Collins, M. and Grogg, J. E. (2011) Building a Better ERMS, *Library Journal*, http://lj.libraryjournal.com/2011/03/digital-resources/building-a-better-erms/.

Corrall, S. (2012) The Concept of Collection Development in the Digital World. In Fieldhouse, M. and Marshall, A. (eds), *Collection Development in the Digital Age*, Facet Publishing, 3-25.

Davenport, T. H. (1992) *Process Innovation: reengineering work through technology*, Harvard Business School Press.

Devenney, A. and Stone, G. (2013) *HIKE Report: to evaluate the suitability of Intota and KB+ for the UK higher education marketplace*, University of Huddersfield, http://eprints.hud.ac.uk/17976/.

Dowdy, B. and Raeford, R. (2014) Electronic Resources Workflow: design, analysis and technologies for an overdue solution, *Serials Review*, **40** (3), 175-87, www.tandfonline.com/doi/pdf/10.1080/00987913.2014.950040.

Emery, J. and Stone, G. (2014) Introduction to OAWAL: open access workflows for academic librarians, *Serials Review*, **40** (2), 83-7, http://pdxscholar.library.pdx.edu/cgi/viewcontent.cgi?article=1156&context=ulib_fac.

Feather, C. (2007) Electronic Resources Communications Management: a strategy for success, *Association for Library Collections and Technical Services*, **51** (3), https://journals.ala.org/lrts/article/view/5158/6260.

Havey, M. (2005) *Essential Business Process Modelling*, O'Reilly.

Khan, Z. A., Odeh, M. and McClatchey, R. (2006) *Digital Libraries: from process modelling to grid-based service oriented architecture*, paper presented at the 2nd International Conference on Information and Communication Technologies from Theory to Application (ICTTA06), Damascus, Syria, 24-28 April 2006, http://arxiv.org/ftp/cs/papers/0602/0602082.pdf.

Kont, K. R. (2015) What do Acquisition Activities Really Cost? A case study in Estonian University Libraries, *Library Management*, **36** (6/7), 511-34.

Lewis, N. (2001) Redefining Roles: developing an electronic journals collection at the University of East Anglia, *Information Services and Use*, **21** (3-4), 181-7.

Lin, F.-R., Yang, M.-C. and Pai, Y.-H. (2002) A Generic Structure for Business Process Modelling, *Business Process Management Journal*, **8** (1), 19-41.

Liu, K., Alderson, A. and Qureshi, Z. (1999) *Requirements Recovery from Legacy Systems by Analyzing and Modelling Behaviour*, paper given at the 15th IEEE International Conference on Software Maintenance, Oxford, 30 August – 3 September 1999,
https://www.computer.org/csdl/proceedings/icsm/1999/0016/00/00160003.pdf.

Lynch, B. P. and Smith, K. R. (2001) The Changing Nature of Work in Academic Libraries, *College and Research Libraries*, **62** (5), 407-20.

Mortimore, J. M. (2005) Access-informed Collection Development and the Academic Library: using holdings, circulation, and ILL data to develop prescient collections, *Collection Management*, **30** (3), 21-37.

Ould, M. (1995) *Business Processes: modeling and analysis for re-engineering and improvement*, Wiley.

Ould, M. (2005) *Business Process Management: a rigorous approach*, The British Computer Society.

Parsons, A. (2010) Academic Liaison Librarianship: curatorial pedagogy or pedagogical curation, *Ariadne*, **65**, www.ariadne.ac.uk/issue65/parsons/.

Pinfield, S. (2001) The Changing Role of Subject Librarians in Academic Libraries, *Journal of Librarianship and Information Science*, **33** (1), 32-8, http://eprints.nottingham.ac.uk/33/3/jolis.pdf.

Rau, E. P. (2007) Managing the Machine in the Stacks: operations research, bibliographic control and library computerization, 1950-2000, *Library History*, **23** (2), 151-68.

Rosemann, M. (2006) Potential Pitfalls of Process Modeling, Part A, *Business Process Management*, **12** (2), 249-54.

Scigliano, M. (2000) Serial Use in a Small Academic Library: determining cost-effectiveness, *Serials Review*, **26** (1), 43-52.

Siddiqui, M. A. (2003) Management for Change in Acquisitions in Academic Libraries, *The Electronic Library*, **21** (4), 352-7.

Stanford University (2005) Discussion on process changes. In *Stanford University Libraries Redesign Report*, http://web.stanford.edu/dept/SUL/library/prod/depts/ts/about/redesign/report/sect10.html.

Tbaishat, D. (2010) Using Business Process Modeling to Examine Academic Library Activities for Periodicals, *Library Management*, **31** (7), 480.

Tbaishat, D. (2016) *Business Process Modelling Using Riva and ARIS, Part 1: process architecture development: comparative study*, paper given at the 21st UK Academy of Information Systems (UKAIS) Conference on Information Systems Comes of Age, Oxford, 12-13 April 2016.

Urquhart, C. and Tbaishat, D. (2016) Reflections on the Value and Impact of Library and Information Services, Part 3: towards an assessment culture, *Performance Measurement and Metrics*, **17** (1), 29-44.

Warwick, J. (2008) Modelling the Demand for Learning Resources in Academic Libraries, *Library and Information Research*, **32** (101), 23-38.

CHAPTER 8

Workflow analysis and process mapping in US academic libraries

Christine Urquhart

COMMENTARY: DINA TBAISHAT

This chapter investigates systems analysis, focusing on the workflow for processes and process mapping. Although there is a lot written on the need to change academic libraries, there is little published analytical research that investigates processes and how such investigations can lead to recommended improvements. When measuring library performance, the emphasis is more on outcomes and outputs (what is done) rather than internal processes (how things are done). However, it is important to understand both processes and roles in academic libraries, especially now when roles are changing and more intertwined. Processes are possibly more interdependent than they were, so it is necessary to focus on identification and analysis of discrete processes and responsible staff roles involved.

The chapter compares workflow analysis and process mapping in detail, following a well structured development of ideas. It starts by summarising two studies and then compares four aspects of them: aims and objectives, methods, analysis methods and findings. This comparative analysis study adds value to the field of systems analysis, specifically in librarianship, as managing change and embedding innovation is a key theme in academic libraries. It is important to identify gaps between current work (reality) and future intentions as stated in aims or strategies, as any mismatches indicate required improvements. This can be achieved by modelling processes that demonstrate the workflows, and discussing the findings with staff.

The framework adopted for comparison uses a 'rich picture' method to define stakeholders, their interrelationships and their concerns. This views a problem situation and provides a basis for analysis to reveal problems in some processes or communications. The framework included the job satisfaction fit areas identified by Mumford (1995), along with the type of participation (consultative, representative or consensual). The elements used in the framework helped express the problem situation and how communications were managed, according to the two studies under comparison.

This chapter relates to Chapter 5, which provides a detailed illustration of library processes in the form of a process architecture diagram, and Chapter 7, which presents a role activity diagram to model the book acquisitions process as an example of seeking process improvements. The part of the framework used for comparison, embracing Checkland's soft systems methodology, supports proper definition of the problem through analysis of the 'rich picture', and deriving the root definition for the relevant system using the mnemonic CATWOE (customers, actors, transformation process, world view, owner, environmental constraints). The process architecture diagram provided in Chapter 5 and the 'rich picture' tool in soft systems methodology (used here) have some things in common: representation of work context; revealing problems, since they should both act as a searchlight for missing, contradictory or unnecessary repetitive elements (communications and data); and organising and reasoning about the information provided. However, the process architecture diagram focuses on the interrelationship between existing processes; CATWOE and soft systems methodology are more of an enquiry tool.

When discussing business processes, Ould (2005, 11) refers to three types of processes. These can loosely be referred to as the set of activities to get a task done; a process that monitors, reports and prioritises that set of activities; and another process that takes a strategic view of the set of activities around a task. To set up workflows it is probably not enough to rely on the basic process mapping, as there will be ongoing development and refinement, and changes in other related processes will have an impact on an existing process. Process mapping does not stop once the workflows have been mapped, problems identified and changes made. There has to be an infrastructure to ensure that the workflows and processes remain relevant.

References

Mumford, E. (1995) *Effective Systems Design and Requirements Analysis: the ETHICS approach*, Macmillan Press.

Ould, M. A. (2005) *Business Process Management: a rigorous approach*, British Computer Society.

8.1 Introduction

This chapter compares and contrasts two different applications of process analysis techniques to resolve management problems in two US academic libraries. The first study, at Duke University (Dowdy and Raeford, 2014), examined the problems of electronic resources management and aimed to improve workflows by using business process management software. The second study, at the University of Michigan (Barbrow and Hartline, 2015), used process mapping to help embed a culture of organisational assessment at the University of Michigan library.

The two studies represent different aspects of systems thinking around information systems. The study by Dowdy and Raeford (2014) emphasises the use of a technical solution to a recognised problem, or rather set of problems, with the management of electronic resources. Their approach could be described as socio-technical, as one of the aims of the workflow analysis was to improve communication among the staff, and help staff do their jobs better. The existing electronic resources management system had not worked well, but the library staff decided that simply replacing one electronic resources management solution with another was not necessarily the solution. The problems required a more holistic approach, one that required an analysis of how the work of managing electronic resources was (or was not) achieved. The published paper describes how a team drawn from across the library, not just those involved in technical services, set about documenting and analysing the workflows associated with e-resources. The study by Barbrow and Hartline (2015) could also be described as socio-technical, as one of the aims of the exercise was to improve library processes, and capture expertise of existing members of staff. However, there is a much stronger emphasis on participative processes by Barbrow and Hartline, as the aim was to empower staff with process mapping skills, to enable staff to recognise where improvements would be made, thus supporting an organisational culture that recognised the importance of questioning existing practice, analysing existing practice and recommending improvements. Process mapping often goes hand in hand with job redesign, or at least that is how process mapping can be seen by staff. In many ways, the approach by Barbrow and Hartline echoes the early work of Enid Mumford on job design in information systems development. Mumford (1995) discusses the various fits that should exist in an employee's job, e.g. to allow staff to use and extend their knowledge and skills (knowledge fit), to allow for some task differentiation and job interest (task structure fit).

The framework used to compare and contrast these studies therefore focuses on the people involved, the staff in the library and the 'customers', those accessing and using the information services provided as well as the processes, and their description.

Chapter 1 alluded to the ways in which technology changes the work of the professions, and chapters 5–7 explained some of the technicalities of business process analysis and systems analysis thinking. Chapter 8 looks more closely at the human side of such analyses.

The next section, Section 8.2, briefly reviews the literature of related studies, and Section 8.3 then outlines the framework used for comparison of the two studies considered in detail. Section 8.4 summarises both studies. Section 8.5 compares aims and objectives of both studies, Section 8.6 compares the methods, Section 8.7 compares the analysis, and Section 8.8 evaluates the findings. Section 8.9 considers what the framework comparison reveals, and Section 8.10 draws conclusions.

8.2   Background

Management of e-resources has become a challenge for many academic libraries, but hopes of a commercial solution in the form of an electronic resources management system are often dashed. Commercial systems may be expensive, time-consuming to set up and do not seem to reflect the workflows of many academic libraries. After carrying out a survey, Collins and Grogg (2011) noted that data maintenance became a headache, and in fact the systems required additional staffing, rather than making the processes of electronic resources management more efficient and effective. Feather (2007) conducted an informal audit of communications associated with e-resources management at Ohio State University, examining inward and outward communications for two months for the e-resources management staff. She classified four types of communication: darts (tasks to be done), lobs (complex communication that bounces between individuals for information and decision making), shadows (archived information and informal information stored to memory) and spotlights (one-way communication from the unit staff to the outside world). Feather noted, 'Informal conversation, which in many ways is the communication channel that maintains the teamwork spirit and cohesiveness of the unit, often spreads knowledge about resources and operations that is never recorded outside human memory.' Workflow analysis needs, ideally, to capture how that knowledge is generated, maintained and updated. Unfortunately, many business process mapping techniques are not equipped to do that. See also discussions in chapter 5 (process architecture) and chapter 7 (on process mapping).

A review of workflow analysis for electronic resources management (Anderson, 2014) notes the different strategic approaches taken by libraries, based on their attitude to e-resources management (replacing print, purchased versus subscribed resources, user oriented with emphasis on a type of acquisition). The review concludes that good communication with staff is vital, particularly as problematic situations and transitions need to be identified. The review refers to two major reports, the Digital Library Federation Electronic Resource Management Initiative (DLF ERMI) report (Jewell et al., 2004) and the Techniques for Electronic Resource Management (TERMS) project report (Pesch, 2008). The electronic resources management system solution needs to fit the library, and Anderson (2014) stresses that workflow analysis should help identify whether there is a suitable electronic resources management system available or not.

Good relations with staff seem essential for the smooth implementation of any information system and McKinnon (2016) emphasises that communication between the electronic resources team and the frontline staff also needs to be good to ensure that problems are identified quickly and solutions found. McKinnon examined how frontline staff at McGill University behaved, in particular how errors (including queries) were reported and how the responses from the collections team were perceived. Such error reporting should be included in the workflow analysis, as such processes are part of the ongoing monitoring of the business processes, and providing support is as much a business process as acquisition and dealing with licences.

8.3   Framework for comparison

Many different methodologies may be used for information systems development, which could be adapted to create a framework for comparing the two studies, and learning from the comparison. The notable effects on staff working directly or indirectly with electronic resources of any changes made in academic library working patterns suggest that methodologies focused on people or organisational effects should provide the most appropriate assistance. Accordingly, the framework uses elements from ETHICS (Mumford, 1995) and soft systems methodology (Checkland, 1981) to help compare the ways in which the problem situation was defined and expressed, and how relations with staff were managed, based on the information provided in the papers.

The job satisfaction fit areas identified by Mumford (and derived from earlier work on a theory of action) are the knowledge fit (recognising that employees have different expectations of competence gains), the psychological fit (general work interest), efficiency fit (including work and supervisory controls), task structure fit (how demanding and fulfilling the tasks are) and ethical fit (whether values of the employee match those of the employer organisation) (Avison and Fitzgerald, 2003, 450). Mumford also examined the type of participation (consultative, representative or consensual).

Checkland's methodology examines a problem situation from as many people's perspectives as possible, and usually includes a 'rich picture', a visual representation of what is involved, to help people talk about the situation. The problem solver and the problem owner need to discuss which viewpoint on the problem situation yields the most relevant system. A root definition is derived for the relevant system using the mnemonic CATWOE - customers, actors, transformation, world view (assumptions), owner, environment.

The framework for comparing the two studies therefore examines and asks the following questions:

● Which of the job fit satisfaction areas were included (and which appear to be omitted)?
● What type of participation process was used?
● How was the problem expressed, and can a root definition be obtained?

Table 8.1 shows the framework in more detail with the questions asked by Mumford (1995) and Checkland (1981).

Table 8.1 *Framework for comparing the process mapping and workflow analysis of Mumford (1995) and Checkland (1981)*

Source	Question	Notes
Mumford (1995)	Knowledge fit?	Some staff aspire to gain greater competence, others do not. Are these differences recognised?
	Psychological fit?	How might an improved system change work to be more interesting (or less interesting) for staff?
	Efficiency fit?	How is the work organised and how are staff supervised?
	Task structure fit?	How demanding and fulfilling are the work tasks for individual members of staff?
	Ethical fit?	Are the values of individual members of staff likely to vary from the values of the organisation?
	What type of participation process was used?	Were views of staff taken into account (consultative)? Were representatives of different staff groups invited to take part (representative)? Were staff actively involved in discussions about the possible changes (consensual)?
Checkland (1981)	How was the problem situation expressed? Whose viewpoints are important?	Is the problem represented as one shared by different stakeholders? Why are some viewpoints more important than others? Is the approach to problem analysis narrowly focused or do the researchers look widely – take a 'rich picture' approach?
	What is the root definition of the system or service?	What is the system or service for? Who is operating it and for whom? What are the basic assumptions? Who owns the system? What are the environmental constraints?

8.4   Summaries

This section summarises the aims and objectives of both projects, the methods used, findings and the conclusions.

The aims and objectives of the project at Duke University (Dowdy and Raeford, 2014) were to improve the effectiveness and efficiency of processes to manage electronic resources. The methods used included formation of a cross-library team that was responsible for the documentation and analysis of all existing e-resource workflows. The team developed a staff responsibility matrix, conducted interviews with staff and then completed workflow diagrams that were analysed to identify weak points. Then they reviewed IT solutions to workflow and data management. The findings of the workflow analysis showed there was ineffective communication (around use of e-mail and human memory), inaccessible information about e-resources, and poor standards (resulting in lost information and duplication). The review of IT solutions found that a combination of IBM Blueworks Live (a collaborative browser-based environment for generating workflows) feeding into IBM's Business Process Manager platform should resolve the workflow problems and the platform SharePoint could be used for document storage.

The aims and objectives of the project at the University of Michigan (Barbrow and Hartline, 2015) were to instil a culture of organisational assessment through providing training and support for process mapping. The methods used were workshops for staff (short introductory session with later more intensive sessions – boot camps). Most participants at the introductory workshops were able to apply the basics of process mapping they had learnt to practise. The Special Collections Library staff were the first team to carry out the more intensive training, with more emphasis on how maps were created than training in Microsoft Visio skills. The workshops appeared to encourage a greater shared understanding of processes, workflows and potential breakdowns.

8.5   Comparison of aims and objectives

Dowdy and Raeford (2014) detail many of the problems with the management of e-resources at Duke University. The LibQual survey of 2011 placed information control, responsible for e-resources and their access, last among all sections of library services for satisfaction and many primary users judged the e-resource services unacceptable. The primary aim was to take control of the processes as there was uncertainty among staff over the complicated workflow, duplication of work, no sense of cohesion or transparency, and reactive troubleshooting. The objectives concerned depiction and analysis of the existing workflows, and review of solutions.

Barbrow and Hartline (2015) are more concerned with the process mapping technique, and how process mapping can help staff be more aware of possible improvements that can be made to the way library services operate. The objectives concern the development and evaluation of training workshops.

On job satisfaction fit, Dowdy and Raeford (2014) seem primarily concerned with the efficiency fit (work controls and supervisory controls) and the knowledge fit (whether skills of staff are adequately used). Depending on the solution finally chosen, there might be task structure fit questions to be answered – how much autonomy will a staff member have, and how demanding and fulfilling will the new tasks for a revised workflow be? In setting out the initial aims and objectives, the participation process appears to have been consultative. The working root definition at the outset could be 'an e-resources management system operated by library services to provide e-resources to students and faculty promptly, without errors in access, in a setting where demand is likely to increase'.

Barbrow and Hartline (2015) are concerned with different types of fit: the social value fit (match between the values of the employee and that of the library) and the knowledge fit (assuming, however, that all staff are interested in increasing skills in process mapping). The aim was consensual participation, at least for the introductory workshop, to involve as many staff as possible. The working root definition is a little more difficult to derive, as the study is more about the preliminary training to support a culture of organisational assessment, rather than a system itself. Perhaps the working root definition for a system supporting a library assessment culture would be 'activities performed by staff to suggest and support improvements in the operation of library services to benefit all library users'. If the viewpoint for the relevant system only refers to the training, then the root definition would be 'a training programme by library staff for library staff on process mapping to help staff initiate improvements in library operations'.

8.6   Comparison of methods

Dowdy and Raeford (2014) used document analysis of existing evaluation reports, and reviewed the published literature on electronic resources management systems. An electronic resources workflow analysis and process improvement team was formed from experts across the library (representative participation) and tasked with documenting and analysing all existing workflows. A staff responsibility matrix was derived to guide the interviews and 40 staff interviewed (representative participation). The guiding principle for the interviews was that they should be consensual, as a supervisor could not interview someone who reported directly to them and no judgements were made over how well a member of staff did their job. Although some details about the knowledge fit must have been apparent in the interviews, the original emphasis seems to be on the efficiency fit. The authors comment that the interviews were 'laborious but necessary'; certainly process documentation for in-depth analysis requires care, as well as consideration for the staff involved.

Barbrow and Hartline (2015) reviewed the literature on process mapping and process improvements and concluded that attention to processes was vital, and that staff had to be included in process mapping before designing process improvement. They therefore took a staged approach to the training programme, with a short introductory workshop before providing a longer one. The short workshop was apparently consensual in approach, as the workshop was short. The title was changed to make it more attractive (a better ethical job satisfaction fit for this group), and activities were participative and consensual, with an emphasis on group work and discussion. The longer boot camp for the Special Collections Library included diverse viewpoints, possibly more by chance than by design, but the authors confirm that varied viewpoints and experience helped them to question some of the assumptions some of the participants might have had. The boot camp was consensual in approach. A colour coded dot system made it possible to identify areas of breakdown in processes, sub-processes that were out of scope, opportunities to improve, areas where consultations with other stakeholders were required, and 'parking lots' where disagreements were parked until there was a time to return for further discussions. In the fourth session the draft workflow was discussed with the participants, and there was an opportunity to reflect on some of the 'parking lots'.

8.7   Comparison of analysis methods

The first objective of the team in Dowdy and Raeford (2014) was drawing the workflow diagrams, and then analysing these diagrams to identify weak points (no definitions are provided in the paper of what a weak point might be), whether the workflow was logical and whether some tasks could be automated or moved. The staff in this library were overwhelmed by the existing workload and the automation of some tasks might be welcomed, but some staff are likely to be concerned that if there is a technical solution to their tasks they will no longer be required. Moving a task to a different workflow may also affect psychological job fit satisfaction, if some staff believe that their status or motivation will be affected, and the task structure fit should, ideally, remain fulfilling, with some control for staff over the tasks involved. The authors do not mention whether they checked back with the interviewees, as they might have done for a consensual approach. The approach seems consultative, with the data from the interviewees used to reach conclusions about the main problems with the e-resource management workflows. Once those problems were identified, the team sought solutions, but not from existing library vendors of electronic resources management systems. They appear to have used the following main criteria: ability to design and manage more complicated workflows, required expertise to support the system, and ability to tackle the main problems with e-mail and knowledge sharing. Clearly there seems to have been a basic problem with the knowledge fit job satisfaction, and what some, though not all, staff may have expected to learn and share with others.

The analysis task for Barbrow and Hartline (2015) was the evaluation of the introductory workshops identifying what had worked well, what staff had valued about their learning, and how staff applied the knowledge acquired. The results of the evaluation helped in planning the later and longer sessions that had been part of the original programme plans. A group that wished to apply for a longer training or set of sessions (boot camp) filled in an application form that encouraged the group to take responsibility for what they wanted to learn, and the group chose a team captain who dealt with the communication with the workshop facilitators. This very neatly emphasised the original aim of empowerment and saved the time of the facilitators, and was an example of consensual participation. The authors note that they could have trained the team involved in the boot camp in Visio, but this would have required extra time and the sessions therefore focused on the process mapping, generating the map through teamwork and discussions. The facilitators themselves produced the Visio map that was used in later sections, to help refine and clarify the workflow.

8.8   Comparison of findings and conclusions

The Duke University team reviewed the options for a business process management system and decided that an IBM-based solution should provide most of the answers to the problems (Dowdy and Raeford, 2014). The IBM solution consisted of Blueworks Live, a collaborative, browser-based environment that allows teams to generate workflows and add documents. Activity boxes may be moved, rearranged, stacked and grouped. Once a draft workflow has been created the system offers multiple views of the workflow.

The mapping view shows potential problems, as the process is documented. After a map has been created and an initial analysis made, the process diagram is generated. All the work may be imported into IBM's Business Process Manager. This management platform provides the tools and a runtime environment for process design, monitoring and optimisation. IBM Business Process Manager could integrate with other systems, a useful feature. An important aspect of the platform was its transparency, so that staff could see where any particular e-resource was and collaborate through the social tools provided. There were good reporting features that allowed identification of bottlenecks and addition of metrics to assess efficiency. The Duke team added SharePoint for document storage. Implementation required a thorough understanding of how the various tools worked, and how the inclusion of documentation equated to programming specifications that dictate how the process will work. There was much liaison between an IBM team and Duke University library staff to ensure the set-up worked well. For example, both sides worked on a Quick Win Pilot on the database workflow, the least complicated workflow, to ensure that the 'To Be' or future workflow would work in Business Process Manager. The authors describe how a database trial would be initiated at a suitable time, with the checklist of tasks to be completed by the trial manager, and how the purchasing (or not) decision would proceed.

The authors conclude that finding solutions to the problems was not easy. 'Looking at the dirty laundry', as they term the analysis, was not pleasant but necessary to develop a holistic view of the situation, and identify appropriate solutions. It appears that representative participation by staff in discussing the framework helped provide a solution that will allow for later consensual participation from all staff in the ongoing development of the system. It is interesting that at several points during the paper the authors stress the importance of staff understanding the big picture. This emphasis reflects the soft systems methodology use of 'rich pictures' to explain the different perspectives and how the pieces fit together. Libraries have often operated in functional silos but the introduction of e-resources has forced a change of perspective.

The final root definition comes after reviewing the analysis, discussion of the 'rich picture' and the CATWOE. Here the final root definition of the business process management arrangements could be phrased as 'a system for electronic resource management workflows that makes for prompt access for library users and that allows staff to track e-resources, to design, monitor and suggest amendments to workflows, with appropriate integration into other library management systems, in the expectation that e-resource management requirements such as licensing, and user demands, will increase in the future'. The earlier root definition, based on the text in the paper, was 'an e-resources management system operated by library services to provide e-resources to students and faculty promptly, without errors in access, in a setting where demand is likely to increase'. As the development work progressed, the need to integrate with other library systems and the data storage provided by SharePoint became apparent. At first, the participation was partly consultative, partly representative, but it seems that consensual participation by staff (as long as they are trained to use the business process management systems) is possible for future refinements of the workflows.

Barbrow and Hartline (2015) note that the basic two-hour workshop on process mapping was sufficient for some staff to begin creating process maps that were discussed with colleagues, including those in other library departments that shared part of a process, or were 'customers' of a process in another department. Even these small steps could help instil a mindset of possible process improvement, sharing knowledge and improving communication. The results of the boot camp with the Special Collections team were many workflow improvements that included movements of responsibility for particular actions and an assessment of the 'gifts-in-kind' process that improved communications between the recipient departments and the development officer. The authors base their conclusions on their lessons learned during the various workshops: training and documentation should emphasise processes, so that library tasks and their contribution to a process may be appreciated better. They suggest that a shared understanding of the current process should precede attempts at assessment, gap analysis and process improvement. Process improvement is a distinct step, after process mapping. The visual product is valuable, although process understanding is more important than learning how a tool such as Visio works. The revised root definition for a process mapping training programme might be: 'a programme with staged training options that allows library staff to acquire and apply process mapping to their own work tasks, and that permits groups of staff to produce maps that are the basis for discussing improvements, to enhance an organisational assessment culture'. The earlier root definition did not make the distinction between the process mapping step and the later steps to discuss process improvement, but these are distinct and will require different levels of management support and infrastructure to sustain process improvement. Barbrow and Hartline started off with a very consensual approach to participation, but to implement process improvement a management structure is necessary, and that is likely to require representative participation (to ensure improvements appear fair to different stakeholders) and consultative participation with library users and senior university management.

8.9   Discussion

Both Barbrow and Hartline (2015) and Dowdy and Raeford (2014) confirm the conclusions of the review by Anderson (2014) that workflow analysis should help identify whether there is a suitable electronic resources management system, and that good communication with staff is vital. It is easy to pronounce on the need for good communication but practical guidelines that bring this about may be more difficult to find. The depth of detail provided by Barbrow and Hartline on the colour coding of processes, to illustrate the type of agreement (or disagreement) reached on the mapping, is both unusual and illuminating. The technique reflects the observation by Checkland (1981) that a visual technique (in his case 'rich pictures') allows for identification of a problem and bringing some of the hidden aspects into view in as neutral a way as possible. Conflicts are shown, and become a point of discussion, but they should not be aggravated. Authors of both studies comment on the extent of work involved in process mapping, but it is important to dig deep, to be aware how people are making the current system work. When identifying four types of communication in e-resources management, Feather (2007) found evidence of 'lobs', complex communication bouncing between individuals for information and decision making. Unpicking these requires much more care than documenting simple 'darts', tasks to be done.

The type of participation differed in Barbrow and Hartline (2015) and Dowdy and Raeford (2014) at the start of their work, but this was not surprising given their different starting points. Dowdy and Raeford (2014) were working 'top-down', from an initially consultative position, gathering evidence about the problem situation, through to representative participation of different expertise and viewpoints on the team formed for the workflow analysis. For the ongoing maintenance and refinement of the workflow it seems that a consensual approach may be used, involving more staff trained in business process mapping and use of the software, to help maintain the 'big picture' of electronic resources management. Barbrow and Hartline (2015) worked 'bottom-up' with a highly consensual approach in the design and operation of the training programme, but for ongoing development, and actual implementation of improved workflows, management approval at various levels would be necessary. At that stage, consultative and representative participation come into play.

Few published studies of process mapping go into much detail about the obvious problem of automating processes (with consequent impact on staffing levels), or the changes that might take place to the mix of activities and tasks a member of staff is expected to do, supervise or manage. These are complex, dependent on the situation and the individuals, and may require a lot of negotiation. Mumford's categories of job satisfaction fit form a useful checklist for many process mapping and process improvement exercises. The need for a knowledge fit - when staff believe that their skills and expertise are being nurtured - and a psychological fit - to suit status, the career ladder and work interest - may become part of later negotiations around new roles when some processes are supported wholly or partly by software. Dowdy and Raeford (2014) focused on the efficiency fit, as their existing workflows were inadequate and user dissatisfaction levels high. The difference between the knowledge fit and the task structure fit (how challenging and fulfilling the employee's tasks are) is blurring as technology increasingly supports some library processes, but job satisfaction is still important. Feather (2007) identified the need to capture the 'shadows' type of communication, the informal information stored to memory, and Dowdy and Raeford (2014) also commented on the prominence of e-mail and human memory in their existing workflows. Capturing that knowledge and avoiding errors in communication was a key concern. Dowdy and Raeford intended to use SharePoint for document storage, to provide an archive of documentation for future access as and when necessary. Whether this is sufficient for a knowledge repository is difficult to judge at this stage, but it seems that there should be some place to record decisions and the reasons for them for future reference and reflection. Business process mapping may help deal with some types of communication identified by Feather (2007), such as the darts (tasks to be done), lobs (complex communication that bounces between individuals for decision making, but this type of communication can usually be streamlined through changes to roles and processes) and spotlights (communication outwards from the unit). However, McKinnon (2016) studied another type of communication with an electronic resources team, that of how errors and queries from frontline staff to the electronic resources team were handled. The description suggests that the pattern of response was similar to that of Iobs, although the frontline staff often tried to contact an individual that they knew, in the hope of obtaining a response, rather than being given a brush-off. Error reporting and queries may be reduced through better workflows but there remains a need to incorporate a monitoring workflow that deals with the handling of support, a help-desk type of routine.

8.10   Conclusions

The comparison of process analysis techniques to resolve management problems depended on the material provided in the published journal articles, and the application of the framework could only go as far as the information provided. The framework helped to illuminate some of the aspects of business process mapping and the effects on staff that might not have been immediately apparent from just reading the articles. As both studies conclude, changing work practices or culture is not easy, but involving staff as early as possible in the change programme seems highly desirable.

References

Anderson, E. K. (2014) Workflow Analysis. In *Electronic Resource Management Systems: a workflow approach*, Library Technology Reports, **50** (3), American Library Association.

Avison, D. and Fitzgerald, G. (2003) *Information Systems Development: Methodologies, Techniques and Tools*, McGraw-Hill.

Barbrow, S. and Hartline, M. (2015) Process Mapping as Organizational Assessment in Academic Libraries, *Performance Measurement and Metrics*, **16** (1), 34–47.

Checkland, P. (1981) *Systems Theory, Systems Practice*, John Wiley & Sons.

Collins, M. and Grogg, J. E. (2011) Building a Better ERMS, *Library Journal*, **136** (4), 22–8.

Dowdy, B. and Raeford, C. (2014) Electronic Resource Workflow: design, analysis and technologies for an overdue solution, *Serials Review*, **40** (3), 175–87.

Feather, C. (2007) Electronic Resources Communication Management: a strategy for success, *Library Resources and Technical Services*, **51** (3), http://dx.doi.org/10.5860/lrts.51n3.204.

Jewell, T. D., Anderson, I., Chandler, A., Farb, S. E., Parker, K., Riggio, A. and Robertson, N. D. (2004) Electronic Resource Management: report of the DLF ERM initiative, Digital Library Federation, Section 4.3.2 and Appendix B.

McKinnon, D. (2016) Using Perceptions and Preferences from Public Services Staff to Improve Error Reporting and Workflows, *Library Resources & Technical Services*, **60** (2), https://www.journals.ala.org/lrts/article/view/5964/7588.

Mumford, E. (1995) *Effective Systems Design and Requirements Analysis: the ETHICS approach*, Macmillan Press.

Pesch, O. (2008) Library Standards and e-Resource Management: a survey of current initiatives and standards efforts, *Serials Librarian*, **55** (3), 482, doi:10.1080/03615260802059965.

CHAPTER 9

A theoretical framework for designing and evaluating semi-structured document triage interfaces

Fernando Loizides and Aekaterini Mavri

COMMENTARY: CHRISTINE URQUHART

The authors of this chapter (Fernando Loizides and Aekaterini Mavri) consider several topics that will be of interest to readers. A notable feature of it is that they back up their recommendations with references to research evidence. Instead of the usual 'how to' guidelines that can be found in manuals of information architecture, this chapter explains why designers should pay attention to certain elements of information architecture, for example, and refers to the research evidence. As the authors themselves emphasise, 'user studies' is a huge area of research, and it is impossible to refer to all the underpinning evidence. Another problem is that 'user studies' means different things to different disciplines with an interest in the information user.

The dialogue project (Dervin and Reinhard, 2006; Dervin, Reinhard and Shen, 2006) examined convergences and divergences in how three fields (library and information science, human–computer interaction and communication and media studies) looked at users and each other. The authors concluded that proper shared dialogue was desirable, but rare. The structures for communication across research and practice, and between the disciplines, did not make for mutual understanding, easy discussion, or – frankly – the understanding of users or audiences that the researchers (and practitioners) truly want. Power, prestige and a dependence on 'authority' get in the way. With that in mind, and without taking away from the excellent presentation of research evidence in this chapter, you should remember that you may need to approach the evidence in this chapter (and other chapters in this book) with the sense-making questions set out in the introduction. What are my reactions to this evidence? What do I agree with? What do I disagree with? What else do I need to know or experience to make further progress with this topic?

There are several themes in this chapter. First, there is the idea of the semi-structured document. The authors' emphasis is on journal articles, patents and similar research study formats, and how these may be presented to readers to help them evaluate their contents quickly and successfully. There is considerable research on the difference in comprehension of reading text (usually linear text) on screen versus paper (e.g. Mangen, Walgermo and Brønnick, 2013). On-screen reading is different as it seems to be more difficult for readers to navigate some types of documents, to check whether they are moving around effectively, and whether they have a good spatial mental representation when reading on screen. Semi-structured documents such as journal articles usually have a standard format – introduction, methods, results and discussion – which can support navigation. Readers know what to expect in particular sections, and the order in which they expect to find things. Nevertheless, readers may have all sorts of different purposes when trying to find and extract information from an online semi-structured document and this chapter discusses the importance of providing a table of contents alongside the full text, and the need to deal with captions, images, tables and figures. It provides an overview of the research evidence and covers information architecture, external factors such as accessibility, and assistive tools.

References

Dervin, B. and Reinhard, C. D. (2006) Researchers and Practitioners Talk about Users and Each Other: making user and audience studies matter, Paper 1, *Information Research*, **12** (1),
http://informationr.net/ir/12-1/paper286.html.
Dervin, B., Reinhard, C. D. and Shen, F. C. (2006) Beyond Communication – Research as Communicating: making user and audience studies matter, Paper 2, *Information Research*, **12** (1),
http://informationr.net/ir/12-1/paper287.html.

Mangen, A., Walgermo, B. R. and Brønnick, K. (2013) Reading Linear Texts on Paper Versus Computer Screen: effects on reading comprehension, *International Journal of Educational Research*, **58** (1), 61–8.

9.1 Introduction

Interface design, with consideration of how people work with the information they access, is an important element of information architecture. Chapter 2 provided an overview of the components of information architecture and how some information behaviour research might help design of navigation. Chapters 5–8 examined process analysis and process modelling – what actually happens with interactions among work roles, and how information may be sought, checked or monitored in a more formal way. Workflows are considered in chapters 13 and 14 as well. This chapter bridges the gap between what could be termed 'formalised' information behaviour seen in workflows and process models, and the informal, casual information behaviour that is the expectation of information architects for many websites. Often users have to work with documents on screen, and pick up clues from the way the documents are structured.

With the advent of more ubiquitous technology and advances in information technology, we are able to locate more information at a faster rate than before. This speed is increasing exponentially to the point where we no longer have a problem with how slowly the information is presented to us or how little information we can find, but with that of information overload (Bawden and Robinson, 2009). This can lead to frustration at the lower side of the severity scale, and to business or safety critical mistakes being made at the other. Most of the information we see and interact with is still heavily textual in nature. Furthermore, this information is also often not formatted or structured in a helpful way. Databases are examples of information in a very structured setting. At the other end of the spectrum we have completely unstructured data, such as an e-mail sent by a student. In the e-mail there are no headings, no paragraphs to distinguish themes and almost no punctuation marks to distinguish between sentences; there are simply ten lines of words, wrapping due to the automatic characters per line allowance. This would be classified as an unstructured document. In this work, we focus on a middle ground: semi-structured documents. These documents are not based on a specific detailed template, but have a loosely arranged structure resembling that of other documents with a similar purpose. An example of documents that are semi-structured is academic articles. One would expect an academic article to include a title, an abstract, an introduction towards the beginning of the article and references towards the end of the article. Not all academic documents have a section on previous studies though. The term semi-structured accounts for documents with a non-rigid structure, in that the labels and contents of particular structural elements may not be consistent or even present (Draper, Christianson and Komissarchik, 2002). Other such document types include legal resources, intellectual property documents (patents) and patient case-history reports for evaluation and prioritisation based on the emergency severity (Van Veen and Moll, 2009).

It is easier (conceptually) to search through structured information than semi-structured and non-structured information. For example, when using structured query language one can return all the records in a database with the surname 'Smith'. Usually, one's information need while searching through structured data is also very ordered and specific. One such query could be 'How many customers are male and how many are female?'. In other cases, the search need is less defined, and acquires a much broader range of information. For example, one may want to learn more about the NEK1 gene in ALS (amyotrophic lateral sclerosis or motor neurone disease) patients. Several variables are present in this information need. How technical are the information seekers and will they understand every single article they read? How much information is enough before they are content? Triage interfaces should thus be designed in order to cater for both well structured and ill defined information queries.

Thus far, interfaces built to assist users in searching for information on semi-structured documents have tended to be generic and not user-centred in their design. The focus has been on the searching algorithms in order to detect 'relevant' documents to be ranked and returned to the information seeker. The user is then expected to search manually through the results and, with minimal assistance, make relevance decisions on documents. This process is dubbed 'document triage' (Bae et al., 2006). It is a sub-process of information seeking, a visual type of search whereby users often rapidly skim and assimilate inform-ation, rather than read it systematically. It typically occurs in a limited amount of time, which is often disproportionate to the volume of documents available.

This chapter suggests a framework to provide guidelines for the creation and evaluation of interfaces with the aim of triaging semi-structured documents such as academic articles, patents, medical studies and legal cases effectively. It aims to help familiarise readers within the information-seeking area by providing a foundation through further reading and examples from various disciplines. It builds on several studies on information seekers, regarding their visual attention, cognitive workings and behavioural patterns, all of which is integrated and referenced. The framework can then be used as a powerful tool in order to accompany and guide designers, developers and user experience consultants by using heuristics to situate the level of perceived effectiveness of the interfaces they are creating or evaluating.

Section 9.2 follows with an explanation of the framework used, and Section 9.3 examines the main concerns of information architecture and how the framework is applied. Section 9.4 considers the external factors and Section 9.5 considers suitable assistive tools. Section 9.6 discusses examples using the framework and Section 9.7 draws conclusions.

9.2   Framework

When designing an interface, especially one that deals with large amounts of information and is highly interactive, the user experience is often neglected and the focus remains on content. With today's powerful web technologies, such as Web 2.0, the capabilities of user interfaces can be considerably enhanced to provide richer information presentation and interaction. Science Direct (www.sciencedirect.com/), a popular online academic document repository, for instance, has recently facilitated advanced features such as thumbnail images in content overview, indication of the user's location within a reading pane, bibliographic information export, related articles and the author's vitae. Without guidance, however, these systems can be limited in aiding information seekers. Furthermore, several competing interfaces make the user experience factor vital in attracting information seekers. The user's choice is often ultimately based on their overall experience of the interface, which should therefore be taken into consideration.

In an effort to build functional triage environments and since specialised heuristics are absent, interface designers are forced to draw from adjacent disciplines such as human–computer interaction and web design to develop triage interfaces.

A design framework for triage interfaces responsible for large collections of documents with at least some regulated structure is presented in Figure 9.1. The framework concerns three primary areas:

- information architecture
- external factors
- assistive tools.

Subsections within this framework present respective design guidelines and principles. The first section is labelled information architecture and looks into the organisation, presentation and aesthetic aspect and interactive behaviour of information architecture elements. The second section presents the influence of external factors, such as the perceived credibility and reliability of the information and the availability and the information load. The third presents a more technical side to the equation with assistive tools that can improve the information seeker's experience.

The reader should note that this may not count as an exhaustive list of factors that need to be taken into account. Throughout the chapter we highlight the role of psychological (cognitive) factors spanning through all the framework findings. These can be less quantifiable and very case (or user) specific. During document triage, information seekers get involved in an interplay of cognition (thoughts), emotion (feelings) and action (physicality) to make sense of the information encountered in order to form the necessary assertions. They often deal with confusion and uncertainty during this process (Kuhlthau, 1991). Apart from possible usability difficulties, issues such as information credibility, availability (document download) and currency of data may also affect the information-seeking process (Loizides et al., 2014). A dedicated design framework should aim to guide creators of triage interfaces in making user-desired actions as coherent and easily perceivable as possible in order to minimise the likelihood of such (negative) issues or feelings (Norman, 2002).

The framework shown in Figure 9.1 opposite allows the designer to self-assess the interface. Using a point-based system, the designer can go through all the principles for each of the three areas and give a score (out of 100). By mapping that score to the circle grid, a triangle graph is produced showing a rating and giving a direction to the designer of where the most significant amount of improvement is needed. The point system of the framework is adaptive and the designer can also adjust the principles or even remove them. In the next section, we present the principles in each of the three areas and produce examples of what potential evaluations of interfaces can look like within the framework (see Figure 9.7).

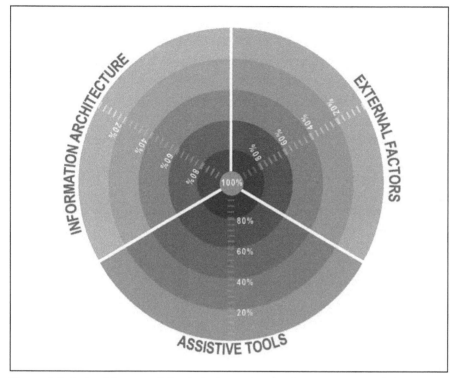

Figure 9.1 *A visual framework for designing and evaluating semi-structured document triage interfaces*

9.3   Information architecture

Being a highly visual process, document triage is influenced by factors such as the structural and presentational properties of the elements it contains. User triage behaviour is therefore not only influenced by the content made available, but also by the visual properties of that content (Shneiderman, 1989) and the interaction affordances it communicates. Although such properties are governed by various principles, which most of the time are interdependent and overlap one another, this work classifies them in four categories:

- content
- layout
- formatting
- behaviour (affordances).

9.3.1   Principles of content

9.3.1.1 Provide key elements in snippets and full-text views (C1)

The first principle of content (C1) is to provide the key elements in snippets and full-text views. Users tend to rely on and heavily scrutinise key elements that present significant information for developing relevance decisions in semi-structured documents (Brady and Phillips, 2003). In academic documents, for example, these key elements are the abstract, introduction and conclusion (Figure 9.2). These should be prioritised and readily appear at the initiation point of the triage activity in dual form as a few-line text previews (content snippets) catering for fast-scanning relevance inspections, and the corresponding full-text content for detailed reading, on user click on a snippet (Loizides and Buchanan, 2009).

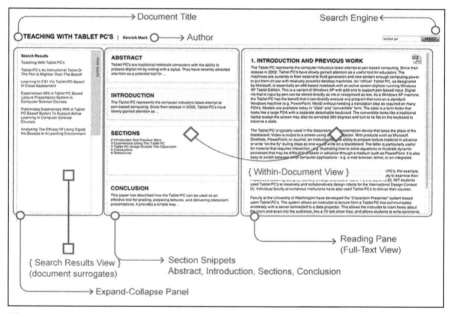

Figure 9.2 *A TriDoc academic document triage application* (from Mavri et al., 2013, reprinted with kind permission from John Benjamins Publishing Company, Amsterdam/Philadelphia. [www.benjamins.com])

9.3.1.2   Provide access to all sections of the document (C2)

The second principle of content (C2) is to give access to all sections of the document. Certain elements are considered most critical (see C1) in providing important cues of the document's worth against an information need. Nonetheless, users regard all document content as useful in forming their concluding relevance judgements. Information seekers are known to engage in a triage pattern of alternating between the section headings (table of contents) and their respective full-text versions (see L2, below), following user selection, as it enables them to navigate and explore the various elements within the document effortlessly.

9.3.2   Principles of layout

9.3.2.1   *Provide integration and linear visual flow of surrogate and within-document views for scanning or reading (L1)*

The first principle of layout (L1) is to provide integration and linear visual flow of surrogate and within-document views for scanning or reading. Information seekers typically engage in three levels of behaviour during triage: 'surrogate' activity, 'within-document' activity and 'in-depth reading' (Loizides and Buchanan, 2013). 'Surrogate' level activity refers to viewing or interacting with the search results (see L3) returned by the system after a user query. 'Within-document' level activity comprises fast skimming of excerpts (information snippets) from key elements in the document (see C1), while 'in-depth' reading denotes linear, systematic reading though the entire contents of a document. Although information seekers largely engage with the first two levels of behaviour for forming their initial relevance judgements, an effective interface should cater for all three by integrating them onto a single screen (Figure 9.2). More specifically, a preferable arrangement involves the layout of important content 'snippets' in a hyperlinked 'table-of-contents' style, appearing on the side of a dedicated reading pane, which displays a full-text version for each snippet, allowing for a more linear and systematic type of reading. A characteristic example is that of an e-book's chapters appearing below one another, side-by-side to a reading window, facilitating a left-to-right and top-to-bottom navigation flow (Figure 9.2).

9.3.2.2   *Supply a dedicated full-text reading area (L2)*

The second principle of layout (L2) is to supply a dedicated full-text reading area. In line with layout principle L1, full-text reading can be accommodated in a standalone reading pane, appearing at the side (generally the right) of document results and text snippets (Figure 9.2). Access to the full contents of a document is possible via vertical scrolling within the reading pane itself. This allows users to gain control by deciding to move linearly or incrementally through 'jumps' (Shneiderman, 1996). Additionally, the scrollbar button's position and size help reduce memory load by indicating the current viewing position within a large block of information as well as implying the length of the information, providing an overview-plus-detail-view interface (Hearst, 1999).

9.3.2.3 Provide a visibly accessible title within reasonable proximity to content (L3)

The third principle of layout (L3) is to provide a visibly accessible title within reasonable proximity to content. In evaluating a document's suitability to an information need, users typically return to reassess the document's title against the information they have scrutinised from sections further into the document. This behaviour is recurring in forming relevance judgements as interaction progresses and more information is assimilated (Clarke et al., 2007; Loizides, 2012). Critical identity elements, such as the title of a book in a digital library for instance (Figures 9.3 and 9.4 opposite), should therefore be constantly visibly accessible and in close proximity to the full-text reading pane, thus minimising the eye-gaze travel distance between the two.

9.3.2.4 Show the visual proximity between related items (L4)

The fourth principle of layout (L4) is to show the visual proximity between related items. Semantically similar items are expected to appear spatially close to one another and share common visual characteristics (like form, shape, colour, graphical treatment). This principle draws from the two Gestalt laws of proximity and similarity coexisting in harmony (Kaplan and Moulthrop, 1994) – a recommended approach for effective triage interfaces. Likewise, users normally expect to find all hyperlinked text snippets or section headings such as the 'front page', 'drawings', 'specifications' and 'claims' from a patent document for instance (Figure 9.5, page 156), in close proximity and visual likeness to one another.

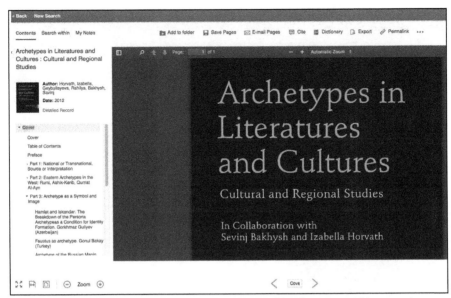

Figure 9.3 *An EBSCOhost online research directory table of contents with top-to-bottom and left-to-right navigation flow and a dedicated scrollable full-text reading window* (from EBSCOHost Online Research Directory, 2016, www.ebsco.com)

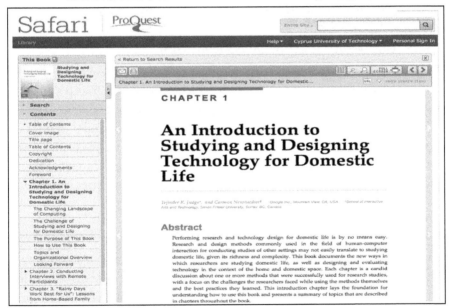

Figure 9.4 *Example of a Safari Books Online Digital Library item with book title and table of contents positioned on the left of the dedicated full-text reading pane* (from Safari Books Online Digital Library, 2016, www.safaribooksonline.com)

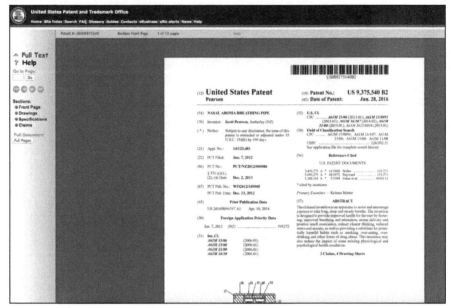

Figure 9.5 *A patent from the US Patent and Trademark Office online repository showing the spatial and visual proximity of relevant items such as the left menu links* (from US Patent and Trademark Office online repository, 2016, www.uspto.gov)

9.3.2.5   *Offer vertical search results orientation (L5)*

The fifth principle of layout (L5) is to offer vertical search results orientation. Information seekers are accustomed to exploring search engine result pages assembled in a vertical manner on pages (Nielsen and Loranger, 2006). The left side is also reportedly where users typically look to find navigation options on a web page (Nielsen, 2008). These can appear on the far-left area of the screen real estate, to the side of section snippets and full-text reading window, facilitating simultaneous 'surrogate' and 'within-document' views during triage (Figure 9.2).

9.3.2.6   *Keep the document structure intact (L6)*

The sixth principle of layout (L6) is to keep the document structure intact. Interface layout can have an impact on the users' triage patterns. Empirical evidence indicates that information seekers prefer to encounter the document sections (such as the 'patient information', 'history' and 'medication' sections in a medical record for instance) in the same order and hierarchy as these would normally occur in the original document (Loizides et al., 2014).

Interfaces that reflect the document structure as closely as possible can provide the required level of familiarity and thus ease of use for information seekers.

9.3.3   Principles of formatting

9.3.3.1   *Harmonise font size and type with recommended ranges (F1)*

The first principle of formatting (F1) is that font size and type should accord to recommended ranges and be fine-tuned based on the unique typographic variables of the interface. Previous studies indicate that body text (full-text reading) falls between the recommended 12–16px range (Sheedy et al., 2005). Relative font sizes (like 'em' or 'percent') should be employed, as text can then be resized by the user agent (e.g. browser) (w3c.org, 2017). However, the font size should be decided, not in isolation, but in reference to the chosen typeface as well (Figure 9.6). It is worth noting that 'designed for screen' fonts typically

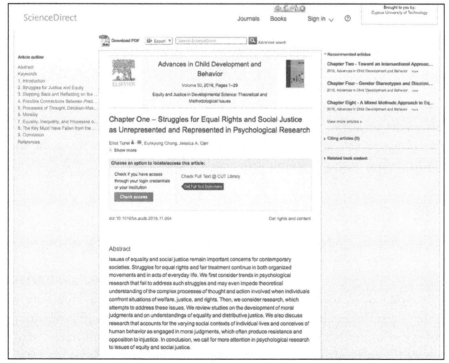

Figure 9.6 *Example of Science Direct Digital Library body text and table-of-contents text in Arial, in 16px and 13px sizes respectively; line heights also differ between the two, as characters per line numbers increase or decrease* (from Science Direct Online Digital Library, 2016, www.sciencedirect.com)

have a taller x-height and larger counter forms (the internal space created by the font outline) (Boyarski et al., 1998) than 'designed-for-print' fonts. Respective adjustments are therefore necessary in order to ensure maximum legibility in triage interfaces.

9.3.3.2   Define line-height values in reference to line-length (F2)

The second principle of formatting (F2) is to define line-height values in reference to line-length. Similarly to the font size or type co-dependency, line-height and line-length variables are also inter-reliant: longer lines are warranted for taller line heights and vice versa, because of the steeper angle sweeps required to locate the beginning of the next line (Dyson, 2004). Consequently, shorter lines, like those in the section snippets (see also C1) for example, should naturally adopt a lower line-length value than the wider lines found in the full-text reading pane, as Figure 9.6 illustrates.

9.3.3.3   Make captions legible and easy to scan (F3)

The third principle of formatting (F3) is to make captions legible and easy to scan. Captions for images, figures and tables are information-rich elements, which effectively summarise important messages. A primary principle for effective interfaces is to display distinct and readily 'scannable' captions, since they play a key role in the users' understanding of a document's scope and end results during triage (Chen, Blostein and Shatkay, 2006).

9.3.4   Principles of affordances

9.3.4.1   Provide on-demand, scalable thumbnail images in close proximity to relevant text (Af1)

The first principle of affordances (allowing actions to be performed) (Af1) is to provide on-demand, scalable thumbnail images in close proximity to relevant text. Images have the ability to communicate important information, faster and more concisely than linguistic means in the information-seeking process (Chen, Blostein and Shatkay, 2006). Large, full-sized versions facilitating exhaustive inspection are necessary during triage. Depending on the context, these may be critical – like in the case of electronic health record systems –

where patients' x-rays and scans offer the required level of detail and precision demanded for medical triage. On-demand image enlargement is suitable for economising space, when available screen area is limited in information- and navigation-heavy screens. In fact, the benefit of such functionality is twofold as it also provides concurrent viewing of text content and accompanying imagery (like in printed media), something which is typically required in order to benefit from the combination of textual and respective pictorial information.

9.3.4.2   Have prominent cues (Af2)

The second principle of affordances (Af2) is to have prominent cues, especially when these lead to further triage activity. Interactions should be easily identifiable, particularly when their activation may lead to additional triage activity. For example, users should quickly become aware of the section snippets' (see C1) clickability, usually through a different colour like hyperlink blue or other distinct typographic characteristics (Figure 9.2), just by looking at the interface and before any interaction. Clicking will lead to the discovery of further information (e.g. the full-text version), an altered triage behaviour and possibly different overall relevance judgements. It is typical for text-dense environments (such as semi-structured documents) to be deprived of graphical artefacts (colours, buttons, icons, graphical treatment), which are important for exposing affordances more noticeably.

9.4   External factors

9.4.1   Providing specialised or adaptive views that can be customised to user needs (EF1)

Other principles concern consideration of external factors governing the provision of specialised or adaptive views that can be customised to user needs (EF1). Different information seekers may require various distinct pieces of information in order to make a judgement. This is the personalised browsing or searching strategy of every individual (Marchionini, 1997), which is formed based on contextual factors. These may be formed for various reasons, such as company search policy. For example, a paralegal may be instructed to filter cases before they are passed on to the attorney by scrutinising only specific parts of a claim and looking for very targeted information. In this case, such specificity allows for the designer to acquire the user requirements to produce the interface easily. The more likely scenario is when the elements of a document are known but the search strategy can vary between different users. For this a more adaptive user interface is required and the constraints should be explored (Lavie and Meyer, 2010).

9.4.2   Providing markers of reliability and credibility (EF2)

Other external factors are markers of reliability and credibility (EF2). Information assimilated by the seeker is often provided from different sources and in different formats. Furthermore, contradicting information makes it necessary to judge which source is more credible and therefore which one to select. Elements such as the origins of the information are crucial for this judgement. These can be publishers, publishing dates and the ability to filter results by author. Evidence shows that such characteristics are usually also exploited when information seekers are not interested in the text at hand and seek further criteria to validate their decisions (Cool, Belkin and Kantor, 1993). It also indicates the need to verify the quality and 'cognitive authority' of information, and how recent and credible the information and its sources are (Rieh, 2002). The added benefit to this method is that it can address the external factor of time constraints as the user can focus on the perceived important elements first and choose to 'ignore' the rest in a satisficing method (Simon, 1956). Satisficing is the theory claiming that users will often settle for an adequate solution rather than the optimal one during an information search.

9.4.3   Ensuring accessibility (EF3)

Another very important external factor (EF3) is to ensure accessibility. The information and the interactions should be made available to people with disabilities. Accessibility is unfortunately still an area that is often neglected in user interfaces, one which is highly researched, however, and several guidelines exist to help authors (Petrie and Bevan, 2009).

9.4.4   Reducing information overload (EF4)

The final external factor (EF4) is the reduction of information overload. A common problem searchers face is that of too much information being returned and presented to the seeker. Our framework deals with the latter: it assists the information seeker and not with the information retrieval aspect of the search system. When dealing with a text-heavy interface, the user can often struggle to distinguish relevant material. The interface needs to become uncluttered without losing vital information.

9.5   Suitable assistive tools – based on user requirements and the norm

This section discusses various forms of technical and interactive elements in interfaces, which aim to assist information seekers in performing faster and more efficient triage processes. Although these are embedded in and interrelate with areas such as external factors (credibility and reliability of information) or information architecture (layout or behaviour), for example, they are presented separately in this standalone section, so that they comprise a set of distinct guidelines for designers and developers of triage interfaces.

9.5.1   Direct link to references and an external bibliography (A1)

The first assistive tool (A1) links directly to references and external bibliography. Citations in within-document sections should be hyperlinks pointing to the respective items in the 'references' section (and vice versa). This allows for faster and more efficient user interactions, with little or no compromise of user experience (Conklin, 1987). Additionally, a bibliography is deemed important by information seekers, as it provides evidence for evaluating the current document's credibility and locating other suitable sources. Within a structured document the references section should point to the respective external online bibliographic sources, whenever available. This poses a few technical challenges, however, when making such content available to users (Amitay, 1997).

9.5.2   A within-document search field and highlighted search keywords in text (A2)

The second assistive tool (A2) provides a within-document search field and highlighted search keywords in text. A search tool for basic or advanced text searches with highlighted keyword pointers should be included in structured document triage interfaces, as it enables faster access to various elements and thus enhances triage processes. This is particularly important for standalone, non-browser-based interfaces, which lack the built-in keyword or phrase facility.

9.5.3   Enhancement of triage interfaces (A3)

The third assistive tool (A3) allows users to operate further triage on their selected search result items. When identifying relevant documents, triage interfaces should present the means by which information seekers can mark specific results items (documents) for further consideration – faster future retrieval whenever necessary. Such means can be as minor as simply numbering the search results, or more facilitative such as by providing checkboxes for sorting, printing, saving and exporting capabilities.

9.5.4   Extraction via visual elements (A4)

The fourth assistive tool (A4) allows extraction via visual elements. Images, figures and tables typically receive elevated amounts of the information seeker's attention, for example patent examination (Loizides and Diallo, 2014), for reasons explained in Section 9.3.4, on behaviour (affordances). Drawing from common examples such as Google's image-search service, triage systems for semi-structured documents should allow for similar provision, across and within-document functionality. This principle recommends the design of interfaces that enable users to decide on the inclusion (or not) of images, customise their presentation, or view them in isolation from the rest of the document content – similar to Google Scholar's treatment in the interface of intellectual property documents. Such interfaces cater to specific needs or user personas, who are either visual by nature or whose triage requires a search for visual information.

9.5.5   A full-text download option (A5)

The fifth assistive tool (A5) provides a full-text download option. Although information seekers typically tend to rely on 'metadata-only document representations' (Marshall, 1998), a full-text document (for example the full PDF) download link should be in place, to support users who wish to view the document in its original form and read or skim through the file in a linear manner, similar to traditional offline reading behaviour. Additionally, information seekers often judge the validity of a source based on its native design, structure and formatting (Davis, Davis and Dunagan, 2012). This is subject to the availability of the document in a full version.

9.5.6   Menus, tools and provisions in close proximity to the content elements they support (A6)

The sixth assistive set of tools (A6) provides menus, tools and provisions in close proximity to the content elements they support. To ensure maximum efficiency, rich, supportive interface functionality such as text search fields, scale or view buttons, personalisation tools (for customised font-type) and paging controls, for example, should be located in close functional proximity to the information content they are designed to facilitate.

9.6   Framework examples

Figure 9.7 (a, b, c and d overleaf) demonstrates different assessments that can result from an evaluation of an interface. Figure 9.7a presents an evaluation which shows that improvement is needed on all three areas on the interface. The triangle has a large surface area and all three vertices of the triangle are close to the circle circumference. Figure 9.7b shows an evaluation where the interface scores high in all areas. The triangle has a small surface area and all three vertices are close to the centre of the circle. Figure 9.7c shows an evaluation in which the interface needs more attention on one of the three areas. Two vertices of the triangle are close to the centre of the circle while the third vertex (external factors) is close to the circumference of the circle. Figure 9.7d shows an evaluation where more work is needed on two areas of the interface. There are two vertices (for assistive tools, information architecture) close to the circumference of the circle while the third (external factors) is close to the circle's centre.

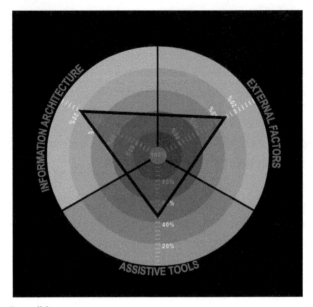

Figure 9.7a *Overall low score*

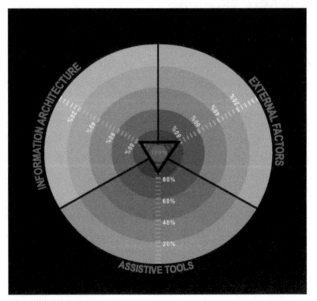

Figure 9.7b *Overall high score*

Figure 9.7 *The Microsoft Amalga Unified Intelligence System facilitating independent image viewing and manipulation functionality for detailed inspection* (no longer available online)

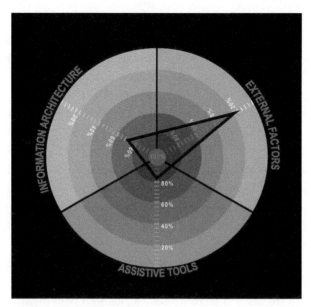

Figure 9.7c *Low score in external factors*

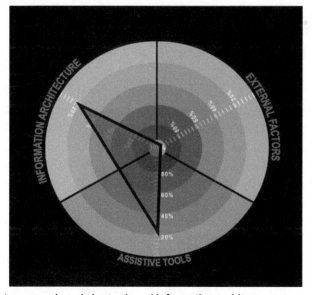

Figure 9.7d *Low score in assistive tools and information architecture*

9.7   Conclusions

In this chapter we presented a framework to visually assist with the design and evaluation of interfaces for the information triage of semi-structured documents. The framework presents three key areas (information architecture, external factors and assistive tools), which are then presented into a finer granularity by specific principles. Visual representation tools that assist in the design and evaluation of specialised interfaces are provided, indicating improvement directions and focus for the interface. The framework is an initial guide and model, which designers and developers can adapt to their specific needs. Principles can be added or deleted to represent the case by case interface implementation and needs. Finally, suitable weighting for each principle can also be applied to maximise the return on time invested by the interface developer versus the benefits it generates for users.

Information architecture guidance may often seem to lack evidence to back up design decisions. This chapter provides pointers to the research evidence that underpin information triage of semi-structured documents, to help users work with such documents.

References

Amitay, E. (1997) Hypertext: the importance of being different, HCRC Research Paper.

Bae, S., Marshall, C. C., Meintanis, K., Zacchi, A., Hsieh, H. Moore, J. M. and Shipman, F. M. (2006) Patterns of Reading and Organizing Information in Document Triage, *Proceedings of the American Society for Information Science and Technology*, **43** (1), 1–27.

Bawden, D. and Robinson, L. (2009) The Dark Side of Information: overload, anxiety and other paradoxes and pathologies, *Journal of Information Science*, **35** (2), 180–91.

Boyarski, D., Neuwirth, C., Forlizzi, J. and Regli, S. H. (1998) A Study of Fonts Designed for Screen Display. In *Proceedings of the SIGCHI Conference on Human Factors in Computing Systems* (87–94), ACM Press and Addison Wesley Publishing Co.

Brady, L. and Phillips, C. (2003) Aesthetics and Usability: a look at color and balance, blog, Software Usability Research Laboratory, Wichita State University, http://usabilitynews.org/aesthetics-and-usability-a-look-at-color-and-balance/.

Chen, N., Blostein, D. and Shatkay, H. (2006) *Biomedical Document Triage Based on Figure Classification*, paper given at the First Canadian Student Conference on Biomedical Computing, Kingston, Ontario.

Clarke, C., Agchtein, E., Dumais, S. and White, R. (2007) The Influence of Caption Features on Lickthrough Patterns in Web Search. In *SIGIR '07 Proceedings of the 30th annual international ACM SIGIR Conference on Research and Development in Information Retrieval.*

Conklin, J. (1987) Hypertext: an introduction and survey, *IEEE Computer Society*, **20** (9), 17–41.

Cool, C., Belkin, N. J. and Kantor, P. B. (1993) Characteristics of Text Affecting Relevance Judgments. In *Proceedings of the 14th National Online Meeting* (77–84), Learned Information.

Davis, M., Davis, K. J. and Dunagan, M. (2012) *Scientific Papers and Presentations*, Academic Press.

Draper, D. L., Christianson, D. B. and Komissarchik, K. L. (2002) US Patent No. 6,449,620, US Patent and Trademark Office.

Dyson, M. C. (2004) How Physical Text Layout Affects Reading from Screen, *Behaviour & Information Technology*, **23** (6), 377–93.

Hearst, M. A. (1999) User Interfaces and Visualization. In *Modern Information Retrieval*, 257–323,
http://people.ischool.berkeley.edu/~hearst/irbook/10/chap10.html.

Kaplan, N. and Moulthrop, S. (1994) *Where No Mind has Gone Before: ontological design for virtual spaces*, paper given at ACM European Conference on Hypermedia Technology, 206–16, ACM,
https://www.researchgate.net/publication/238519908_Where_no_mind_has_gone_before_Ontological_design_for_virtual_spaces.

Kuhlthau, C. C. (1991) Inside the Search Process: information seeking from the user's perspective, *Journal of the American Society for Information Science*, **42** (5), 311–88.

Lavie, T. and Meyer, J. (2010) Benefits and Costs of Adaptive User Interfaces, *International Journal of Human-Computer Studies*, **68** (8), 508–24.

Loizides, F. (2012) *Understanding and Conceptualising the Document Triage Process Through Information Seekers' Visual and Navigational Attention*, PhD thesis, City University, London.

Loizides, F. and Buchanan, G. (2009) *An Empirical Study of User Navigation During Document Triage*, Lecture Notes in Computer Science, 138–49, Springer-Verlag.

Loizides, F. and Buchanan, G. (2013) Towards a Framework for Human (Manual) Information Retrieval. In Lupu, M., Kanoulas, E. and Loizides, F. (eds), *Proceedings of the Multidisciplinary Information Retrieval: 6th Information Retrieval Facility Conference, Limassol, Cyprus, 7-9 October 2013*, 87–98, Springer.

Loizides, F. and Diallo, B. (2014) Using Eye-Tracking to Investigate Patent Examiners' Information Seeking Process. In Lamas, D. and Buitelaar, P. (eds), *Proceedings of the Multidisciplinary Information Retrieval: 7th Information Retrieval Facility Conference, Copenhagen, Denmark, 10-12 November 2014*, 76–81, Springer.

Loizides, F., Photiades, T., Mavri, A. and Zaphiris, P. (2014) On Interactive Interfaces for Semi-Structured Academic Document Seeking and Relevance Decision Making, *New Review of Information Networking*, **19** (2), 67–95.

Marchionini, G. (1997) *Information Seeking in Electronic Environments*, Cambridge University Press.

Marshall, C. C. (1998) Making Metadata: a study of metadata creation for a mixed physical-digital collection. In *Proceedings of the Third ACM Conference on Digital Libraries*, 162–71, ACM.

Mavri, A., Loizides, F., Photiades, A. and Zaphiris, P. (2013) We Have the Content . . . Now What? The role of structure and interactivity in academic document triage interfaces, *Information Design Journal*, **20** (3), 247–65.

Nielsen, J. (2008) Right-Justified Navigation Menus Impede Scannability, Nielsen Norman Group, www.nngroup.com/articles/right-justified-navigation-menus.

Nielsen, J. and Loranger, H. (2006) *Prioritizing Web Usability*, New Riders.

Norman, D. A. (2002) The Psychopathology of Everyday Things. In Levitin, D. J., *Foundations of Cognitive Psychology: core readings*, MIT Press, 417–43.

Petrie, H. and Bevan, N. (2009) The Evaluation of Accessibility, Usability and User Experience. In Stephanidis, C. (ed.), *The Universal Access Handbook*, CRC Press, 10–20.

Rieh, S. Y. (2002) Judgment of Information Quality and Cognitive Authority in the Web, *Journal of the American Society for Information Science and Technology*, **53** (2), 145–61, doi:10.1002/asi.10017.

Sheedy, J. E., Subbaram, M. V., Zimmerman, A. B. and Hayes, J. R. (2005) Text Legibility and the Letter Superiority Effect, *Human Factors: The*

Journal of the Human Factors and Ergonomics Society, **47** (4), 797–815, doi:10.1518/001872005775570998.

Shneiderman, B. (1989) Reflections on Authoring, Editing, and Managing Hypertext. In Barrett, E. (ed.), *The Society of Text: hypertext, hypermedia, and the social construction of information*, MIT Press.

Shneiderman, B. (1996) The Eyes Have It: a task by data type taxonomy for information visualizations, https://www.cs.umd.edu/~ben/papers/Shneiderman1996eyes.pdf.

Simon, H. A. (1956) Rational Choice and the Structure of the Environment, *Psychological Review*, **63** (2), 129.

Van Veen, M. and Moll, H. A. (2009) Reliability and Validity of Triage Systems in Paediatric Emergency Care, *Scandinavian Journal of Trauma, Resuscitation and Emergency Medicine*, **17** (1), 1.

W3C.ORG (2017) www.w3.org/QA/tips/font-size.

CHAPTER 10

Resource discovery case studies

Karen Colbron and Christine Urquhart

COMMENTARY: CHRISTINE URQUHART
This chapter discusses three Jisc-funded resource discovery projects at academic libraries throughout the UK: a photograph project at Queen's University Belfast, the use of the balanced value impact model for stakeholder and audience analysis at Middlesex University's Museum of Domestic Design and Architecture, and building a better content management system at the Museum of English Rural Life (MERL) and Special Collections at the University of Reading. This tries to meet the needs of casual visitors, and bring more visitors to the site.

The Queen's University project was designed jointly by library staff and the academics from the School of Modern History and Anthropology. One of the reasons for this collaborative approach was the benefit of dissemination among academic networks by academics, so project outputs could be used and reviewed by faculty elsewhere. Importantly, the project outputs were cited in other publications, which in turn led to discovery of resources by other academics and doctoral students. In a comparison of the referencing behaviour of doctoral students and faculty members, Larivière, Sugimoto and Bergeron (2013) found that doctoral students generally tend to cite more documents per article than do faculty, and that the literature that they cite is generally more recent. This is not surprising, but what was surprising was that faculty in social sciences and the humanities were far more likely to cite theses than the doctoral students.

The authors suggest that through their academic networks, including the examination process for doctoral students, faculty are likely to be aware of relevant research by doctoral students elsewhere – and such research may take a long time to get published in books or journals, if it is published at all.

Academic partners in the project added annotations for the photographs. Roles and responsibilities for the various elements of the work could probably be fairly well defined. When reviewing the history of library–faculty collaboration, Cunningham (2010) suggests that digital humanities projects present good opportunities for collaboration as the projects may be multidisciplinary – or at least produce material that is of interest to several fields of research. Collaboration between faculty and library staff is essential as digital humanities scholars may not appreciate the importance of guidelines for preservation – nor the need for metadata for preservation. Some of the information schools (I-Schools) in the USA have created digital humanities internships to help prepare students for a variety of work on digital humanities projects. Conway et al. (2010) mention technology and systems training, preservation reformatting and legal issues.

Other digital humanities projects are concerned with textual material, and large corpora of textual material provide several possibilities for analysis. Heuwing, Mandl and Womser-Hacker (2016) describe a participative design process for a large text corpora (almost 3000 school textbooks in history and geography during the period of the German Empire). The research team started by interviewing academic researchers in their offices (contextual interviews) discussing how they worked on recent projects, their methods for access and retrieval, what tools they used, what type of documents they created, and the type of analysis and verification (use of contextual clues) they attempted. They used activity models to present their research findings in participatory workshops. The activity models are similar in principle to 'use cases' – bringing together the discrete tasks and activities that comprise an accepted research work goal. Chapter 5 provides more details about use case descriptions and use case diagrams. Setting out the activity model in this way allows participants in the design process to comment on the model, and helps to identify any missing activities or problems for research work on the text corpora. Researchers at Penn State University (Antonijević and Cahoy, 2014) used an online survey, but combined that with in-depth interviews, conducted in the respondents' university offices, to find out more about the personal information management practices of staff, including access and browsing (often using Google Scholar), use of bibliographic software tools, and ways of storing documents and data, including security measures taken. Their findings confirm the need for research tools that support a continuous research workflow as existing tools often support just parts of the process.

For Oxford University, Athenaum21 Consulting Research (Madsen and Hurst, 2015) took a broader view of resource discovery, aimed at understanding how and why Oxford University staff and students used resources, how such searching connected people in different parts of the university who might need to share expertise or resources, and how to make the resources more accessible internally and externally. The research team conducted interviews (45 with users, 30 with collection providers, 16 with vendors and suppliers), had 22 consultations with external institutions, made site visits to seven Oxford libraries and museums, and carried out three literature reviews. Their findings confirmed that searching practices change as users are more familiar with their subject domain, and suggested that it is important to find where the boundaries lie. Visualisation tools would be helpful for novice users. The research team recommended that collection level metadata should be used to produce Venn diagrams showing what exists at Oxford. More expert users want to search across relevant collections in different disciplines; cross collection searching would be easier for them if they used a Lucene-based technology such as Elasticsearch to index and expose an individual item's metadata. Such visualisation techniques would also help novice searchers be more adventurous – but in a bounded way – and find items outside their immediate disciplinary collections. Exposing metadata for indexing by Google and Google Scholar helps university staff and students, and makes resources, or information about resources, available to external users.

One method that is intended to help library staff understand how humanities scholars work uses 'personas' – fictional academic researchers whose experience, responsibilities and information seeking and information requirements are based on interviews with real people and the research evidence on information seeking among this group of scholars (Al-Shboul and Abrizah, 2016). Analysis of the qualitative interview data made it possible to identify common patterns of needs and behaviour, the type of events that trigger information seeking, and the type of activities undertaken to meet the information need and manage the information retrieved.

The MERL team found the concept of 'digital visitor' or 'digital resident' useful when trying to work out how students could really engage with the collections, rather than simply using the collections as a supermarket, picking up items and then leaving. White and Le Cornu (2011) present and discuss the digital visitor-resident continuum, suggesting that the digital immigrant–native division is not suited to the situation with social media. They stress the importance of appreciating that users may be in different communities, and different virtual places, digital visitors in some, but digital residents in others, and that motivation needs to be considered. Davis (2014) suggests that when students use the technology as a tool, behaving as a visitor, their experience is transient. If the student enjoys working in the virtual environment they may be more likely to develop a social presence within the environment. The extent to which students are willing and able to do this depends on other factors. Perhaps those who are intellectually curious and already sociable are more likely to become digital residents. Some strategic learners with other external (e.g. family) responsibilities may not value being a digital resident, and prefer to remain digital visitors.

The idea of engagement with learning spaces is not new, and predates social media. Urquhart et al. (2004) discusses a comparison of various frameworks for pedagogical evaluation of virtual learning environments and learning management systems. A conversational framework is useful for examining the interactions between student and teacher, but a viable systems model is useful for considering the management of groups of learners. Examination of student interviewee comments on the benefits of the virtual learning environment (at different higher education institutions) showed that some perceived the virtual learning environment as a learning framework that definitely supported their learning, and was essentially a classroom extension for them, to allow more conversation between student and teaching staff, and some interaction, to allow reflection on learning. Doing exercises helped students to monitor their own learning, for example. The observation that students' use of the virtual learning environment often did not progress beyond a basic level is reminiscent of White and Le Cornu's (2011) description of the 'digital visitor' phenomenon – academics left some basic resources for students to pick up (or not) as they pleased. Progressing to proper engagement, and individualisation of learning for the student, demands more planning by teaching staff. It is challenging for teams in special collections to collaborate with academic staff, and probably requires staff in special collections to look carefully at not only the module content for students, but also how students are assessed.

References

Al-Shboul, M. K. and Abrizah, A. (2016) Modes of Information Seeking: developing personas of humanities scholars, *Information Development*, **32** (5), 1786–805.

Antonijević, S. and Cahoy, E. S. (2014) Personal Library Curation: an ethnographic study of scholars' practices, *Portal: Libraries & the Academy*, **14** (2), 279–98.

Conway, P., Fraistat, N., Galloway, P., Kraus, K., Rehberger, D. and Walter, K. (2010) Digital Humanities Internships: creating a model ischool-digital humanities center partnership. In *Proceedings of the Digital Humanities Conference*.

Cunningham, L. (2010) The Librarian as Digital Humanist: the collaborative role of the research library in the digital humanities, *Faculty of Information Quarterly*, **10** (2), http://fiq.ischool.utoronto.ca/index.php/fiq/article/view/15409.

Davis, J. (2014) Dimensions of Identity and the Student Experience of Networked Learning. In Bayne, S., Jones, C., de Laat, M., Ryberg, T. and Sinclair, C. (eds), *Proceedings of the 9th International Conference on Networked Learning 2014*, www.lancaster.ac.uk/fss/organisations/netlc/past/nlc2014/abstracts/pdf/davis.pdf.

Heuwing, B., Mandl, T. and Womser-Hacker, C. (2016) Combining Contextual Interviews and Participative Design to Define Requirements for Text Analysis of Historical Media, *Information Research*, **21** (4), http://InformationR.net/ir/21-4/isic/isic1606.html.

Larivière, V., Sugimoto, C. R. and Bergeron, P. (2013) In Their Own Image? A comparison of doctoral students' and faculty members' referencing behaviour, *Journal of the American Society for Information Science and Technology*, **64** (5), 1045–54.

Madsen, C. and Hurst, M. (2015) *Resource Discovery @ The University of Oxford*, Athenaum21 Consulting Research, https://www.bodleian.ox.ac.uk/__data/assets/pdf_file/0009/197118/

Oxford-Resource-Discovery-Final-Report.pdf.
Urquhart, C., Spink, S., Thomas, R., Yeoman, A., Durbin, J., Turner, J., Fenton, R. and Armstrong, C. (2004), Evaluating the Development of Virtual Learning Environments in Higher and Further Education. In *Blue Skies and Pragmatism: learning technologies for the next decade, ALT-C 2004, 11th International Conference*, 14–16 September 2004, 157–69, http://hdl.handle.net/2160/237.
White, D. S. and Le Cornu, A. (2011) Visitors and Residents: a new typology for online engagement, *First Monday*, **16** (9), http://firstmonday.org/ojs/index.php/fm/article/view/3171/3049.

10.1   Introduction

This chapter discusses some resource discovery projects at academic libraries throughout the UK. The projects were all part of Jisc's programme Spotlight on the Digital (https://digitisation.jiscinvolve.org/wp/spotlight-on-the-digital/). The programme aimed to explore and highlight the challenges of digitised collection discovery and to provide and suggest solutions accordingly. The projects selected for this book all examined aspects of information searching by potential users of the resources or collections, and explained how resource discovery was managed by the project. The first project, in Special Collections and Archives, Queen's University Belfast, used Flickr to promote a collection of photographs from the Sir Robert Hart manuscript collection. The second project, at the Middlesex University's Museum of Domestic Design and Architecture, examined how to use the balanced value impact model (Tanner, 2012) to help analyse the possible purposes of the collection for various stakeholders, and how to choose appropriate social media for particular audiences. The third project examined how to build a better content management system at the MERL and Special Collections at the University of Reading, to try to meet the needs of casual visitors, and bring more visitors to the site, by capitalising on social media.

As Section 6.2.1 notes, one of the changes in resource discovery in many academic libraries from 2011 onwards is the use of social media. Instead of trying to direct students to use library discovery systems directly, when social media is used creatively it can help libraries bring students, and casual visitors desired by many special collections, to the library system. This type of activity is an additional responsibility for electronic resources librarians, who have been involved more with acquisition, troubleshooting access and organising e-resources through cataloguing. To cater fully for resource discovery using social media involves more than promoting selected resources via the library's Facebook pages, however. As Weller (2010, 351) points out, we may need to mediate among different knowledge organisation systems to provide for a knowledge organisation systems ontology. There are simpler approaches that may provide workable solutions for many situations, such as use of collaboratively built structured folksonomies (Yoo et al., 2013) or methods for search engine optimisation (Onaifo and Rasmussen, 2013). This chapter often emphasises the use of social media to help promote collections to more occasional users, without adversely affecting use of existing databases for research purposes. The evaluation of the website architecture is effectively integrated into the design.

Section 10.2 discusses the first case study – on using Flickr to promote a photograph collection – and Section 10.3 describes how resource discovery was enhanced. Section 10.4 discusses the second case study – on using the balanced value impact model to help analyse possible purposes of a collection – and Section 10.5 looks at the social media analyses involved. Section 10.6 discusses the third resource discovery project – on building a better content management system for a new website – and Section 10.7 describes how audience needs were assessed. Future developments for the revised website are outlined in Section 10.8. Section 10.9 draws conclusions.

10.2 Using Flickr to promote a photograph collection

The case study for Jisc supported a research project collaboration between Special Collections and Archives, the School of Modern History and Anthropology (both at Queen's University Belfast) and the Institute of Modern History and the Chinese Academy of Social Sciences in Beijing (Queens University Belfast, 2015). The Robert Hart collection related to 19th century and early 20th-century China. As part of the collaboration project a photobook was created comprising around 100 photographs with an accompanying narrative to show Hart's life in China.

Special Collections and Archives aimed to increase awareness of the digitised manuscript and archival resources in the University, both within the university and to external researchers (Mitchel and Costelloe, 2015). When the project started, Special Collections and Archives had their own web pages, a Twitter account and a blog. The team wanted to have a presence on general online resources such as Wikipedia and Flickr, as these rank highly on search engine retrieval results.

One of the problems was rights management, as the collections are research assets of the University and the University's rights in them had to be protected. Some digital resources put online by different cultural organisations are available on open licences, or Creative Commons CC0 licences, which allow resources to be placed in the public domain, often because copyright has expired. However, this was not possible for this project and one of the reasons for choosing Flickr was the ability to license images in a way that suited the needs of the project. Flickr allowed the upload of watermarked images. The 'all rights reserved' licence was chosen, and all the images selected for the Flickr site were watermarked with the Queen's University logo, with the help of computing services staff.

10.3   Helping resource discovery for a photograph collection

One very practical aspect of resource discovery is ensuring that digital resources can be cited consistently in the research literature. If links to the digital resources are broken, the URL is no longer valid, and the reference lacks valid access information. If scholars only cite the original collection to avoid problems with broken links with the digitised resource, then other researchers may not realise that the resource is available online.

After assessing various options, the team decided to create a site on Flickr for the photographs, as Flickr is a very popular photo-sharing site on the internet, used by many institutions. The high Google ranking of Flickr made it more likely that searchers would return the Robert Hart site in a Google search, and images could be licensed as desired when using a Flickr site (see above).

The team created a professional profile page that allowed them to describe Special Collections and Archives at Queen's University Belfast, and provide links to their website and Twitter. An album was created for the photograph collection, allowing description of the resource, plus the ability to add further collections in the future.

10.4   Use of the balanced value impact model at the Museum of Domestic Design and Architecture

The project at the Museum of Domestic Design and Architecture (MoDA) at Middlesex University was part of the planning of the new website. Problems to be overcome included a static website and inflexible content management system, with poor search engine optimisation, and therefore little use of the online collections (Smith and Panaser, 2015). Many people could be expected to be interested in the collections – scholars researching the development of suburbia and town planning, jewellery designers and other designers looking for inspiration from the wallpaper collection, and members of the public interested in interior design. The collections include the Silver Studio (designs, textiles, photographs and archival material), the Crown Wallpaper collection, a domestic design collection and books on architecture and town planning.

At the start of the project, the aim was to analyse whether the social media output suited the needs of the user groups, and then to develop a social media policy. From the social media policy, a content strategy for the website could be developed and the discovery activities for the various collections united within a coherent digital strategy.

10.5 Social media analyses and use of the balanced value impact model

The team examined Instagram, Periscope, Vimeo and Storify as possible social media to improve the discoverability of the collections. Despite the apparent attraction of Instagram for a student audience, the app in fact strips out the metadata from the images. This is not ideal in making the collections easy to discover. In addition, Instagram was not available as an app on the iPad, a basic tool used in the Museum. The team believed that use of social media had to chime with institutional aims, stakeholders and audiences.

Periscope was judged useful for live events, but not for functions that require longer term use. Vimeo, on the other hand, has licensing options that suited MoDA, as the team wished to embed Creative Commons licensing into content, to allow others to share content (and therefore send traffic to MoDA), but with awareness of their rights. The range of analytics appeared helpful. The main advantage might be the storage of content, allowing collection-based content to be embedded in the new website and Storify.

Storify can quickly show readers what kind of reaction an event or topic is getting on social media, and allows MoDA to embed Vimeo and tweets within contextual information to tell a story through a social media campaign. Storify is also compatible with Blogger. Stories told about the collections using Storify and Blogger could be reappropriated later through the new website.

In the first stage of developing the balanced value impact model the team performed a SWOT analysis of the current situation. Strengths included the highly visual collection and a small team, able to move fast and innovate. Weaknesses included the lack of content or social media strategies, problems with the current website and the feeling that students were not engaged. Opportunities presented themselves through use on new media, events that offered outreach to a wider community (e.g. pop-up Hasler Gallery in North Finchley), and existing arrangements with developments in the museums sector (e.g. Culture 24 project). Threats included the need to deal with copyright, maintaining continuity of the activities, intellectual property issues, and the need for buy-in from contributors for certain projects.

In the second stage the team identified and grouped the stakeholders, dividing them into primary stakeholder groups (those directly affected by the resource) and secondary stakeholder groups (those indirectly affected). For example, university teaching staff are classed as primary stakeholders, of the partners and collaborators group with the following attributes: internal (users and influencers). Writers, authors and artists may form one of the producers and creative groups with the attributes (users, influencers, external). Secondary stakeholders included the Chinese and international audience, a marginalised non-user group, with the attribute 'potential user'. Writers, authors and artists (less involved) may also be secondary stakeholders (champions, partners and collaborators groups) with the attributes of 'potential users', 'opinion leaders' and 'potential supporters'. Artists' relatives could belong to commentators, consumers, champions groups with the attributes of 'potential users', 'potential supporters', but also 'potential opponents'.

Four balancing perspectives were then identified: social (audience, stakeholders and wider society affected and benefits obtained), economic (demonstration of economic benefits to the organisation and society), innovation (digital resource enabling innovation that sustains the social and economic benefits) and internal (processes within the organisation benefitting by the innovation).

The value drivers assigned to the perspectives and mapped to the stakeholders completed the analysis. The identified value drivers were:

- education (people aware how digital resources contribute to their own and other people's sense of culture, education, knowledge and heritage – and therefore value them)
- community (people benefit from the experience of being part of a community afforded by the digital resource)

- existence or prestige (people appreciate and value the fact that others in their community cherish the resource, even if they do not use it personally)
- inheritance or bequest value (people value the potential direct benefit to their descendants and future members of their community).

Doing the analysis helped the team to identify possible projects for particular stakeholder groups, with an idea of what the outputs should be.

10.6   Improving resource discovery at the Museum of English Rural Life and Special Collections, University of Reading

The MERL had a large amount of digitised material but found it difficult to make it widely available. Alongside the Heritage Lottery Fund project, the improvement project Digging Deeper aimed to provide more intuitive pathways into the collection that did not involve use of the Adlib database (Hilton and Koszary, 2015). The majority of MERL's collections are catalogued and available online through the Adlib database, but the user interface is more suited to professional users.

The main aims of the website improvement project were:

- to integrate the Digging Deeper work into the social media presence
- to implement the new digital asset management system so that the tagging function was compatible with Digging Deeper
- to research the needs of academics for teaching so that resources can be presented by themes of interest for learning
- to allow for a variety of access points to allow for different audience needs
- to use Google Analytics to ensure that the website works well with Google searches.

10.7   Assessing audience needs

The team was already interested in tracking use of MERL's digital collections across the internet. Some analytics were already performed on Twitter, Pinterest, Facebook and Tumblr, but the team believed that more professional tools such as Hootsuite might be useful.

Research into academic needs and preferences started with a review of the relevant curricula at the University of Reading, to check which resources might be useful to faculty, and assess whether some subject packages would be valued.

To test out how a wider audience might use the collections, the team planned to upload the low-risk object collection photographs on Wikimedia Commons. There are third party rights in many of the collections, which limits what can be made available under a Creative Commons licence.

10.8   Future developments for the Museum of English Rural Life

The revised website was launched in September 2016 (Hilton and Koszary, 2017) after meeting some but not all of the original aims. This was largely because of staff time problems, as the redevelopment also involved changes to the physical galleries and the website. The museum started an Arts Council England project in November 2016, working with Reading Museum and building on the work conducted with Jisc.

As no decision had been made on a new official content management system for the University, the project team built the MERL website using the content management system Activedition, with Google Analytics tags, goals, tracking, interactions and filters built in. Staff and volunteers tested the initial design and structure. The Discover section of the website allows users to browse objects, archives and books (categorised into themes and categories), as envisaged in the Digging Deeper aims and objectives. Each object is linked to a specific collections page and a gallery page if the object is on public display. Each page is designed to have a visual impact and function similar to a blog page with high quality photos and text. This type of page is far more useful for linking to social media than the object records on the Adlib database (which still perform a useful function for researchers).

The teething problems included the search function, which is difficult to navigate and not very intuitive. There should be more objects in the section but working with Activedition is time-consuming and the objects need to have professional photographs. Time problems are exacerbated by the need to put in manual entries as the information cannot be pulled from the digital asset management system (one of the objectives of the Arts Council project is to deal with this problem).

Work on social media is ongoing, and visitors are invited to share their visit through social media. Staff are exploring new platforms such as Instagram.

10.9   Conclusions

The case studies of resource discovery and interaction with social media are projects in progress, and the case study descriptions explain that changes were made to the original plans. These projects are dealing with potential users, who are much more difficult to profile than existing faculty staff, researchers and students. As the descriptions illustrate, there are often time and funding problems for such pilot projects. They emphasise the importance of thinking at an early stage in designing website architecture how and what to evaluate when trying to determine whether the website has successfully met its aim of satisfying the needs of existing and potential users.

References

Hilton, A. and Koszary, A. (2015) Implementing Resource Discovery Techniques at the Museum of English Rural Life and Special Collections, University of Reading: using resource discovery techniques to create a user friendly web presence,
https://digitisation.jiscinvolve.org/wp/files/2015/09/case_study_resource_discovery_merl.pdf.

Hilton, A. and Koszary, A. (2017) Implementing Resource Discovery Techniques at the Museum of English Rural Life and Special Collections, University of Reading: using resource discovery techniques to create a user friendly web presence,
https://digitisation.jiscinvolve.org/wp/files/2017/02/case_study_resource_discovery_MERL_update.pdf.

Mitchel, U. and Costelloe, L. (2015) Implementing Resource Discovery Techniques in Special Collections & Archives, Queen's University Belfast: using Flickr to promote special collections,
https://digitisation.jiscinvolve.org/wp/files/2015/09/case_study_resource_discovery_queens.pdf.

Onaifo, D. and Rasmussen, D. (2013) Increasing Libraries' Content Findability on the Web with Search Engine Optimization, *Library Hi-Tech*, **31** (1), 87–108.

Queens University Belfast (2015) Sir Robert Hart Project,
http://blogs.qub.ac.uk/sirroberthart/sir-robert-hart-project/.

Smith, S. and Panaser, S. (2015) Implementing Resource Discovery Techniques at the Museum of Domestic Design & Architecture,

Middlesex University: social media and the balanced value impact model, https://digitisation.jiscinvolve.org/wp/files/2015/09/case_study_resource_discovery_moda.pdf.

Tanner, S. (2012) *Measuring the Impact of Digital Resources: balanced value impact model*, King's College London, https://www.kdl.kcl.ac.uk/fileadmin/documents/pubs/BalancedValueImpactModel_SimonTanner_October2012.pdf.

Weller, K. (2010) *Knowledge Representations in the Social Semantic Web*, De Gruyter Saur.

Yoo, D., Choi, K., Suh, Y. and Kim, G. (2013) Building and Evaluating a Collaboratively Built Structured Folksonomy, *Journal of Information Science*, **39** (5), 593–607.

CHAPTER 11

Increasing social connection through a community-of-practice-inspired design

Catherine M. Burns and Adam Euerby

COMMENTARY: CHRISTINE URQUHART

Catherine Burns and Adam Euerby used cognitive work analysis to help design a website intended to foster community of practice principles in order to improve networking. First, we need to appreciate the history of cognitive work analysis, and where the ideas about the work domain analysis come from. It's important to recognise that both cognitive work analysis and communities of practice have evidence behind their concepts, and that they are not merely theoretical frameworks that seem to work.

Cognitive work analysis comes from studies conducted by Rasmussen and colleagues at the Risø National Laboratory in Denmark in the early 2000s (Naikar, 2017). They were tasked with improving the safety of nuclear power plants in Denmark. Observations confirmed that the hardware was indeed reliable, but that, despite this, accidents could still happen. Human error appeared responsible, when workers were confronted with unfamiliar circumstances. However, the research indicated that had the workers known fully the state of the system, they could have formulated an appropriate response. Later research examined six professional technicians, problem-solving with different types of instruments, which each had a particular fault. Detailed analysis of the verbal protocols (think-aloud protocols) produced a coding scheme that revealed patterns in the reasoning used by the technicians. The technicians reasoned at different levels of abstraction (from the physical properties to the general functional purpose) and at different levels of decomposition (whole system through to a component). This formed what they termed the two-dimensional abstraction-decomposition space. Generally, the technicians started in the most abstract (purpose)/whole system corner and worked through to the opposite corner (physical form/component) – although the line of working could zig zag a little. These findings led to the first stage of cognitive work analysis modelling – the work domain analysis. This was developed by Vicente (2002) (among others) for design of interfaces that displayed three modes of cognitive reasoning: skill-based, rules-based and knowledge-based behaviour. The aim of systems designed through CWA is often to support workers in dealing with unexpected situations. Workers should be able to explore a number of ways of dealing with the situation while remaining within the boundaries of acceptable performance (Naikar, 2017). The system is there to assist the human to explore, to learn, improve skills and to avoid error, through providing constraints.

In the example presented by Catherine Burns and Adam Euerby, the most abstract level is that of functional purpose, then the value and priority measures, followed by processes, and finally: people, relationships, projects and events. Within the cell for value and priority measures, the idea of constraints and boundaries is evident – that the external network should not be extended too much if this is going to adversely affect the strength of connections, for example. The categories of processes supported are to do with strengthening connections or partnerships. And finally, the least abstract cell details the type of roles and events involved – the very practical physical outcomes.

Early work by Lave and Wenger on communities of practice (1991) emphasises the social nature of much learning (see Chapter 12) – the learning that takes place informally in the workplace, or in leisure activities. We are all likely to be members of different communities of practice and at different levels in each community. An interested beginner in some, and more involved, with a greater leadership role in others. Wenger (1998, Chapter 10) discusses learning architectures along two dimensions. One dimension concerns modes of belonging (engagement, imagination and alignment) and the infrastructure needs to provide for those modes of belonging through, for example, tools for participation (for engagement), scenario development (for imagination) and feedback and audit mechanisms (for alignment). The other dimension reflects the ways in which such learning could be situated within the community.

Mapping the community of practice ideas to the work domain analysis produces complementary labels to those for the work domain analysis but the emphasis is on learning. The top level is the desired state of the learning community, and the next level reflects some of the ideas from Wenger on the four dualities of the way learning can be situated within the community. The first duality is participation/reification: active participation versus the congealment of certain aspects of practice (in stories, tools and documents) – 'a certain understanding is given form' (Wenger, 1998, 59). The second is designed versus emergent (results of a design versus response to a design). The third is local/global – for learning, communities of practice need to access other practices, although the community is primarily responsible for its own learning. The fourth duality is identification/negotiability, which essentially looks at the way power is negotiated and what participation means and involves in that setting.

The level of the work domain analysis of processes maps to 'practices' of the communities of practice, the types of activity that need to be supported. Catherine Burns and Adam Euerby have merged the lowest (least abstract) levels together. These are the roles, and type of objects, events and documents that need to be considered in the design.

Research on communities of practice, and their use of tools and stages of evolution, stresses that communities may move backward and forward or stick at a particular stage. Work for the National Electronic Library for Health in the UK in the early 2000s (Urquhart, Yeoman and Sharp, 2002) used the stages identified in an IBM evaluation of communities of practice, to determine whether the 'virtual branch libraries' were developing as intended. The stages are: potential (main function to connect individuals), building (allowing core members to learn about each other, share experiences and knowledge, and create norms), engaged (main function to support access and learning), active (engagement of community members in real work) and finally adaptive (where new products and services, and even new communities are developed). The framework helped to evaluate how well some of the communities of practice were developing and what some of the problems were. These were 'designed' communities and the modes of belonging (engagement, imagination, audit and feedback) had to be clear to members of the community.

References

Lave, J. and Wenger, E. (1991) *Situated Learning: legitimate peripheral participation,* Cambridge University Press.

Naikar, N. (2017) Cognitive Work Analysis: an influential legacy extending beyond human factors and engineering, *Applied Ergonomics,* **59** (Part B), 528–540.

Urquhart, C., Yeoman, A. and Sharp, S. (2002) *NeLH Communities of Practice Evaluation Report.* Prepared for NeLH team, NHS Authority.

Vicente, K. J. (2002) Ecological Interface Design: progress and challenges, *Human Factors: The Journal of the Human Factors and Ergonomics Society,* **44** (1), 62–78.

Wenger, E. (1998) *Communities of Practice: learning, meaning and identity,* Cambridge University Press.

11.1   Introduction

Today's internet technology is as much about connecting people as it is about providing access to information. However, we have relatively few tools that reveal social interaction requirements and measure the social effect of new technology. There are several approaches from the fields of human factors engineering and human–computer interaction that have examined how to design for teams (for example Salas et al., 1992; Naikar et al., 2000; Endsley, Bolte and Jones, 2003; Cooke, 2005). The Computer Supported Collaborative Work community has generated many interesting examples of how technology can change the way people interact and work together (e.g. Malone and Crowston, 1990). But again, these are primarily examinations of how tightly connected people work effectively together through technology to achieve specific goals. The design of technology to support a community is somewhat different. In this case the ties between people are looser and interaction is optional for users. We believe that building an understanding of how communities interact through technology is an important and under-explored direction for human–computer interaction.

Communities are social systems that are much less tightly connected than teams. While communities may not work on tight tasks together, having an effective community can generate several benefits to an organisation. Effective communities over time build practices and expertise within their members and promote the flow of information and practice between their members. The recent emergence of social networking technologies, particularly in the workplace, has made developing effective social communities an important goal for organisational success. Those creating design methods need to consider how communities function and recommend designs that have a measurable influence on social effectiveness.

Those working with the concept of communities of practice have recognised some features of effective communities; Wenger (1998) considers the framework of a learning architecture for organisations and education. However, the concept does not lend itself so well to the design of community supporting systems that operate across organisations. We suggest that this approach presents an opportunity to integrate communities of practice principles with a more relevant design method. We propose that a design built from this communities-of-practice-inspired method should demonstrate clear improvements in community functioning over time.

In this work we used a human factors method with which we had experience, cognitive work analysis (Vicente, 1999), and modified the approach by using principles from the concept of communities of practice as developed by Wenger (1998) and Wenger, McDermott and Snyder (2002) to design a new website for a community. We studied the influence of this new design on the behaviour of the community, taking a longitudinal approach where we examined the community before the new design was introduced, shortly after its introduction, and then again several months later.

Like the authors of several of the chapters in this book, we are concerned with websites that users work with. Chapter 9 considered semi-structured document architecture, Chapter 10 compared the needs of researchers and casual visitors, Chapter 13 considers clinical document architecture, and Chapter 14 discusses the needs of systematic reviewers for collaborative working. Cognitive work analysis is an established method for studying the work domain. The working of a community of practice is examined in Chapter 12, and communities of practice theory has been applied to several examples of virtual communities - very relevant to much professional work and study today.

Section 11.2 describes the methodology used in the study. Section 11.3 sets out the results, and Section 11.4 discusses them. Section 11.5 draws conclusions.

11.2   Method

In this section we discuss the community under study, the design approach that we followed and how the new design was evaluated to assess changes in community behaviour.

11.2.1 The community

The University-Community Partnership for Social Action Research (UCP-SARnet) was launched in 2008. It is an organisation based at Arizona State University with a mission to 'educate, engage and empower communities' by facilitating global partnerships between universities, local governments and community organisations. These partnerships are aimed at creating new opportunities for joint action to realise the United Nations Millennium Development Goals (MDGs).

UCP-SARnet maintains a partnership with 42 organisational partners and 971 members, including university students, university faculty, community activists and members of local government. Seven volunteer regional coordinators, located in Argentina, Australia, Ghana, India, Nigeria, Poland and South Africa, act as ambassadors for UCP-SARnet, facilitating collaborations between local community organisations, universities and governments in efforts towards achieving the MDGs. The partners, members and regional co-ordinators, led by a leadership team of 43 volunteers, work together to organise events promoting the MDGs, source new strategic partnerships, and contribute directly to MDG-related projects.

To support its distributed activities, UCP-SARnet does much of its work through an online social networking portal powered by Igloo Software (www.igloosoftware.com/). The Igloo platform provides a suite of features including member profiles, blogging, discussion forums, wikis, calendars, document sharing, status updates and e-mail notifications. A site manager allows administrators of UCP-SARnet to customise the navigation and display of these features using a drag-and-drop Site Manager and Page Editor. This combination of features allows UCP-SARnet administrators to choose how to stream activities in any of these features through virtually any site structure and page layout. For instance, the administrator can stream new blog and discussion forum posts by dragging and dropping those components and arranging them on the page using the Page Editor.

In July 2010, UCP-SARnet began to revamp its social networking portal on the Igloo platform with the broad goal of making it 'more attractive and alive'.

11.2.2 Design approach

From meetings with core members of the UCP-SARnet leadership team, and considering the intentions of cognitive work analysis (Vicente, 1999) with the principles for supporting communities of practice, a work domain analysis was developed. This process is described fully in Euerby and Burns (2010, 2012). Table 11.1 shows the work domain model. It should be noted that two views of the domain are presented, one specific to the purpose of the community (Domain) and the other related to the purpose of being a community (Community). In the left-hand column, traditional work domain levels are shown. The far right-hand column shows levels that were proposed to be more consistent with the principles for supporting communities of practice.

Table 11.1 *View of a community-of-practice-inspired work domain analysis* (from Euerby and Burns, 2012, republished with permission of Sage Publications; permission conveyed through the Copyright Clearance Center, Inc.)

Level of work domain analysis	Domain	Community	Community of practice intentions
Functional purpose	Achieve the UN MDGs	Agreed on role in the larger context; strength in relationships to actively discuss differences with domain and practice Established what knowledge should be shared and how to share it	Desired state of the learning community
Value and priority measures	Span of the external network vs strength of the connections Social action vs research results Power of the researcher vs power of the communities Mobilise knowledge and mobilise communities Bring awareness about MDGs and drive collective social action to achieve them Educate, engage and empower communities	Participation vs reification Designed vs emergent Identification vs negotiability Local vs global Increase alignment, engagement and imagination	Tradeoffs and priorities of the negotiation of meaning

(continued)

Level of work domain analysis	Domain	Community	Community of practice intentions
Processes	Build formal partnerships, host networking and public outreach events, collaborate with partners	Building connections between the core participants, identifying opportunities to provide value in the larger context, finding the ideas and insights that are worth sharing with other members, identifying gaps in the knowledge, refining the role of communities of practice in the larger context	Practices
People, relationships, projects, events	Network facilitator, executive team members, regional coordinators, peripheral members, knowledge partners, organisational partners, memorandums of agreement with organisational partners, executive meetings, stand-up against poverty events, bridging the world virtual events		People, relationships, projects, events

The overall result of taking the communities-of-practice-inspired approach was closer consideration of the tactics of building the community, alongside the strategic view of purposes provided by the work domain analysis.

11.2.3 New design

As a result of the analysis, several changes were made in the redesign of the website. These changes are summarised in Table 11.2 and discussed in more detail in Euerby and Burns (2012).

Table 11.2 *Key design changes made to a website after a work domain analysis* (from Euerby and Burns, 2012, republished with permission of Sage Publications, permission conveyed through Copyright Clearance Center, Inc.)

Components	Design concept	Community support
Home page	External facing page focuses on presenting activities and successes of UCP-SARnet's efforts to achieve the MDGs Congregates information and artefacts relevant to meeting the MDGs Provides a space for communication to prospective members and partners, and other stakeholders in the larger context of the MDGs	Staying current in the external communications provides members with a way to view and reflect on UCP-SARnet's role in meeting the MDGs; in doing so, members may begin dialogue to refine and agree on the role of communities of practice in the larger context of meeting the MDGs (Desired state of the learning community)

(continued)

Components	Design concept	Community support
Photo banner rotator	Displays specific efforts to achieve MDGs Presents examples of member participation	Providing a visual image of how UCP-SARnet is providing value in the MDG efforts helps members identify new ways in which they may provide value (Practices)
UCP-SARnet in action blog	Provides a communication stream for potential members, partners and other stakeholders in the larger context	Allowing members to monitor the outgoing communication helps create an orientation towards providing value in the external context (Practices) This orientation makes it easier to identify gaps in knowledge and thus provide a productive meeting for the MDGs, of value to all. (Practices) Focusing the design on transient kinds of communication features (blogs) rather than static communication features (wikis) was a trade-off of reification for participation, which was seen to best serve alignment, engagement and imagination in UCP-SARnet (Tradeoffs and priorities)
Members area	Internal facing page focuses on content authoring, sharing and exchanging dialogue Provides a central space for informal dialogue about the MDGs and UCP-SARnet as a community of practice Congregates internal information and artefacts relevant to the internal operations of UCP-SARnet	Focusing on content authoring, sharing and dialogue helps to give members experience with using the knowledge, so over time UCP-SARnet members may learn what knowledge should be shared and how to share it (Practices) Setting a more informal context for dialogue helps members build the strength in relationships to discuss differences in domain and practice (Desired state of the learning community)
Members area blog	Provides a communication stream for internal dialogue about the MDGs and how the community of practice can improve its efforts towards them	Providing a flexible and informal medium for internal dialogue supports all of the practices (Practices)
Recent activity or latest comments bar	Provides a historical view of the internal communication streams and comments and the exchange of documents and other artefacts Encourages revisiting the site by showing what is new and allows members to catch up with any unfolding dialogue Encourages message reciprocation by making comments more visible to the whole community of practice	By providing a historical view of the dialogue, members are better able to track conversations so they learn what knowledge should be shared and how (Practices, people and relationships) Encouraging message reciprocation inclined the core team to build a variety of connections through shared content matter, personal exchanges, etc. (Practices, people and relationships)

(continued)

Components	Design concept	Community support
Facilitator's frame	Recognises the role of facilitators in supporting the internal activities of UCP-SARnet	By recognising these shared roles and their similar relationship to the UCP-SARnet community of practice, this component helps to build connections between facilitators (Practices, people and relationships)

11.2.4 Evaluation

The influence of the new website design was evaluated longitudinally over six months at three times. A baseline measure was taken before the new site was implemented (at or around 1 January 2011); the new site was launched on 16 January 2011; then the effect of the new site was measured at two points, once two months after the new site went online (around 12 March 2011) and once several months later (around 29 May 2011). The intent of this approach was to try to identify transient changes that may have occurred with the new site, and longer term more sustainable changes, and to be able to observe changes shortly after implementation of the new site and longer term changes.

Figure 11.1 shows a timeline of the evaluation and when survey responses were received. The triangle above each cluster of circles indicates the average respondent submission date for each survey.

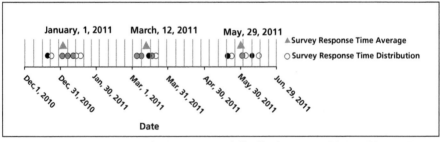

Figure 11.1 *Survey response time average and distribution, 1 Dec 2010 to 29 Jun 2011* (from Euerby and Burns, 2014, 370, reproduced under the terms of the Creative Commons Attribution-NonCommercial 3.0 License [CC BY-NC 3.0]).

11.2.5 Surveys

Three identical surveys were conducted with the UCP-SARnet leadership team at each of the evaluation points. The surveys were built to assess the social presence and usability of the site. There were also questions on various social connections between members that will not be reported in this chapter.

Of the 43 members on the UCP-SARnet leadership team, there were 26 respondents to the first survey, 24 respondents in the second survey and 17 respondents in the third survey; 14 base respondents completed all three surveys. Because of these differing numbers, the analyses below were based on the respondents who completed all three surveys.

11.2.5.1 Social network analysis

Social network analysis was used to examine the connections between members of the community. These results have been previously reported in Euerby and Burns (2014) and are included here in summary. To look at the social network, members of the leadership team were given a list of the other team members and asked to report whether they felt they did not know the person, knew them somewhat, or knew them well. This intuitive sense of knowing was a deliberate part of this study in order to capture the sense of community. Network graphs and social network analysis statistics could be calculated from this data (Euerby and Burns, 2014).

11.2.5.2 Website usage

Website usage data was evaluated in order to see whether or not the community was actively using the site. Google Analytics (www.google.com/analytics/) was set up for the UCP-SARnet web portal, which allowed the researcher to track various usage metrics over time. Google Analytics allowed tracking of both return users and new users to the UCP-SARnet website. When tracking usage by UCP-SARnet leadership team members, return users were of particular interest. To find out the extent of social engagement of the UCP-SARnet leadership team, we tracked how often return users visited the site, how many pages they looked at during each visit to the site, and the time they spent during their visit.

Similar to the social presence measures, the website usage analysis helped to determine if there was a relationship between UCP-SARnet site traffic that corresponded to changes in the design of the site. In order to compare the site usage data with the survey data we selected three periods of ten weeks corresponding to the three survey (S) dates: Period 1 (P1) ten weeks before the release of the website on 16 January 2011, corresponding to S1; Period 2 (P2) ten weeks leading up to near the end of S2; and Period 3 (P3) ten weeks leading up to near the end of S3.

This was the main hypothesis when analysing website usage:

The redesign of the UCP-SARnet social networking portal at the end of Period 1 will change overall website usage by the UCP-SARnet leadership team over time.

11.2.5.3 Website communication

The activity not the content of communication was examined, in order to see whether the new site was encouraging participation, one of the key community of practice principles. The website communication analysis examined the blog and comment posts made on the UCP-SARnet web portal through P1, P2 and P3. Similar to the website usage analysis, the communication analysis consisted of a count of the blog posts, comment posts and unique bloggers and commenters over each week. These metrics were chosen to provide a view of how the UCP-SARnet members were using the redesigned UCP-SARnet website, which featured a community blog stream.

This was the main hypothesis when analysing the count of posts to the website:

The redesign of the UCP-SARnet social networking portal at the end of Period 1 will increase the number of blog posts, comments and unique weekly posters to UCP-SARnet over time.

11.3 Results

The results are set out in three sections, looking at the social network analysis, website usage and website communication over the three time periods. As mentioned previously, only respondents who completed all three surveys were included in the analysis.

11.3.1 Social network analysis

Actor–actor social network analysis results are shown in Figure 11.2 opposite at the times of surveys 1, 2 and 3. Overall there was an increase in the number of neighbours and connections, and establishment of a denser network structure. Social network analysis examines the vertices (nodes) in the network, and looks at the lines (called edges, Figure 11.2) connecting vertices together. One vertex may be connected to several adjacent vertices (its neighbours) and the degree of a vertex is the number of ties (lines between vertices) in which the

Network Diameter	3	Network Diameter	4	Network Diameter	3
Avg. Number of Neighbors	4.1 5	Avg. Number of Neighbors	5.4 3	Avg. Number of Neighbors	6.1 4
Number of Nodes	14	Number of Nodes	14	Number of Nodes	14
Number of Edges	41	Number of Edges	57	Number of Edges	69
Network Density	0.23	Network Density	0.31	Network Density	0.38
Multi-edge Node Pairs	14	Multi-edge Node Pairs	19	Multi-edge Node Pairs	26

Figure 11.2 *Social network analysis results at the times of surveys 1, 2 and 3* (from Euerby and Burns, 2014, 374, reproduced under the terms of the Creative Commons Attribution-NonCommercial 3.0 License [CC BY-NC 3.0]).

vertex is involved. The density of a network may be defined as the number of lines in a simple network, expressed as a proportion of the maximum possible number of lines, but often the degree of a vertex is a better measure. Vertices with higher degrees have more ties (more neighbours) (see multi-edge node pairs, Figure 11.2) and will be in denser sections of the network. These changes were statistically significant.

11.3.2 Website usage

Website usage was measured by weekly site visits (Figure 11.3), weekly page views (Figure 11.4) and weekly average time on site (Figure 11.5, page 199). Each figure shows the mean results over periods 1–3 (P1, P2 and P3), with the standard error of the mean. The statistical analysis uses 'returning users' because this item most closely describes the site usage of the UCP-SARnet leadership team; however, the results for 'all users' were shown to provide more context for the reader. In general, the results showed an increase in weekly site visits, a decrease in weekly page views and a decrease in weekly time spent.

A multivariate analysis of variance (MANOVA) was conducted using the

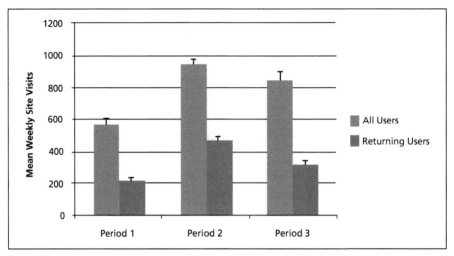

Figure 11.3 *Mean weekly site visits during each period for all users and returning users* (Euerby, 2012)

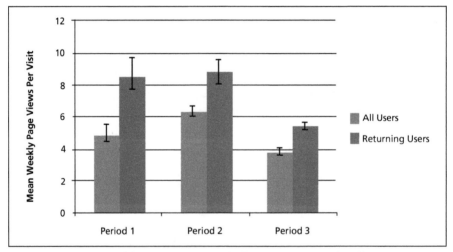

Figure 11.4 *Mean weekly page views per visit during each period for all users and returning users* (Euerby, 2012)

returning user data with weekly site visits, weekly page views per visit and weekly average time on site as dependent variables, and P1, P2 and P3 as the independent variable. To use MANOVA, one of the assumptions to be met is that the population covariance matrices within each group of independent variables are equal. The Box M test indicated that this assumption was met.

The MANOVA showed that there was a statistically significant difference in

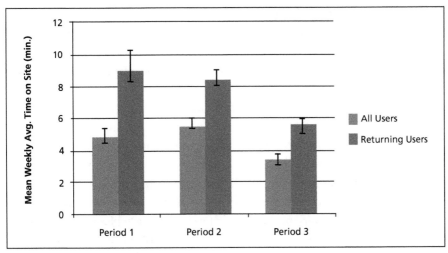

Figure 11.5 *Mean weekly average time on site during each period for all users and returning users* (Euerby, 2012)

website usage variables between periods (ε^2 (6, 50) = 9.72, p < 0.05, Wilks' λ = .213, *partial* ε^2 = 0.538). Follow-up univariate analysis of variance (ANOVA) tests were conducted using the returning user data. The univariate ANOVAs showed that there was a significant effect over the three periods on weekly site visits (F(2, 27) = 26.25, p < 0.05, *partial* ε^2 = .660), page views per visit (F(2, 27) = 6.138, p < 0.05, *partial* ε^2 = 0.313) and weekly average time on site (F(2, 27) = 5.057, p < 0.05, *partial* ε^2 = 0.273). Post-hoc tests between periods were conducted using the Tukey HSD (Honest Significant Difference) test. Mean scores for weekly site visits were different between P1 and P2 (p < 0.005), P2 and P3 (p < 0.05) and P1 and P3 (p < 0.005). Mean scores for page views per visit were not different between P1 and P2 (p = 0.957), but were different between P2 and P3 (p < 0.05) and P1 and P3 (p < 0.05). Finally, mean scores for weekly average time on the site were not different between P1 and P2 (p = 0.881), marginally different for P2 and P3 (p = 0.050), and significantly different between P1 and P3 (p < 0.05). Considering that the results showed an increase in weekly site visits, a decrease in weekly page views, and a decrease in weekly time spent, this could suggest that while users were returning more frequently to the site, their time spent on the site was becoming more efficient as they spent less time and explored fewer pages.

11.3.3   Website communication

The website communication analysis consisted of statistics based on number of content posts to the UCP-SARnet site over each period, in particular the number of blog posts and comments, as well as unique bloggers and commenters each week.

Figure 11.6 shows the content statistics based on number of posts to UCP-SARnet over P1, P2 and P3. Overall, a strong increase was seen in P2, followed by a strong decrease by P3. Similar to the website usage analysis, a MANOVA was conducted with weekly blog posts, weekly comments and weekly unique users as dependent variables and P1, P2 and P3 as independent variables. Box's M Test for equality of covariance matrices was significant at the accepting the null hypothesis that covariance matrices of web usage variables are equal across periods, which did not satisfy the assumption of homoscedasticity for MANOVA. Therefore the overall effect of the period on the three website content statistics could not be determined.

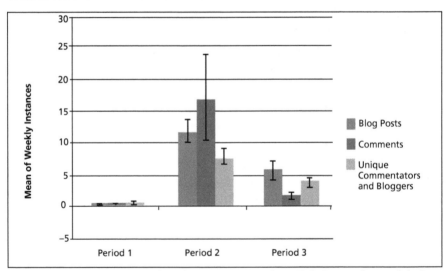

Figure 11.6 *Content statistics based on post type on the UCP-SARnet web portal during each period* (Euerby, 2012)

Follow-up univariate ANOVA tests were conducted for each of the website content analysis variables. The univariate ANOVAs showed that there was a significant effect over the three periods on weekly blog posts ($F(2, 27) = 16.630$, $p < 0.05$, *partial* $\varepsilon^2 = .552$), weekly comment posts ($F(2, 27) = 5.747$, $p < 0.05$, *partial* $\varepsilon^2 = 0.299$) and weekly unique commenters and bloggers ($F(2, 27) = 20.247$, $p < 0.05$, *partial* $\varepsilon^2 = 0.600$).

Post-hoc tests between periods were conducted using the Tukey HSD test. Mean scores for weekly blog posts were different between P1 and P2 ($p < 0.005$), P2 and P3 ($p < 0.05$) and P1 and P3 ($p < 0.05$). Mean scores for weekly comments were different between P1 and P2 ($p = 0.05$) and P2 and P3 ($p < 0.05$), but were not different between P1 and P3 ($p < 0.960$). Finally, mean scores for weekly unique commenters and bloggers were different between P1 and P2 ($p < 0.05$), P2 and P3 ($p < 0.05$) and P1 and P3 ($p < 0.05$). In general these results supported the idea that over time website content had increased, though there was a noticeable transient increase as a result of the release of the new site.

11.4 Discussion

Overall there were several interesting results from this study. Using communities of practice with a human-factors engineering approach, cognitive work analysis, added new perspectives on how to design websites to encourage community building and communication. On evaluation, there is some evidence that the new design achieved some of the goals of communities of practice. Overall, connections between members of the community increased. Weekly site visits increased and there was an increase in the amount of communication through comments and blogs and the number of unique communicators. There were, however, some interesting observations that we had not expected, notably short-term transient effects and longer term more sustained activity effects.

The social network analysis was a useful measure to look at social and organisational development. In this work, we took a primarily structural look at connections. Since this work, other authors have also examined function–actor networks, using the cognitive work analysis models more deeply (Houghton et al., 2015). This approach could continue the cycle of generating new design insights.

There was a strong transient effect observed as site users communicated far more often after the new site was released, with this activity dropping over time. This may have been a result of experimentation and exploration of the features of the new site. Over time, however, users still reverted to a higher rate of communication than before the site redesign, suggesting the new site had some effect.

When looking at website use we observed an increase over time in weekly page visits, but at the same time a decrease in the final observation period in page views per visit and the average time spent on the site. This could reflect several things, from more efficient scanning of the site for key information, to possible effects directly from the redesign (the redesign could have made the most frequently accessed information available through the first pages thereby reducing both page views and time spent). From a usability perspective this would not be a bad thing, but there are emerging ideas in interaction and persuasive design that may be able to exploit more context aware data and analytics to develop a more responsive and participating community (Abdelnour-Nocera, Oussena and Burns, 2015).

There are two limitations to be considered in this study. First, the community under study may be naturally evolving over time so while it is tempting to attribute the changes we observed to the new website we designed, there could have been other factors involved. For example, a short-term issue of great interest could easily influence the rate of communication. Second, the design of the site itself could have influenced the number of page views or time taken to access information on the site. Overall, however, there is some evidence that over time the new website had a positive influence on the community.

11.5   Conclusions

This work explored the use of a community building approach from communities of practice in sociology, together with a cognitive work method, to inspire a new website design in order to encourage community building. The community of practice approach was useful to focus the discussion of design needs and to provide a rationale for the various design elements that were chosen. Evaluated over time, there was evidence that the design approach had some success. Overall, this study points to the need for further exploration of methods that can influence the social interaction of people with each other through technology.

Acknowledgements

We are thankful to the members of the UCP-SARnet leadership team for participating in this study. We also acknowledge the support of the Natural Sciences and Engineering Research Council of Canada. We thank Tim Rodgers for helping with the data analysis.

References

Abdelnour-Nocera, J., Oussena, S. and Burns, C. M. (2015) Human Work Interaction Design of the Smart University. In Abdelnour-Nocera, J., Barricelli, B. R., Lopes, A., Campos, P. and Clemmensen, T. (eds), *Human Work Interaction Design: work analysis and interaction design methods of pervasive and smart workplaces*, IFIP Advances in Information and Communication Technology, Springer.

Cooke, N. J. (2005) Measuring Team Knowledge. In Stanton, N., Hedge, A., Brookhuis, K. and Salas, E. (eds), *Handbook on Human Factors and Ergonomics Methods*, CRC Press.

Endsley, M. R., Bolte, B. and Jones, D. G. (2003) *Designing for Situation Awareness: an approach to user-centered design*, Taylor & Francis.

Euerby, A. (2012) *Designing for Social Engagement in Online Social Networks Using Communities of Practice Theory and Cognitive Work Analysis: a case study*, Unpublished Master's thesis, University of Waterloo, Canada.

Euerby, A. and Burns, C. M. (2010) Advancing Complex Sociotechnical Systems Design Using the Communities of Practice Framework. In *Proceedings of the 54th Annual Meeting of the Human Factors and Ergonomics Society*, 428–32.

Euerby, A. and Burns, C. M. (2012) Designing for Social Engagement in Online Social Networks Using Community of Practice Theory and Cognitive Work Analysis: a case study, *Journal of Cognitive Engineering and Decision Making*, **6** (2), 194–213.

Euerby, A. and Burns, C. M. (2014) Improving Social Connection Through a Communities-of-Practice-Inspired Cognitive Work Analysis Approach, *Human Factors*, **56** (2), 361–83.

Houghton, R. J., Baber, C., Stanton, N. A., Jenkins, D. P. and Revell, K. (2015) Combining Network Analysis with Cognitive Work Analysis: insights into social organisational and cooperation analysis, *Ergonomics*, **58** (3), 434–49.

Malone, T. W. and Crowston, K. (1990) What is Coordination Theory and How Can it Help Design Cooperative Work Systems? In *Proceedings of the 1990 ACM Conference on Computer Supported Cooperative Work*, 357–70.

Naikar, N., Drumm, D., Pearce, B. and Sanderson, M. P. (2000) Designing New Teams with Cognitive Work Analysis. In *Proceedings of the Fifth Australian Aviation Psychology Symposium, Manly, Australia*.

Salas, E., Dickinson, T. L., Converse, S. A. and Tannenbaum, S. I. (1992)

Toward an Understanding of Team Performance and Training. In Swezey, R. W. and Salas, E. (eds), *Teams: their training and performance*, Ablex Publishing.

Vicente, K. J. (1999) *Cognitive Work Analysis: toward safe, productive, and healthy computer-based work*, Lawrence Erlbaum Associates.

Wenger, E. (1998) *Communities of Practice: learning, meaning, and identity*, Cambridge University Press.

Wenger, E., McDermott, R. and Snyder, W. (2002) *Cultivating Communities of Practice: a guide to managing knowledge*, Harvard Business School Press.

CHAPTER 12

Methods for studying information provision, networking and communication in patient support groups

Cristina Vasilica and Paula Ormandy

COMMENTARY: CHRISTINE URQUHART

In the evaluation of the patient support portal, Cristina Vasilica and Paula Ormandy used activity theory, which was originally proposed by Russian psychologist Alexey Leontiev, and is rooted in early 20th century Russian psychology. There are two main ideas: the social nature of the human mind, and the inseparability of human mind and activity, the former idea elaborated by Vygotsky, and the latter by Rubinshtein (Clemmensen, Kaptelinin and Nardi, 2016). Vygotsky's theories of learning emphasise the social far more than those of Piaget, and Vygotsky's ideas about scaffolding, social interactions and learner support are used in the design of distance learning platforms and virtual learning environments (e.g. Boettcher, 2004; Huang, Rauch and Liaw, 2010). The version of activity theory commonly presented is based on the work of Engeström and team (Engeström, Miettinen and Punamäki, 1999), which added the notion of community to the subject–object interaction. An activity is seen as a system of human 'doing' in which a subject works on an object in order to obtain a desired outcome. To do this, the subject employs tools, which may be external to the subject, or internal. The common representation of activity theory shows one inner triangle with apices for subject, object and community, and an outer triangle that has apices for the mediating tools. Between subject and object, the mediating artefacts are tools (as mentioned), between community and object there is a division of labour (to allow distribution of activity), and between subject and community there are rules.

For example, in a study that used activity theory to examine web application requirements, the tools included the internet, books and methodologies; the rules included trading standards and policies; and the division of labour included roles such as the warehouse despatcher and the web developer (Uden, Valderas and Pastor, 2008). The subject was the customer; the object was the product to be purchased; and the community included managers, customers and software companies. Pretty straightforward, seemingly, but the value of using activity theory to frame the later analysis of activities into actions and operations, and hence the task model, is that the interactions between people, their tools and resources are described (unlike most examples of hierarchical task analysis). Activity theory allows for a better understanding of cultural and historical factors, and the dynamic, changing nature of activities – as customers use the web application more, for example.

In the doctoral research by Cristina Vasilica the activity theory triangle (Figure 12.1) helped to prompt thinking about the way the tools had to meet the needs of the subjects, principally the patients with chronic kidney disease. The community was considered to be the patients with chronic kidney disease, their families and the professionals involved in their care. Between the subject and the community there are rules, and ethical codes of practice. The latter might be a particular concern for health professionals contributing to the portal, with the need to preserve patient confidentiality. There is a possible confusion between tools and the output afforded by the tools in Cristina's diagram – it might be clearer to indicate that the function of the tools was to allow deposition of content created by the users, for information sharing and information exchange.

Unlike some other studies of engagement, that contrast the active members of the network with those who are merely 'lurkers', Chapter 12 demonstrates that there were different levels of engagement that were more reminiscent of behaviour in a community of practice (Wenger, 1998, Chapter 3 on learning). There were evolving norms of behaviour for how to engage, how to disengage (often temporarily), coming to a consensus on how to use the network and how to respond, telling stories about experience of living with the condition, that would be helpful to others. The community of practice leaders were the 'influencers', who helped to keep the community active; 'conversationalists' provided feedback and new content; and 'browsers' may not have provided much input but were at the same time 'legitimate peripheral participants' as they read and collected information.

References

Boettcher, J. V. (2004) Design Levels for Distance and Online Learning. In Howard, C., Schenk, K. and Discenza, R. (eds), *Distance Learning and University Effectiveness: changing educational paradigms for online learning*, Information Science Publishing.

Clemmensen, T., Kaptelinin, V. and Nardi, B. (2016) Making HCI Theory Work: an analysis of the use of activity theory in HCI research, *Behaviour & Information Technology*, **35** (8), 608–27.

Engeström, Y., Miettinen, R. and Punamäki, R.-L. (1999) *Perspectives on Activity Theory*, Cambridge University Press.

Huang, H. M., Rauch, U. and Liaw, S. S. (2010) Investigating Learners' Attitudes Toward Virtual Reality Learning Environments: based on a constructivist approach, *Computers & Education*, **55** (3), 1171–82.

Uden, L., Valderas, P. and Pastor, O. (2008) An Activity-Theory-Based Model to Analyse Web Application Requirements, *Information Research*, **13** (2), paper 340.

Wenger, E. (1998) *Communities of Practice: learning, meaning and identity*, Cambridge University Press.

12.1 Introduction

The chapter provides an overview and critical analysis of the methods used to study information behaviour in the context of online communication. In a healthcare paradigm, traditionally focused on offline communication models such as leaflets or face-to-face information provision, advances in mobile and online technologies provide new communication channels (Atkinson and Castro, 2008). Information-seeking behaviour, new models of engagement and communication using social media are discussed, drawing on real-life social experiences of people managing a long-term condition, and their engagement in an online peer support group. For example, one individual, managing chronic kidney disease, is part of a local online peer support group designed for renal patients: the Greater Manchester Kidney Information Network (GMKIN). Don (a pseudonym) realised after reading online about other people's experiences of managing the disease that 'My journey has not been easy but it has been absolutely a piece of cake compared to what other people [have] gone through and that has made me realise that perhaps my quality of life is better than what I was perceiving it' (Vasilica, 2015b, 202). Throughout the chapter, patients' experiences like this highlight the impact real-life patients' stories have on other people's perceived quality of life. In Don's view, and the views of other patients that we followed in a longitudinal study for almost two years, the narratives shared on the network were novel and informative. They uncovered different coping mechanisms and ways of managing symptoms, and helped patients to live well with the condition.

In reality, the engagement of patients remains a challenge, despite the technological developments and excitement associated with them. The chapter examines how engagement with social media is sustained as a result of empowering patients to become co-producers of health information, increasing the novelty of information shared, the sociability and continuous peer support. Indeed, using social media within the technological mix enables researchers or practitioners to involve patients in the co-production and sharing of information that is relevant, timely, understandable and accessible, to satisfy their information needs. Activity theory is used to connect the key concepts explored: information needs, information behaviour and social connections, and the power of social media.

This chapter emphasises the co-creation of information and knowledge for an online peer support group. As Chapter 1 has mentioned, one of the future roles that information professionals could play is that of moderator, or at the very least training of future moderators of online communities. This is information systems architecture for a purpose, to help oversee and ensure the quality of the content, encourage and edit (if necessary) contributions, so that practical expertise is available to all those in the online community who would benefit. Information behaviour, as discussed here, is much more than the simple navigation pathways considered for some website architecture. Chapter 11 discussed how communities of practice theory was integrated into the design and evaluation of a website that supported an online community working across organisations. This chapter focuses on what individuals do, working together to solve problems associated with health care, and thus co-creating knowledge for sharing with others, providing expertise online.

Section 12.2 outlines the main research on information behaviour that relates to the design of the website, and Section 12.3 sets out the main aspirations of the project for social connectivity. Section 12.4 discusses the website design, and Section 12.5 compares the levels of engagement observed. The use of activity theory to analyse the use of the site is discussed in Section 12.6, and Section 12.7 draws conclusions.

12.2 Information behaviour

Evidence suggests that an information need occurs when an individual recognises that they lack particular information, which they perceive to be essential to accomplish a goal (Case, 2007). People managing a long-term condition use information to achieve goals to foster self-management, promote independence, improve self-esteem and live a normal life which, coupled with symptom management and treatment, prevent further complications, improving the chances of survival (Davies, 2010; Ormandy and Hulme, 2013). They attempt to find information at different points of their illness. Extensive research has been carried out to understand the information behaviour process (Robson and Robinson, 2013); this section mainly outlines the key theoretical frameworks developed to capture information need, information seeking and information searching. These models act as a basis for other research in the field.

Cole (2011) conceptualises an information need as a black box underpinned by three categories: information behaviour, context and human condition, the latter seen as a holistic approach to information need. Overall, Cole's theory is presented in the context of information retrieval (Savolainen, 2012), where information behaviour is concerned with seeking, (awareness of need or gap, and actions taken to deal with the gap), searching (which may be passive, active, ongoing) and using information (that may then affect further information seeking). Over the years, Wilson has introduced a series of frameworks or models, which portray information behaviour as the interplay of theoretical concepts (1999, 2004, 2006, 2007). Information need develops, then the searching process and the contextual factors inhibit or support the seeking process (Wilson, 1999). The models have been expanded to include a list of characteristics within information seeking (Ellis, 1989), and findings drawn from consumer research and health information management (Wilson, 2007). Ellis (1989) adopted Glaser and Strauss' (1967) grounded theory approach to establish the information-seeking steps: starting, chaining, browsing, differentiating, monitoring and extracting. Kuhlthau's information search process adds a new dimension, focusing on the interrelationships between cognitive factors (thoughts), affective factors (feelings) and physical factors (brainstorming, browsing) that occur at each stage of the search process (Kuhlthau, 2004).

While Ellis (1989) and Kuhlthau (1993) focus primarily on the information-seeking process (cognitive aspects), Dervin is concerned with what users 'really think, feel, want and dream', stressing how individuals need to make sense of the situation they are in (Dervin, 1998, 39).

Researchers have attempted to develop health-specific information-seeking models focused on either patients or practitioners. Gorman (1995) sought to clarify the information seeking to inform patient care of clinicians in primary care and explored the concepts of unrecognised need, recognised need, pursued and satisfaction of information need. Other researchers expanded on Gorman's concepts and revealed that patients have recognised, unrecognised and deferred needs (Alzougool, Chang and Gray, 2008; Ormandy, 2008a, b).

In the renal field, Ormandy (2008a) developed an information need study building on the work of theorists such as Wilson (1981), Dervin (1992) and Case (2007). The study identified that for patients such as Don the main priorities were related to information about illness self-management, complications and physical symptoms. In Ormandy's research, the information concerned how the illness impacts on daily activities, the treatment available and how coping with life was considered by patients as less important than psychological concerns and coping strategies, which activated other information needs. The findings resonate within research on patient need (Rutten et al., 2005; Astin et al., 2008; Franssen et al., 2009; McNair et al., 2013; van Weert et al., 2013).

The growth of digital technology is believed to change the information-seeking patterns of users (Xie, 2007). Wilson (2004) suggested that users are adopting simple search strategies and that systems must be designed to reduce the complexity of the topic searched or provide an interactive search process for complex requirements. Patients find it easier to access health information via the internet, and similarly information providers found the internet useful as a means of distributing information in different ways. More recently, the rise of social media has created digital tools that enable patients to share and rate their experiences of health care, and actively access information (Rozenblum and Bates, 2013). While patients demonstrate increased trust in the accuracy of medical institutions and information from health professionals (McMullan, 2006), online technologies have become a popular resource to access health information (Beaudoin and Hong, 2011; Song and Chang, 2012). Approximately 80% of internet users seek information online (Gruzd, Staves and Wilk, 2012). Patients search the web for information related to nutrition or diet, medication side effects, symptoms, alternative treatment options and second opinions. Social media, for example networks such as Facebook and Twitter, is beneficial in reaching a wide patient population, from different ethnic backgrounds, to provide education, enable social engagement and change behaviour (Shaw and Johnson, 2011).

12.3   The powerful future – social connectivity and information provision

Mark Zuckerberg, founder of Facebook, has stated that his original idea for creating social media derived from an ambition to achieve social change and a connected world: 'I'd love to improve people's lives, especially socially. . . Making the world more open is not an overnight thing. It's a 10–15 year thing' (Zuckerberg, n.d.). Don reinforced the significance of social connectivity for patients: 'I think I just needed that reassurance that I wasn't alone, I drew an awful lot from that' (Vasilica, 2015a).

The entire internet started as a bulletin board system, which enabled users to share information (Kaplan and Haenlein, 2010). Then the original idea of user-generated content began with Wikipedia, but key to its expansion was the 'like' button introduced by Facebook in 2008. Over the years the use of social technologies has expanded, from just information exchange to developing friendship, connections, social movements and social support: a movement to harness collective intelligence (O'Reilly and Battelle, 2009), although, most organisations do not yet use social media at full capacity.

The term Web 2.0 was first introduced in 2004 to set the boundaries of a new technology, which encompassed platforms continuously updated by users, creating combinations (or mashups) from one or multiple sources, then adding their own knowledge and perspective, generating a network effect (O'Reilly, 2005). User-generated content was the general term coined in 2005 to describe the various forms of digital content created by Web 2.0 users (Kaplan and Haenlein, 2010). Social media technology blurs the boundaries between reception and production of information (Betsch et al., 2012), and user-generated content relates closely to the concept of 'word of mouth', but in an electronic context (Smith, Fischer and Yongjian, 2012). User-generated content takes a variety of forms including tweets (Twitter), status updates (Facebook), videos (YouTube, Vimeo), limited time availability information (Snapchat) and blogging. It fulfils three basic requirements: it must be publicly available to a group of people; the content must be innovative and not copied directly from a different source; and it must be created separately from professional routines.

The body of social media research emerged from various research studies on friendship (Boyd, 2004, 2006; Boyd and Ellison, 2007; Joinson, 2008), social capital (Ellison, Steinfield and Lampe, 2006, 2011), information and emotional support (Eysenbach et al., 2004; Buchanan and Coulson, 2007; Coulson, Buchanan and Aubeeluck, 2007; Malik and Coulson, 2010) and impact on quality of life and health (Chan and Dicianno, 2011; Roblin, 2011; Merolli, Gray and Martin-Sanchez, 2013; Merolli et al., 2015).

The rise of social media has resulted in many patients no longer relying on information just being given; they like to be part of the information production process by offering solutions to problems, comments and sharing their experiences (Adams, 2011; Hardiker and Grant, 2011; Lober and Flowers, 2011). This does not come as a surprise as health professionals have limited time to respond to patients' queries during a typical interaction (Haase and Loiselle, 2012). Meeting the information needs of different patients is a challenge for modern healthcare (Ormandy, 2008b; Schinkel, Schouten and van Weert, 2013).

Social media researchers have observed very different levels of engagement with the media. Groups commonly contrasted are the active ('posters') and passive ('lurkers'). Their motivations for engagement are very different (Preece, Nonnecke and Andrews, 2004; Rau, Gao and Ding, 2008; Petrovčič and Petrič, 2014). Posters are the members who actively contribute user-generated content (Schlosser, 2005). They expect reciprocity, alongside gaining enjoyment in helping others and new knowledge, which motivate them to post. The user-generated information process is influenced by the enthusiasm of moderators, who offer enjoyable experiences (Lai and Chen, 2014), intimate relationships (Rau, Gao and Ding, 2008) and social capital (Zhao, Ha and Widdows, 2015). Lurkers are defined as passive members who do not post or post fewer messages than posters, and learn by observing (Gray, 2004; Petrovčič and Petrič, 2014). Their main reasons for lurking are having no immediate need to post, the need to know the group better before posting, the belief that they are helpful by not posting, not knowing how to use the software, disliking the group dynamics, and believing that the community does not meet their needs (Preece, Nonnecke and Andrews, 2004). Lurkers may also refrain from posting because they have contradictory views, or are afraid of being criticised or judged by other members of the community (Guan, 2006). In health online communities, lurkers may form over 45% of the users (Nonnecke and Preece, 2000). Interestingly, lurkers refrain from posting or commenting, but with time some become active users because they read the content of messages and become familiar with community norms and values (Schneider, von Krogh and Jäger, 2013).

A more complex classification of levels of engagement is given in the Social Technographics Ladder (Bernoff and Li, 2010) where the ladder represents the hierarchical order of user participation within social media. The most active individuals are creators, followed by critics, collectors, joiners, spectators and the inactive. Participants can satisfy one or more roles on the ladder (Bernoff and Li, 2010).

Brodie et al. (2011) brand the user engagement of online communities as sub-processes, which take different forms: sharing, co-developing, learning, socialising and advocating. Sharing is a behavioural and cognitive engagement sub-process, where users actively generate (co-create) information from personal knowledge and experience, along with learning and acquiring new knowledge from the information. Co-developing is associated with engagement to assist in developing new products, services, brands or brand meanings. Users are socialising because of the benefits of two-direction interaction, in which they develop attitudes, social norms and common purpose, and advocate and recommend the community to others (Brodie et al., 2011).

Schneider, von Krogh and Jäger (2013) identified the role of expert members who contribute to the welfare of the community, actively engage and need new information to discover new ideas, but who are not necessarily actively seeking new knowledge. Evidence denotes that the information spread online, for example patients' personal blogs, forums and wikis, enables patients to prepare for or decide on treatment, manage symptoms and adverse effects, reduce uncertainty and fulfil information need (Bender et al., 2013; Schneider, von Krogh and Jäger, 2013; Vennik et al., 2014).

12.4   The design of the Greater Manchester Kidney Information Network site

The Greater Manchester Kidney Information Network (GMKIN; gmkin.org.uk) is an innovative joint venture between a local kidney patient association and academia, in response to patient demand to develop a mechanism to connect patients. Research suggested that patients' information needs about the reality of managing kidney disease in everyday life were not being met, and talking with peers would be beneficial (Ormandy, 2008a, b). With that in mind, innovative ways to enable patients to access information from the experienced kidney patient community were sought. Meetings with patients and local practitioners informed and shaped the collaborative project, which originated in August 2012.

Drawing on evidence from information need, social media and engagement behaviour theorists it was evident that social media could be used to enable kidney patients to support each other, and to develop a deeper understanding of how patients used the different features and evidence of preferred levels of engagement. The designers of the GMKIN examined the impact of social media on information provision for patients from the outset, and evaluated their self-efficacy (the extent of their belief in their ability to complete tasks) and engagement. Interest focused on the dynamics of social media interactions, how community moderators worked, how patients' roles evolved, and the effects of health practitioner involvement.

The evidence provided in this section comes from the longitudinal study of patients with a chronic kidney disease who had access to GKMIN. The network, set up in 2013, was a user-centred design, eliciting informal feedback on reference and prototype versions of the network (Norman, 1998). From the inception stage, the network and the platform were developed using theory and experience from similar research projects involving social media. The information search process (Kuhlthau, 2004) influenced the design, assuming that users would follow a similar search process online, primarily when they received contradictory information and required support (Warner and Procaccino, 2004). The system was designed to support patients in managing complexity (Wilson, 2004), by directing them to information and offering peer-to-peer support. The informational components addressed the needs identified by Ormandy and Hulme (2013).

It was essential to engage users. The designers of the GMKIN thought engagement would be a positive experience 'characterized by attributes of challenge, positive effect, insurability, aesthetic and sensory appeal, attention, feedback, variety or novelty, interactivity and perceived control' (O'Brien and Toms, 2008, 949). Furthermore, the designers of the GMKIN applied the principles of social capital (Putnam, 2000; Szreter and Woolcock, 2004) in order to build a sustainable community, recognising that ties among members stimulate the process of posting (Law and Chang, 2012). The GMKIN developed into a social and informational intervention using the following social media tools:

- the GMKIN platform: a bespoke online system developed to enable patients to access information and/or register anonymously to post blogs and comments or use the forum to ask or respond to specific questions; clinicians joined the network, submitting blogs and useful information such as diet suggestions, reports on developments at the local hospital, and notification of research opportunities
- the GMKIN on Facebook: patient-to-patient, closed social networking group, initially open to recruit local patients, then closed to protect the confidentiality of those sharing information
- GMKINet: a Twitter account to engage in conversations on health matters including chronic kidney disease, to share and build a follower base to increase patient involvement, give greater access to patient opinion, and raise the profile of the GMKIN.

Chris (pseudonym), a patient involved in the GMKIN, describes the inter-operability of the three different media: 'It's almost like, if you imagine a university campus, Twitter is like the notice board and then Facebook is the student union and then the website is like the resource library. So it kind of depends on what you are looking for' (Vasilica, 2015b, 236).

Crucial to the project was the development of a sustainable community of patients, who share a positive and respectful relationship among themselves. The existing research on social capital exposed that bonding, bridging and linking contribute significantly to online relationships, although not explicitly in reference to the behaviour of community moderators (Kobayashi, 2010). Indeed, there were very few examples of how to achieve the bonding, bridging and linking in practice, particularly how community moderators could manage user comments to build positive relationships, avoid unacceptable language or behaviour and stimulate user-generated content. One of the questions underpinning the project was how to create sustainable patient engagement strategies using social media and social capital constructs.

One of the authors (Cristina Vasilica) adopted the community moderator role, drawing on her expertise of managing online communities. She and her colleagues developed an engagement strategy, influenced by community of practice concepts, which suggest that collective learning occurs in social settings (Lave and Wenger, 1991) and bonding social capital (Putnam, 2000). It primarily focused on observing users, to learn their needs and preferences, adopting a friendly approach, listening to the voice of the community, stimulating leaders and providing content that stimulated their engagement. Designers of the GMKIN posted welcoming messages to get to know new members, asking them to introduce themselves and promoting GMKIN functionalities, which encouraged other members of the group to join and greet new members. It was fundamental to the role to develop meaningful relationships among users through light discussions, sociability and supporting prospective leaders. A classic example of a light discussion involved a simple garden photo, posted by the community moderator during a period of silence, which reverberated with the community members in an unexpected way: 'When you post pictures of your home town and your tomatoes . . . and I think the more you know people the more you are interested in what they say and it's . . . if you start to know someone it's more interesting to know what they are saying than it is if they are just a complete stranger' (Chris) (Vasilica, 2015b, 146).

'And your flowers [picture of garden], I mean it is part of it you don't have to be thinking of dread and doom serious as it is I mean I say thank God I am not on dialysis' (Jon) (Vasilica, 2015b, 146).

'I'll apply for a job in your garden [laughs]' (Mark) (Vasilica, 2015b, 146).

Supporting prospective leaders played an important part in achieving a community that was sustainable beyond the initial period of research. The patient leaders (in the apprenticeship role), who joined the community as newcomers (initially engaged in peripheral participation), gained experience and learnt from the moderator practice and continuous discussions contributing to the growth, establishment and now sustainability of the GMKIN.

12.5 Levels of engagement

Research has categorised the various levels of engagement in creating and distributing content (Section 12.3). The evidence observed within the GMKIN indicated that patients engaged on different levels: at the highest level contribution (as influencers), mid level (as conversationalists) and low level (as browsers) (Vasilica, 2015b). These levels were not distinct segments of the group as influencers also engaged in conversational or browsing activities. (Table 12.1). Despite benefitting from the information shared on the GMKIN, patients who lacked sufficient experience of the illness and had primarily joined to gain new knowledge preferred a passive role. Patients sharing the browser role demonstrated an increased confidence and self-efficacy similar to the influencer and conversationalist, which supports the suggestion that social interaction is linked to behaviour change.

Table 12.1 *Levels of engagement when creating and distributing content on the GMKIN*

Influencer	Conversationalist	Browser
The role involved more responsibility than just advocacy. In particular, the influencer created and shared information while focusing on advocacy and wishing the community to work for the other patients involved in the community.	The role was significant in influencing members' engagement by providing feedback and keeping the conversations flowing.	The browsing mode was the most common mode, associated with reading and collecting information.

Although the focus of the GMKIN was on peer-to-peer support, efforts were made to involve practitioners, who initially expressed concerns that any information they provided may be misunderstood by patients. Some viewed their code of practice as an impediment to sharing information or connecting with patients on Facebook, primarily a personal and friendship platform. When asked, patients did not want practitioners as friends on the GMKIN or expect them to offer medical advice, but preferred them to have an overseeing role providing reassurance that information shared by other patients was accurate. Donna said:

> More direction than actual medical advice, because I feel if I wanted medical advice I will rather wait for my appointment.
>
> (Vasilica, 2015b, 184)

And Lucy agreed:

It is up to them if they want to respond or if they just want to sit back like I do and just take on what is going on rather than answering too many questions.

(Vasilica, 2015a)

Those practitioners who joined the GMKIN contributed to information provision and observed the discussions. Indeed, patient opinion suggested that the presence of health professionals within the community does not stifle patient-to-patient discussion but provides a level of reassurance and credibility on the network. Don said:

There is someone there who understands the technicality of it [makes me] much more comfortable. [I'd] much [prefer to] express an opinion that was wrong and have someone there with authority behind them to actually correct me rather than engage in argument with someone you know who did not have that authority behind them. So I do really welcome the influx of [the] medical profession into it.

(Vasilica, 2015b, 184)

Social media is often overlooked for its potential to provide peer-to-peer support and a positive health outcome, although the GMKIN reinforces confidence in using such media. Health professionals require training to understand social media and Facebook privacy settings, and the ability to create groups with whom specific information can be shared. More importantly, clinicians need to treat social media platforms as a mechanism to connect and communicate with patients and not be intimidated by these 'friendship' venues. Adoption of social media should be treated as an intervention, in which all offline rules (privacy, confidentiality) are maintained.

Engagement with social media does not just happen, but is discussed and influenced by those who manage the community, and the users themselves. For a community to work and be sustainable it requires all three levels of engagement, producing information that is highly regarded by patients and can bring about positive change in the local community. The results of the study revealed that the majority of patients involved in the research increased their self-efficacy, their knowledge to better self-manage their condition, and confidence to seek future employment (Vasilica, 2015b).

12.6   Social media 'connectivism' through activity theory

Activity theory originated from the Russian school of thought pioneered by Vygotsky, Leont'ev and Rubinshtein (Leont'ev, 1977, 1978) and was later continued by the Scandinavian researcher Engeström (1999). Activity theory is a collective activity with norms and rules shared by the community members (community), in which subjects undertake activities motivated by a need (object) and influenced by tools, which enable them to achieve their goals (outcomes). The activity is influenced by the context (a closed group or team or the society) in which it takes place and the influencing mechanisms (norms and the division of labour). The theory acknowledges that the outcome-bounded activity progresses as the knowledge and understanding develops within the mind of the subject involved in the process (Bedny and Karwowski, 2004).

The theory has been applied in various domains – psychology, education, online learning, human–computer interaction, system development, information science, digital library development, information retrieval and information-seeking behaviour (see Wilson's 2006 work, which provides a detailed account of the application of activity theory). Other prolific authors have explored the theory in different contexts (Bødker, 1989; Kuutti, 1991; Hjørland, 1997, 2000, 2004; Kaptelinin and Nardi, 2007).

In the process of providing information and support, people must undertake different activities to transform their goals into desired outcomes. Activity theory appears to provide a conceptual framework to map the journey of social media users from seeking information to obtaining improved health outcomes (Figure 12.1 on the next page).

It was envisaged that by setting up the tools to enable patients to talk to one another and provide health information it would satisfy their information need and increase self-efficacy. Among the tools, the online community set up on Facebook, the GMKIN platform and Twitter enabled patients to access support and share information in the form of blogs, comments and tweets. The information generated within the GMKIN moved beyond patient stories to include biomedical information, and presented new medical advances. Patients acknowledged that information was the main contributor to remaining engaged, confirming studies that indicated that social media should help elicit patient-generated content (Applebaum, Lawson and von Scheven, 2013; Merolli, Gray and Martin-Sanchez, 2013). Kidney patients joined the online groups to obtain information (Buchanan and Coulson, 2007; Mo and Coulson, 2010;

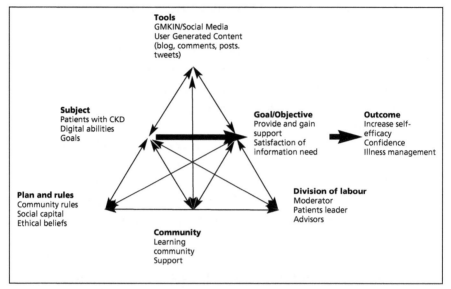

Figure 12.1 *Social Media GMKIN CKD application of activity theory* (adapted from Engeström, 1987, 78)

Welbourne, Blanchard and Wadsworth, 2013). Sharing information can generate problems, with information reliability often a cause for concern within social media communities (Adams, 2010; Fernandez-Luque, Karlsen and Melton, 2012; Moorhead et al., 2013). This problem may be alleviated if healthcare practitioners join the network, and can reassure patients. However, ethical issues associated with practitioners' codes of practice remain one of the most significant challenges faced during the development and running of the GMKIN.

The rules of the community are associated with different levels of use and the division of labour. For example, the community manager's role was to influence the development of relationships among members through implementing social capital concepts (Putnam, 2000; Woolcock, 2001; Szreter and Woolcock, 2004), enabling members gradually to become acquainted with the community norms and regulations. Jon commented:

> Obviously I got more and more involved in it since its [formation]. . . . To be quite honest with you I did not know the difference between HD [hemodialysis] and PD [peritoneal dialysis], I do now but even before dialysis that was it, I did not realise that [these were] different forms of dialysis and this is something I picked up.
>
> (Vasilica, 2015b, 173)

And Don said:

> You reminded me so many times it will develop, it will happen. We find a
> subject that people are interested in. [A] classic example is the photograph of
> your garden and the conversations we had coming out of that, nothing at all to
> do with CKD [chronic kidney disease].   (Vasilica, 2015b, 146)

Community is an important pillar of social media. Indeed, having an
information system without a community is representative of a ghost town.
Today, 'connectivism' suggests that knowledge is directly linked to a network
and the minds of connected people (Siemens, 2005). Information and social
support contribute to sustained engagement, which then triggers learning and
knowledge. Similar to community of practice principles, the domain of
learning and increase in knowledge is distributed over a period of time
(Wenger, McDermott and Snyder, 2002). Members (at all levels of engagement,
especially, conversing and influencing) initially join the community as
newcomers and through engaging in the process of generating information
make the community work (Lave and Wenger, 1991). Patients at different stages
of chronic kidney disease, with varied digital skills, joined the network having
a goal in mind, the majority expressing their readiness to offer something to
others in a similar situation. Vicky said:

> The biggest goal is to show another person that it is possible . . . that even if you
> are suffering from this illness you can still get out there and still do things.
>   (Vasilica, 2015b, 142)

And Jannie agreed:

> If I write a blog and it helps one person it is worth it.
>   (Vasilica, 2015b, 142)

Patients' goals are known to influence engagement (O'Brien and Toms, 2008;
Hollebeek, 2011). At the initial point of engagement, the user has a specific or
experiential goal in mind, triggered by motivations and interest, and is attracted
by the aesthetic appeal or novelty of the system (O'Brien and Toms, 2008).

12.7 Conclusions

This chapter highlighted how emerging technologies could be used to engage patients in online interventions, which in turn triggers positive social and health outcomes.

For this to happen the community moderators (influencers) have to take an active role in stimulating conversations, developing meaningful relationships and understanding the community's needs. The presence of health practitioners increases the level of reassurance and credibility on the network.

By connecting with online communities, patients access informational support, which satisfies their information need (Vasilica, 2015b). Social learning via social media would potentially encourage patients to engage with their condition more than they might do otherwise, improve self-management, and in some cases set them on a path to becoming patient leaders. Connectivism is crucial in alleviating loneliness and enabling patients to find an important lifeline and non-judgemental company. As a result, patients increase confidence with their own competence in dealing with their condition.

References

Adams, S. (2010) Revisiting the Online Health Information Reliability Debate in the Wake of 'Web 2.0': an inter-disciplinary literature and website review, *International Journal of Medical Informatics*, **79** (6), 391–400.

Adams, S. A. (2011) Sourcing the Crowd for Health Services Improvement: the reflexive patient and 'share-your-experience' websites, *Social Science & Medicine*, **72** (7), 1069–76, doi:10.1016/j.socscimed.2011.02.001.

Alzougool, B., Chang, S. and Gray, K. (2008) Towards a Comprehensive Understanding of Health Information Needs, *Electronic Journal of Health Informatics*, **3** (2), 15.

Alzougool, B., Chang, S. and Gray, K. (2015) A New Scale to Measure the State of an Informal Carer's Information Needs: development and validation, *Journal of Consumer Health on the Internet*, **19** (3-4), 200–18, doi:10.1080/15398285.2015.1089396.

Applebaum, M. A., Lawson, E. F. and von Scheven, E. (2013) Perception of Transition Readiness and Preferences for Use of Technology in Transition Programs: teens' ideas for the future, *International Journal of Adolescent Medicine and Health*, **25** (2), doi:10.1515/ijamh-2013-0019.

Astin, F., Closs, S. J., McLenachan, J., Hunter, S. and Priestley, C. (2008) The

Information Needs of Patients Treated with Primary Angioplasty for Heart Attack: an exploratory study, *Patient Education and Counseling*, **73** (2), 325–32, doi:10.1016/j.pec.2008.06.013.

Atkinson, R. D. and Castro, D. (2008) Digital Quality of Life: understanding the personal and social benefits of the information technology revolution, *SSRN Electronic Journal*, doi:10.2139/ssrn.1278185.

Beaudoin, C. E. and Hong, T. (2011) Health Information Seeking, Diet and Physical Activity: an empirical assessment by medium and critical demographics, *International Journal of Medical Informatics*, **80** (8), 586–95, doi:10.1016/j.ijmedinf.2011.04.003.

Bedny, G. Z. and Karwowski, W. (2004) Activity Theory as a Basis for the Study of Work, *Ergonomics*, **47** (2), 134–53, doi:10.1080/00140130310001617921.

Bender, J. L., Katz, J., Ferris, L. E. and Jadad, A. R. (2013) What is the Role of Online Support from the Perspective of Facilitators of Face-to-Face Support Groups? A multi-method study of the use of breast cancer online communities, *Patient Education and Counseling*, **93** (3), 472–79, doi:10.1016/j.pec.2013.07.009.

Bernoff, J. and Li, C. (2010) Harnessing the Power of the Oh-So-Social Web, *IEEE Engineering Management Review*, **38** (3), 8–15, doi:10.1109/emr.2010.5559138.

Betsch, C., Brewer, N. T., Brocard, P., Davies, P., Gaissmaier, W., Haase, N., Leask, J., Renkewitz, F., Renner, B., Reyna, V. F., Rossmann, C., Sachse, K., Schachinger, A., Siegrist, M. and Stryk, M. (2012) Opportunities and Challenges of Web 2.0 for Vaccination Decisions, *Vaccine*, **30** (25), 3727–33, doi:10.1016/j.vaccine.2012.02.025.

Bødker, S. (1989) A Human Activity Approach to User Interfaces, *Human-Computer Interaction*, **4** (3), 171–95, doi:10.1207/s15327051hci0403_1.

Boyd, D. (2004) Friendster and Publicly Articulated Social Networks. In *Proceedings of the Conference on Human Factors and Computing Systems - CHI2004, Vienna, Austria*, ACM Press, 1279–82.

Boyd, D. (2006) Friends, Friendsters, and Top 8: writing community into being on social network sites, *First Monday*, **11** (12), doi:10.5210/fm.v11i12.1418.

Boyd, D. M. and Ellison, N. B. (2007) Social Network Sites: definition, history, and scholarship, *Journal of Computer-Mediated Communication*, **13**

(1), 210–30, doi:10.1111/j.1083-6101.2007.00393.x.

Brodie, R. J., Hollebeek, L. D., Juric, B. and Ilic, A. (2011) Customer Engagement: conceptual domain, fundamental propositions, and implications for research, *Journal of Service Research*, **14** (3), 252–71, doi:10.1177/1094670511411703.

Buchanan, H. and Coulson, N. S. (2007) Accessing Dental Anxiety Online Support Groups: an exploratory qualitative study of motives and experiences, *Patient Education and Counseling*, **66** (3), 263–9, doi:10.1016/j.pec.2006.12.011.

Case, D. O. (2007) *Looking for Information: a survey of research on information seeking, needs, and behavior*, Elsevier and Academic Press.

Chan, W. M. and Dicianno, B. E. (2011) Virtual Socialization in Adults with Spina Bifida, *PM&R*, **3** (3), 219–25, doi:10.1016/j.pmrj.2010.12.002.

Cole, C. (2011) A Theory of Information Need for Information Retrieval that Connects Information to Knowledge, *Journal of the American Society for Information Science and Technology*, **62** (7), 1216–31, doi:10.1002/asi.21541.

Coulson, N. S., Buchanan, H. and Aubeeluck, A. (2007) Social Support in Cyberspace: a content analysis of communication within a Huntington's disease online support group, *Patient Education and Counseling*, **68** (2), 173–8, doi:10.1016/j.pec.2007.06.002.

Davies, N. J. (2010) Improving Self-Management for Patients with Long-Term Conditions, *Nursing Standard*, **24** (25), 49–56, doi:10.7748/ns2010.02.24.25.49.c7562.

Dervin, B. (1992) From the Mind's Eye of the User: the sense-making qualitative and quantitative methodology. In Glazier, J. D. and Powell, R. R. (eds), *Qualitative Research in Information Management*, Libraries Unlimited, 61–84.

Dervin, B. (1998) Sense-making Theory and Practice: an overview of user interests in knowledge and use, *Journal of Knowledge Management*, **2** (2), 36–46.

Ellis, D. (1989) A Behavioural Model for Information Retrieval System Design, *Journal of Information Science*, **15** (4–5), 237–47, doi:10.1177/016555158901500406.

Ellison, N. B., Steinfield, C. and C. Lampe (2006) Spatially Bounded Online Social Networks and Social Capital: the role of Facebook. In *Proceedings of the 56th Annual Conference of the International Communication Association, Dresden.*

Ellison, N. B., Steinfield, C. and Lampe, C. (2011) Connection Strategies: social capital implications of Facebook-enabled communication practices, *New Media & Society*, **13** (6), 873–92, doi:10.1177/1461444810385389.

Engeström, Y. (1987) *Learning by Expanding: an activity-theoretical approach to developmental research*, Orienta-Konsultit Oy.

Engeström, Y. (1999) Learning by Expanding: ten years after (translated by F. Seeger), http://lchc.ucsd.edu/MCA/Paper/Engestrom/expanding/intro.htm.

Eysenbach, G., Powell, J., Englesakis, M., Rizo, C. and Stern, A. (2004) Health Related Virtual Communities and Electronic Support Groups: systematic review of the effects of online peer to peer interactions, *British Medical Journal*, **328** (7449), doi:10.1136/bmj.328.7449.1166.

Fernandez-Luque, L., Karlsen, R. and Melton, G. B. (2012) HealthTrust: a social network approach for retrieving online health videos, *Journal of Medical Internet Research*, **14** (1), e22, doi:10.2196/jmir.1985.

Franssen, S. J., Lagarde, S. M., van Werven, J. R., Smets, E. M. A., Tran, K. T. C., Plukker, J. T. M., van Lanschot, J. J. B. and de Haes, H. C. J. M. (2009) Psychological Factors and Preferences for Communicating Prognosis in Esophageal Cancer Patients, *Psycho-Oncology*, **18** (11), 1199–207, doi:10.1002/pon.1485.

Glaser, B. G. and Strauss, A. L. (1967) *The Discovery of Grounded Theory: strategies for qualitative research*, Aldine.

Gorman, P. N. (1995) Information Needs of Physicians, *Journal of the American Society for Information Science*, **46** (10), 729–36, doi:10.1002/(sici)1097-4571(199512)46:10<729::aid-asi3>3.0.co;2-2.

Gray, B. (2004) Informal Learning in an Online Community of Practice, *Journal of Distance Education*, **19** (1), 20–35.

Gruzd, A., Staves, K. and Wilk, A. (2012) Connected Scholars: examining the role of social media in research practices of faculty using the UTAUT model, *Computers in Human Behavior*, **28** (6), 2340–50, doi:10.1016/j.chb.2012.07.004.

Guan, X. (2006) Reasons for the Formation of Cybernetic Lurkers, *Journal of Huaihai Institute of Technology*, **4**, 79–82.

Haase, K. R. and Loiselle, C. G. (2012) Oncology Team Members' Perceptions of a Virtual Navigation Tool for Cancer Patients, *International Journal of Medical Informatics*, **81** (6), 395–403, doi:10.1016/j.ijmedinf.2011.11.001.

Hardiker, N. R. and Grant, M. J. (2011) Factors that Influence Public Engagement with eHealth: a literature review, *International Journal of Medical Informatics*, **80** (1), 1–12, doi:10.1016/j.ijmedinf.2010.10.017.

Hjørland, B. (1997) *Information Seeking and Subject Representation: an activity-theoretical approach to information science*, Greenwood Press.

Hjørland, B. (2000) Information Seeking Behaviour: what should a general theory look like?, *The New Review of Information Behaviour Research*, **1**, 19–33.

Hjørland, B. (2004) Arguments for Philosophical Realism in Library and Information Science, *Library Trends*, **52** (3), 488–506.

Hollebeek, L. D. (2011) Demystifying Customer Brand Engagement: exploring the loyalty nexus, *Journal of Marketing Management*, **27** (7–8), 785–807, doi:10.1080/0267257x.2010.500132.

Joinson, A. N. (2008) Looking At, Looking Up or Keeping Up with People?: motives and use of Facebook. In Czerwinski, M., Lund, A. and Tan, D. (eds), *Proceedings of the Twenty-Sixth Annual SIGCHI Conference on Human Factors in Computing Systems, Florence, Italy*, Association of Computing Machinery, 1027–36.

Kaplan, A. M. and Haenlein, M. (2010) Users of the World, Unite! The challenges and opportunities of social media, *Business Horizons*, **53** (1), 59–68, doi:10.1016/j.bushor.2009.09.003.

Kaptelinin, V. and Nardi, B. (2007) Acting with Technology: activity theory and interaction design, *First Monday*, **12** (4), doi:10.5210/fm.v12i4.1772.

Kobayashi, T. (2010) Bridging Social Capital in Online Communities: heterogeneity and social tolerance of online game players in Japan, *Human Communication Research*, **36** (4), 546–69, doi:10.1111/j.1468-2958.2010.01388.x.

Kuhlthau, C. (2004) *Seeking Meaning: a process approach to library and information services*, 2nd edn, Libraries Unlimited.

Kuhlthau, C. C. (1993) A Principle of Uncertainty for Information Seeking, *Journal of Documentation*, **49** (4), 339–55, doi:10.1108/eb026918.

Kuutti, K. (1991) Activity Theory and its Applications in Information Systems Research and Design. In Nissen, H.-E., Klein, H. K. and Hirschheim, R. (eds), *Information Systems Research Arena of the 90s*, North-Holland, 529–50.

Lai, H. M. and Chen, T. T. (2014) Knowledge Sharing in Interest Online Communities: a comparison of posters and lurkers, *Computers in Human*

Behavior, **35**, 295–306.

Lave, J. and Wenger, E. (1991) Legitimate Peripheral Participation in Communities of Practice Situated Learning: legitimate peripheral participation. In Lave, J. and Wenger, E. (eds), *Situated Learning: legitimate peripheral participation,* Cambridge University Press.

Law, S. P. and Chang, S. P. (2012) Social Capital and Knowledge Sharing in Online Communities: a mediation model. In *[Proceedings of the] 45th Hawaii International Conference on System Sciences,* 3530–9.

Leont'ev, A. (1977) Activity and Consciousness. In *Philosophy in the USSR: problems of dialectical materialism,* Progress Publishers, 180–202, www.marxists.org/archive/leontev/works/1977/leon1977.htm.

Leont'ev, A. (1978) *Activity, Consciousness, and Personality,* translated by M. J. Hall, Prentice Hall, www.marxists.org/archive/leontev/works/1978/index.htm.

Lober, W. B. and Flowers, J. L. (2011) Consumer Empowerment in Health Care amid the Internet and Social Media, *Seminars in Oncology Nursing,* **27** (3), 169–82, doi:10.1016/j.soncn.2011.04.002.

Malik, S. H. and Coulson, N. S. (2010) Coping with Infertility Online: an examination of self-help mechanisms in an online infertility support group, *Patient Education and Counseling,* **81** (2), 315–18, doi:10.1016/j.pec.2010.01.007.

McMullan, M. (2006) Patients Using the Internet to Obtain Health Information: how this affects the patient–health professional relationship, *Patient Education and Counseling,* **63** (1–2), 24–8, doi:10.1016/j.pec.2005.10.006.

McNair, A. G. K., Brookes, S. T., Kinnersley, P. and Blazeby, J. M. (2013) What Surgeons Should Tell Patients with Oesophago-Gastric Cancer: a cross sectional study of information needs, *European Journal of Surgical Oncology,* **39** (11), 1278–86, doi:10.1016/j.ejso.2013.08.005.

Merolli, M., Gray, K. and Martin-Sanchez, F. (2013) Health Outcomes and Related Effects of Using Social Media in Chronic Disease Management: a literature review and analysis of affordances, *Journal of Biomedical Informatics,* **46** (6), 957–69, doi:10.1016/j.jbi.2013.04.010.

Merolli, M., Gray, K., Martin-Sanchez, F. and Lopez-Campos, G. (2015) Patient-Reported Outcomes and Therapeutic Affordances of Social Media: findings from a global online survey of people with chronic pain, *Journal of Medical Internet Research,* **17** (1), e20, doi:10.2196/jmir.3915.

Mo, P. and Coulson, N. (2010) Empowering Processes in Online Support Groups among People Living with HIV/AIDS: a comparative analysis of 'lurkers' and 'posters', *Computers in Human Behavior*, **26** (5), 1183-93.

Moorhead, S. A., Hazlett, D. E., Harrison, L., Carroll, J. K., Irwin, A. and Hoving, C. (2013) A New Dimension of Health Care: systematic review of the uses, benefits, and limitations of social media for health communication, *Journal of Medical Internet Research*, **15** (4), e85, doi:10.2196/jmir.1933.

Nonnecke, B. and Preece, J. (2000) Lurker Demographics: counting the silent. In *Proceedings of the ACM CHI 2000 Human Factors in Computing Systems Conference*.

Norman, D. A. (1998) *The Invisible Computer*, MIT Press.

O'Brien, H. L. and Toms, E. G. (2008) What is User Engagement? A conceptual framework for defining user engagement with technology, *Journal of the American Society for Information Science and Technology*, **59** (6), 938-55, doi:10.1002/asi.20801.

O'Reilly, T. (2005) Web 2.0: compact definition?, O'Reilly Radar, http://radar.oreilly.com/2005/10/web-20-compact-definition.html.

O'Reilly, T. and Battelle, J. (2009) Web Squared: Web 2.0 five years on, O'Reilly Radar, http://assets.en.oreilly.com/1/event/28/web2009_websquared-whitepaper.pdf.

Ormandy, P. (2008a) *Chronic Kidney Disease: patient information needs, preferences and priorities*, Unpublished PhD thesis, University of Salford.

Ormandy, P. (2008b) Information Topics Important to Chronic Kidney Disease Patients: a systematic review, *Journal of Renal Care*, **34** (1), 19-27, doi:10.1111/j.1755-6686.2008.00006.x.

Ormandy, P. and Hulme, C. (2013) Measuring Patients' Preferences and Priorities for Information in Chronic Kidney Disease, *Information Research*, **18** (3).

Petrovčič, A. and Petrič, G. (2014) Differences in Intrapersonal and Interactional Empowerment between Lurkers and Posters in Health-Related Online Support Communities, *Computers in Human Behavior*, **34**, 39-48, doi:10.1016/j.chb.2014.01.008.

Preece, J., Nonnecke, B. and Andrews, D. (2004) The Top Five Reasons for Lurking: improving community experiences for everyone, *Computers in Human Behavior*, **20** (2), 201-23, doi:10.1016/j.chb.2003.10.015.

Putnam, R. D. (2000) *Bowling Alone: the collapse and revival of American community*, Simon and Schuster.

Rau, P.-L. P., Gao, Q. and Ding, Y. (2008) Relationship Between the Level of Intimacy and Lurking in Online Social Network Services, *Computers in Human Behavior*, **24** (6), 2757-70, doi:10.1016/j.chb.2008.04.001.

Roblin, D. W. (2011) The Potential of Cellular Technology to Mediate Social Networks for Support of Chronic Disease Self-Management, *Journal of Health Communication*, **16** (sup1), 59-76, doi:10.1080/10810730.2011.596610.

Robson, A. and Robinson, L. (2013) Building on Models of Information Behaviour: linking information seeking and communication, *Journal of Documentation*, **69** (2), 169-93, doi:10.1108/00220411311300039.

Rozenblum, R. and Bates, D. W. (2013) Patient-Centred Healthcare, Social Media and the Internet: the perfect storm?, *BMJ Quality & Safety*, **22** (3), 183-6, doi:10.1136/bmjqs-2012-001744.

Rutten, L. J. F., Arora, N. K., Bakos, A. D., Aziz, N. and Rowland, J. (2005) Information Needs and Sources of Information Among Cancer Patients: a systematic review of research (1980-2003), *Patient Education and Counseling*, **57** (3), 250-61, doi:10.1016/j.pec.2004.06.006.

Savolainen, R. (2012) Conceptualizing Information Need in Context, *Information Research*, **17** (4).

Schinkel, S., Schouten, B. C. and van Weert, J. C. M. (2013) Are GP Patients' Needs Being Met? Unfulfilled information needs among Native-Dutch and Turkish-Dutch patients, *Patient Education and Counseling*, **90** (2), 261-7, doi:10.1016/j.pec.2012.11.013.

Schlosser A. E. (2005) Posting Versus Lurking: communicating in a multiple audience context, *Journal of Consumer Research*, **32** (2), 260-5.

Schneider, A., von Krogh, G. and Jäger, P. (2013) 'What's Coming Next?': epistemic curiosity and lurking behavior in online communities, *Computers in Human Behavior*, **29** (1), 293-303, doi:10.1016/j.chb.2012.09.008.

Shaw, R. J. and Johnson, C. M. (2011) Health Information Seeking and Social Media Use on the Internet Among People with Diabetes, *Online Journal of Public Health Informatics*, **3** (1), doi:10.5210/ojphi.v3i1.3561.

Siemens, G. (2005) Connectivism: a learning theory for the digital age, *International Journal of Instructional Technology and Distance Learning*, **2** (1), 3-10, http://202.116.45.236/mediawiki/resources/2/2005_siemens_

Connectivism_A_LearningTheoryForTheDigitalAge.pdf.

Smith, A. N., Fischer, E. and Yongjian, C. (2012) How Does Brand-Related User-Generated Content Differ Across YouTube, Facebook, and Twitter?, *Journal of Interactive Marketing*, **26** (2), 102-13, doi:10.1016/j.intmar.2012.01.002.

Song, L. and Chang, T.-Y. (2012) Do Resources of Network Members Help in Help Seeking? Social capital and health information search, *Social Networks*, **34** (4), 658-69, doi:10.1016/j.socnet.2012.08.002.

Szreter, S. and Woolcock, M. (2004) Health by Association? Social capital, social theory, and the political economy of public health, *International Journal of Epidemiology*, **33** (4), 650-67, doi:10.1093/ije/dyh013.

van Weert, J. C. M., Bolle, S., van Dulmen, S. and Jansen, J. (2013) Older Cancer Patients' Information and Communication Needs: what they want is what they get?, *Patient Education and Counseling*, **92** (3), 388-97, doi:10.1016/j.pec.2013.03.011.

Vasilica, C. (2015a) Personal communication, from data collected for evaluation of GMKIN, unpublished, University of Salford.

Vasilica, C. (2015b) *Impact of Using Social Media to Increase Patient Information Provision, Networking and Communication*, PhD thesis, University of Salford.

Vennik, F. D., Adams, S. A., Faber, M. J. and Putters, K. (2014) Expert and Experiential Knowledge in the Same Place: patients' experiences with online communities connecting patients and health professionals, *Patient Education and Counseling*, **95** (2), 265-70, doi:10.1016/j.pec.2014.02.003.

Warner, D. and Procaccino, J. D. (2004) Toward Wellness: women seeking health information, *Journal of the American Society for Information Science and Technology*, **55** (8), 709-30, doi:10.1002/asi.20016.

Welbourne, J., Blanchard, A. and Wadsworth, M. (2013) Motivations in Virtual Health Communities and their Relationship to Community, Connectedness and Stress, *Computers in Human Behavior*, **29** (1), 129-39.

Wenger, E., McDermott, R. and Snyder, W. (2002) *Cultivating Communities of Practice*, Harvard Business School Press.

Wilson, T. D. (1981) On User Studies and Information Needs, *Journal of Documentation*, **37** (1), 3-15, doi:10.1108/eb026702.

Wilson, T. D. (1999) Models in Information Behaviour Research, *Journal of Documentation*, **55** (3), 249-70, doi:10.1108/eum0000000007145.

Wilson, T. D. (2004) Information Seeking Behaviour and the Digital

Information World, *European Science Editing*, **30** (3), 77-80.

Wilson, T. D. (2006) A Re-examination of Information Seeking Behaviour in the Context of Activity Theory, *Information Research*, **11** (4), www.informationr.net/ir/11-4/paper260.html.

Wilson, T. D. (2007) Evolution in Information Behavior Modeling: Wilson's model. In Fisher, K., Erdelez, S. and McKechnie, L. (eds), *Theories of Information Behavior*, Information Today, 31-6.

Woolcock, M. (2001) The Place of Social Capital in Understanding Social and Economic Outcomes, *Canadian Journal of Policy Research*, **2** (1), 11-17.

Xie, H. (2007) Shifts of Interactive Intentions and Information-Seeking Strategies in Interactive Information Retrieval, *Information Research*, **12** (4), doi:10.1002/(sici)1097-4571(2000)51:9<841::aid-asi70>3.0.co;2-0.

Zhao, J., Ha, S. and Widdows, R. (2015) The Influence of Social Capital on Knowledge Creation in Online Health Communities, *Information Technology and Management*, doi:10.1007/s10799-014-0211-3.

Zuckerberg, M. (n.d.) Mark Zuckerberg quote, www.azquotes.com/quote/685740.

CHAPTER 13

Health information systems: clinical data capture and document architecture

Faten Hamad

COMMENTARY: ALISON YEOMAN

In this chapter, Faten Hamad looks at the challenges facing developers of health information systems. The chapter first provides an overview of how the concepts of information architecture can be applied in the context of healthcare systems. In Chapter 2, the author has explained that the key to successful information architecture is to create a structured, shared environment that is accessible and meets the needs of users. She pointed out that users often have different needs, preferences and behaviour, as noted also by Rosenfeld, Morville and Arango (2015). Consequently, designing a system that works effectively for all users is not easy.

This is particularly true in the case of healthcare, a system that can be viewed as both 'complicated', because of the number of components in the system (e.g. the number of users of a particular computer interface), and 'complex', because of the web of relationships and interactions between healthcare professionals, professionals and patients (Kannampallil et al., 2011). In the introduction Hamad identifies five challenges for developers working in this environment:

- a lack of resources and evidence base
- legacy information systems developed for particular functions, which do not integrate well with other systems

- a lack of information sharing
- the need for rigorous safety management systems and regulatory mechanisms
- the sheer volume of information that healthcare organisations have to manage.

She then considers clinical data management and the importance of data sharing including the challenges of combining information from different sources or in different formats and ensuring that staff enter data correctly.

Hamad cites Almunawar and Anshari (2012), who describe health information systems as sitting at the intersection between the business of healthcare provision and the information systems to support clinical work. She explains that 'clinical research and investigation', where the emphasis is on case reports and 'big data' (the collection of large amounts of data), has benefitted from recent advances in technology and electronic data capture, which is explored in Section 13.4. For general health information systems, on the other hand, the emphasis is on effective information exchange and communication. This leads to a discussion of electronic health records, the challenge of integrating them with electronic data captures, and developing HL7 (Health Level Seven) standards to support the efficient and secure exchange of health information.

As well as providing further context for the issues and challenges faced by information architecture developers (as discussed in Chapter 2), Hamad explains that the HL7 standards are based on an object-oriented model such as one of those examined in Chapter 5. This chapter provides a practical example of some of the theories of classification described in chapters 2 and 3, using International Classification of Disease (ICD) and Systematized Nomenclature of Medicine (SNOMED) codes, and shows the importance of getting this right. This chapter is an interesting contrast to Chapter 12 by Cristina Vasilica and Paula Ormandy, which focused on building bridges between consumers of healthcare by developing an online community.

Vasilica and Ormandy's acknowledgement of the important role health professionals can play in providing reassurance and credibility in such an online community and their call for clinicians to use social media as mechanisms for engaging with patients is an example of the opportunities developments in information technology can bring. Whether their primary interest is in active patient care or in research, health professionals are working in an environment where timely and reliable information is essential and the ideal is fully integrated systems that can share information efficiently, securely and accurately. All this in high-pressure systems in which, along with the five challenges identified by Faten Hamad, there has historically been a culture of reliance on colleagues as key sources of information and where practitioners face barriers such as cognitive load, lack of time and lack of information-skills training (Clarke et al., 2013; Politi et al., 2017).

References

Almunawar, M. N. and Anshari, M. (2012) Health Information Systems (HIS): concept and technology,
https://arxiv.org/ftp/arxiv/papers/1203/1203.3923.pdf.

Clarke, M. A., Belden, J. L., Koopman, R. J., Steege, L. M., Moore, J. L., Canfield, S. M. and Kim, M. S. (2013) Information Needs and Information-Seeking Behaviour Analysis of Primary Care Physicians and Nurses: a literature review, *Health Information and Libraries Journal*, **30** (3), 178–90.

Kannampallil, T. G., Schauer, G. F., Cohen, T. and Patel, V. L. (2011) Considering Complexity in Healthcare Systems, *Journal of Biomedical Informatics*, **44** (6), 943–47.

Politi, L., Codish, S., Sagy, I. and Fink, L. (2017) Balancing Volume and Duration of Information Consumption by Physicians: the case of health information exchange in critical care, *Journal of Biomedical Informatics*, **71** (July), 1–15.

Rosenfeld, L., Morville, P. and Arango, J. (2015) *Information Architecture: for the web and beyond*, 4th edn, O'Reilly Media Inc.

13.1   Introduction

Healthcare is making increasing use of information technology, but there are many difficulties for health information system developers:

- Resource constraints reflect increasing demands on clinical services, and there is also a lack of evidence in health informatics (Rigby and Ammenwerth, 2016, 3-11).
- Different information systems (or modules) have been developed, often

over a period of time, for particular healthcare functional units. Such systems do not necessarily integrate well, even within one organisation.

- A lack of information sharing encourages a silo mentality, which in turn keeps information use at a routine level, with few opportunities to use information effectively to transform clinical processes.
- Healthcare organisations are concerned about risks to patient safety (and possible litigation), which may be greater in information technology systems unless there are proper safety management systems and regulatory mechanisms in place.
- Healthcare organisations have to manage a huge volume of information.

MeSH (Medical Subject Headings) defines a health information system as a system for the collection and/or processing of data from various sources, and using the information for policy making and management of health services. Goldschmidt (2005) has a similar definition that also stresses the retrieval, sharing and use of health care information, data and knowledge for communication and decision making. Kushniruk and Nøhr (2016) list some of the risks of bad design that were identified during a design game for clinicians on preventing adverse drug events. Some information may be missing because information is not integrated, and some measurements out of normal range may not be noticed as a result of misreading and mistakes in analysis. Rigid information system design leads to workarounds, and some duplication of effort. The lack of user input during the design is often a major factor in the failure of systems in healthcare, as the information architecture does not reflect what the clinical users need for effective and safe working (Niazkhani et al., 2009).

People who undertake clinical research and investigation are heavy data consumers of clinical data and case reports. Recent technological advances make the use of and reliance on information systems to collect and organise the required data an added value for clinical institutions. Electronic data capture occurs when systems collect data in electronic rather than paper form. This data can be organised electronically in databases to improve data entry, data validation and reporting for clinical trials. Electronic data capture systems should also save time for clinical analysis. The pharmaceutical industry has established an acceptable electronic data capture performance (Welker, 2007; Walther et al., 2011).

In general health information systems the main emphasis is on communication, information exchange and ensuring that those who need information obtain it in a usable format. One of the major international initiatives on the design of an architecture for health care documentation is HL7, which originally focused on messaging requirements (so that users would know where to look for information required, under headings they recognised). The HL7 clinical document architecture became an ANSI (American National Standards Institution) standard in 2000, a document mark-up standard that covers the structure and semantics of clinical documents such as discharge summaries (Dolin et al., 2006).

Chapter 13 examines the production of the research data that may be discussed, in a different format by the users of the online community, such as those described in Chapter 12. The emphasis is on the workflows for clinical data management (with emphasis on research needs). Clinical document architecture can be contrasted with the general requirements for semi-structured document architecture explained in Chapter 9.

This chapter is organised as follows. Section 13.2 provides an overview of how an information and systems architecture might be used in the health sector. Sections 13.3 and 13.4 continue to discuss clinical data management and electronic data capture, and Section 13.5 considers how electronic data capture works with electronic health record systems. Section 13.6 examines the key features of the HL7 clinical document architecture and general requirements for such standards. Section 13.7 draws conclusions.

13.2   Healthcare systems and information architecture – a top-level view

In the UK, the National Health Service (NHS; www.nhs.uk/pages/home.aspx) is the primary healthcare services provider. The main services that the NHS provides are primary care through general practitioners (GPs), hospital care, community services, mental health and specialist services. Tan, Liu and White (2013) described the information architecture for NHS healthcare services. They define information architecture as a framework that provides the right information (both content and context) to the right person, when and where required. They examined and defined the information requirements at organisational and application level of healthcare organisations in order to propose an appropriate information architecture. At the organisational level, the information requirements dictate the overall information technology architecture. This comprises the organisation context and contents, and system specifications - the databases to build. The application level defines the information requirements for the information system.

These are the six key elements of information architecture (Tan, Liu and White, 2013):

- the six interrogative elements about information: what (data), how (process), where (network), who is (stakeholder), when (time) and why (motivation)
- appropriate document templates based on business activities and processes (see Section 13.6 on HL7 clinical document architecture)
- user-friendly interfaces through suitable labelling and navigation schemes (not covered in this chapter, see Chapter 9 for discussion of interface design)
- information management (setting out how information is stored, organised and accessed)
- change management in order to deal with the changing business and clinical environment (see Chapter 5 on general business process architecture).

Tan, Liu and White (2013) consider information architecture to be a collection of norms and information objects. Norms govern the context, the organisation's activities and practices, where actors are assigned a specific role for certain activities. Norms provide the motivation to use the information and indicate how the data is used. The norms contribute to the technical specification and design of the system. Information objects are the contents of the information system - the meaning, representation, location and value of the information. So an information object contributes to the design of information system, data representation schemes and database design (Tan, Liu and White, 2013). For instance, information objects are the things of interest, the entities of the database, while the meaning, location and representation of the objects will contribute to the properties of tables and the entire database. For relational databases, metadata - the data about and describing the information objects - link the information architecture to the design of the database schemas (and explain and specify aspects of information management).

When recording details about patient conditions and clinical activities performed, ICD codes are widely used in health information systems for classification of conditions. The ICD has developed over decades from a means of recording causes of death to a classification that may support health activities such as public health planning and examining the effectiveness of health interventions. The history and development of the ICD, the increasing complexity of the structure, and the cultural problems in data collection, coding, analysis and interpretation are covered in detail in Bowker and Star (2000, chapters 2–4). Articles examining use of the ICD cover a wide range of topics such as validation of administrative data (e.g. Jolley et al., 2015), or the validity of ICD codes in identifying particular conditions (e.g. Singh et al., 2017) or how ICD codes can be assigned automatically using structured and unstructured data (Scheurwegs et al., 2016). The ICD could be viewed as the language (or more accurately languages) that describe what clinical activity has occurred and for what reason. It is a tool for information management, a list tool – useful, but care must be exercised to understand the level of detail being applied (Bowker and Star, 2000, 137).

Another approach to standardise the terms used to describe clinical conditions and clinical activities is to focus on clinical terminology. A not-for-profit organisation, SNOMED International, is responsible for developing SNOMED clinical terms (www.snomed.org/about). There is no space in this chapter to discuss clinical coding and clinical terminology but those interested in the social and cultural implications of classification should refer to Bowker and Star (2000). For a history of the Read codes and the merger with SNOMED, see Benson (2011).

13.3 Clinical data management

Data sharing is essential to support clinical research. Providing clinical investigators and study personnel access to real-time and longitudinal healthcare data for review can facilitate clinical research, for example, patient follow-up in order to examine the safety and efficiency of drugs and medical products. Lu and Su (2010) stress that clinical data management needs to combine patient data from different clinical systems, and often a mix of paper-based data entry and electronic data capture have been used. In clinical trials, the design of the case report form (in paper or electronic format) is key to ensuring that data is collected according to the protocol, and that collection complies with safety and regulatory requirements. In the course of a trial the clinical data management or quality assurance team needs to assess and verify data collection and the database for completeness. For data management the ideal design should reflect site workflow and use standard-based system integration (Lu and Su, 2010) (see also Section 13.4). A survey of German-speaking radiation oncology units found that 77% used a health information system, all participated in at least one documentation project, but only 52% used specialised documentation systems such as electronic case report forms (Kessel and Combs, 2015). Problems included funding and expertise to implement new documentation systems.

There are some initiatives to incorporate electronic data capture with electronic health record systems (e.g. the project entitled Electronic Health Records for Clinical Research Functional Profile) and work by Roche Pharma Development and Genentech (Gangarapu et al., 2015). The latter projects focus on concept development – mining clinical data for a better understanding of targeted patient populations – protocol design; using current real-world clinical data to determine the impact of specific criteria on the feasibility of a protocol and patient identification; and using electronic health records to identify directly potentially eligible patients for proactive patient recruitment (Gangarapu et al., 2015). In other words, the use of patient data in hospital systems should provide realistic inclusion criteria, help design a workable protocol, and ensure that all eligible patients are approached. Kessel and Combs (2015) found that 13 hospitals of 34 in their survey (38%) were using an electronic health record within the health information system for data capture. The rest of the hospitals have an independent electronic health record system for additional use or as the only system for patient documentation.

The problem is not just the design of the systems for data capture – workflow is also important and staff need to enter data correctly and consistently. For example, Smith et al. (2016) investigated the accuracy of various pressure ulcer monitoring systems against a 'gold standard' pressure ulcer wound audit in a random sample of NHS trusts. The audit collected data on existing and healed ulcers to use to assess the accuracy of existing monitoring systems. Further data on other wounds were collected to explore the possibility of misclassification on monitoring systems. The results suggested that not all patients with pressure ulcers were noted on the systems, grading of severity was sometimes inaccurate, and the audit failed to confirm the reports of a pressure ulcer associated with a patient on some systems.

13.4   Electronic data capture

Traditional clinical trials data collection was by paper-based case report forms, followed by data entry into a relational database by two people to try to ensure data integrity. The process was increasingly inconvenient for the large volume of clinical data generated (Walther et al., 2011). With the increasing number of information and communication technology applications (e.g. electronic health records maintained by healthcare providers and institutions, electronic laboratory reports, and digital medical images from devices), clinical trials research required new information systems to capture and then process the data ready for submission for approval of new drugs or devices. Electronic data capture systems emerged (Walther et al., 2011; FDA, 2013). Electronic data capture systems take over the functions of data entry, data validation and data reporting for analysis.

Electronic data capture may be web-based software that stores participant data collected in clinical trials, generally replacing paper-based case report forms with electronic forms. The Clinical Data Interchange Standards Consortium (CDISC; www.cdisc.org) is a global, open, multidisciplinary, non-profit organisation, which has established standards to support the acquisition, exchange, submission and archive of clinical research data and metadata. CDISC has partners with a large number of pharmaceutical companies and academic institutions that undertake clinical research (CDISC, 2011). Chatterjee, Pawse and Gopalani (2016) explain the importance of data integrity, to avoid claims of fraud, which is the responsibility of the clinical data managers. They suggest that centralised risk-based monitoring will make clinical monitoring more efficient. Electronic data capture has many advantages, for instance it provides immediate access to trial data and trial status reports via the web, and provides an improved quality of data entry (by automatically querying potential errors). Some electronic data capture systems, such as Electronic Data Capture Services of the Société Générale de Surveillance (SGS), can support the adaptive trial design, when a trial changes over time, as the system automatically updates the trial design providing a full control over trial settings (SGS, 2017). The main advantage with electronic data capture is that the data becomes immediately available after collection and accordingly users can monitor data collection, enter, review and analyse data in real time, and perform online data checks to assure data quality at entry point (Walther et al., 2011).

There are many electronic data capture software providers, each offering specialised solutions for certain customer profiles or study phases, and some pharmaceutical companies have developed their own electronic data capture software. Some of the common features of electronic data capture are cloud storage, providing easy access from anywhere, and role-based permissions to ensure that only authenticated users are allowed to have access to the data, as the electronic data capture system creates accounts for users with credentials and designated permissions. A designer of electronic case report forms typically allows users to use and adapt templates for forms, building in edit checks. Visits and other calendar events can be scheduled. A query management system may be installed, which can have an audit trail to track changes to data (Lopienski, 2016).

Data standards are available to make acquisition, exchange, submission and archiving of clinical trial data more accurate on one hand and to provide data in a sharable format on the other, for instance, electronic data capture regulations for Computerized Systems Used in Clinical Trials (CSUCT) for Title 21, Part 11, of the US Code of Federal Regulations (21 CFR Part 11). It deals with Food and Drug Administration guidelines for electronic records and electronic signatures in order to ensure that data records are only processed by an authorised person. There are also standards that the electronic data capture system should adhere to, for example on data interchange. Data interchange standards cover the Operational Data Model, Laboratory Data Model and Study Data Model, which are all CDISC standards. These standards ensure that the collected data can be integrated with other data from other resources with different data standards, and make data migration easier (Kush, 2006; Souza, Kush and Evans, 2007; Shah et al., 2010). Electronic data capture software is being developed to extract patient data directly from electronic health records.

13.5   Electronic health records and electronic data capture

Almunawar and Anshari (2012) described health information systems as the intersection between two fields: the business of healthcare provision and the information systems to support clinical work. Generally, health information systems support many services and sub-modules, and all these need to be coordinated and controlled using efficient communication techniques in order to support high quality services (Al-Sakran, 2015).

The electronic health record is the core of a health information system. An electronic health record usually requires an integrated database to maintain a patient's healthcare history (textual, radiology images, electrocardiograms, audio and waveform data and other media content) within a shared environment (Garrett and Seidman, 2011; Al-Sakran, 2015). In such records, the system stores and maintains the patient's record for future retrieval. With the increasing amount of patient information captured in electronic health records, there is an opportunity to use that data for secondary purposes such as clinical research. The Center for Drug Evaluation and Research encourages seamless exchange of structured, re-usable information between health care and clinical research systems so that data may be entered once at the point of care and used many times without manual re-entry or manual source data verification (FDA, 2015). However, electronic health records and research systems (or electronic data capture systems) have different workflow and regulatory compliance needs. Although both systems have similar data such as medications, test results and problems, they do not have the same purposes and use this data differently. Electronic health record systems are primarily used to improve healthcare delivery, and enhance the quality and safety of patient care. Electronic data capture systems primarily focus on electronic documentation, collection and management of data captured by clinical research sites participating in a given study. In other words, the emphasis in electronic health record systems is on workflow to support the provision of care, while in electronic data capture systems the emphasis is on workflow that enables verification of data integrity and validity (Laird-Maddox, Mitchell and Hoffman, 2014).

The FDA (2015) believes that electronic capture of data associated with the electronic health record and other healthcare devices such as digital imaging, mobile health devices and instruments to collect electronic patient reported outcomes might improve reliability, quality, traceability, provenance and integrity of clinical data to regulatory submission. A report from the policy meeting of the American Medical Informatics Association in 2011 (Cusack et al., 2013) agreed that clinical data could serve other secondary purposes, but stated that the primary purpose of clinical data capture and documentation is to support health and healthcare directly. It recommended that data capture and documentation should be aligned with the clinical team's workflow, and that multidisciplinary and team working should be supported. The focus should be on the patient, who should be seen as the key part of the care team.

A number of organisations have worked to address the challenge of integrating electronic health record and electronic data capture to exchange data. In 2007 the Integrating the Healthcare Enterprise and the CDISC worked with multiple electronic health record and electronic data capture vendors and pharmaceutical companies to develop the Retrieve Form for Data Capture Profile (RFD) (ITI Technical Committee, 2011; Laird-Maddox, Mitchell and Hoffman, 2014). The RFD is 'a method for gathering data within a user's current application context to support the prepopulation of forms retrieved from an external source such as an electronic data capture system' (Laird-Maddox, Mitchell and Hoffman, 2014, 2). It supports the retrieval of a form from another source such as an electronic health record, the display and completion of the form, and then return of an instance of data to the receiving application. It also amends previously captured data (ITI Technical Committee, 2011). For instance, a healthcare provider uses an electronic health record to document patient care. If a research institution requires some data from the healthcare provider from an electronic health record's database, an RFD enables the electronic health record user to retrieve a data capture form from a research institution to fill out the form, and to return the data to them without leaving the electronic health record application.

With the RFD profile, the research institute provides data capture forms in a schema appropriate to its domain. The RFD profile uses XForms technology, which supports co-operation between the form display and form provider systems. In this there is an iterative process to complete the required form with the desired data in case of interruptions, or if the form was only partially filled with data at the first time. The profile also supports a generic polling mechanism that allows the research institution to set out issues with the data that has been captured so that the healthcare provider can correct them.

In order to demonstrate interoperability between electronic health records and RFDs, Florida Hospital (Orlando, Florida) agreed to collaborate with Cerner to implement the RFD workflow in their environment. Florida Hospital is already using the Cerner Millennium record system in its workflow (Laird-Maddox, Mitchell and Hoffman, 2014).

The process of interoperability demonstration works as follows:

- A continuity of care document is generated from the electronic health record. It contains the most recently populated values for the relevant data elements.
- The continuity of care document is an XML-based HL7 standard used in the exchange of clinical data between healthcare providers.

- The continuity of care document is transformed into a format that can be used by the research system with a script of code.
- The electronic case report form is displayed within a new window where values from the electronic health record are prepopulated in the appropriate fields.
- The user can enter additional research-specific data, modify values from the electronic health record, and save the form.

This process can be completed with minimal interruption to the current electronic health record session and data flows from the electronic health record to an electronic case report form without manual re-entry. It appears that Cerner's interoperability demonstrations using RFDs proved to be able to retrieve data for a research data capture system from the Millennium electronic health record (Laird-Maddox, Mitchell and Hoffman, 2014).

Data capture is expensive for clinical trial managers, and it saves time and money if data can be used from electronic health records. Unfortunately, as indicated already, managers of patient care systems and clinical trials have different priorities. A comparison of data elements from case report forms with data elements with electronic health records from hospitals working on the Electronic Health Records for Clinical Research Project (EHR4CR) found differences even for adverse event reporting, an aspect of care of interest to both. The final data inventory identified the 133 data elements most frequently found in clinical trials. There was no serious adverse event documentation available directly for more than half of the possible data exporting sites (hospitals) (Bruland et al., 2016). The information or other indicators may be there within another clinical concept, or described in free text.

Electronic health record data from hospitals has contributed to patient recruitment processes, but an increasing number of trials are conducted in primary care settings. A study examining the proportion of eligibility criteria that could be matched with data from electronic health records in primary care in the UK found that around 74% of electronic health records already contain much of the data required, suggesting that integration with clinical trial management systems should not be too difficult (Ateya, Delaney and Speedie, 2016). Another approach is to use the electronic health record data to create a real-world reference population of uncontrolled patients to supplement a control and placebo group in some long-term studies (in this case a clinical trial in severe asthma, Franzén et al., 2016). The routine collection of large amounts of clinical data (big data) is more common, and these datasets may be used for research – for public health, examination of variation between healthcare providers, and supplementing other sources of data, but the main challenge is to demonstrate data quality and attribution of cause and effect (Cook and Collins, 2015).

Secondary data analysis contributes to clinical research more and more. The preferred searching mode will probably function like Google, with emphasis on free text searching. The University of Michigan's Electronic Medical Record Search Engine (EMERSE) for searching narrative documents stored in electronic health records has similar functions to Google but other functionalities suited to the medical environment to deal with abbreviations (e.g. to avoid removing OR as a stop word as OR in medicine means operating room), plus a medical spellchecker. EMERSE allows users to save search queries as search bundles that may be shared with other users – a similar principle to the development of search filters (see also Section 14.2), but a more collaborative approach. The researchers developed an experimental extension to EMERSE to apply the nomenclatures included in the Unified Medical Language System® Metathesaurus for more comprehensive query expansion (Hanauer et al., 2015). A project examining how to improve the use of social data in medical research compared two user interfaces – a web search, which was Google-like in allowing users to browse, search and view metadata about a study variable, and a traditional search, which in effect expects users to know what they are looking for. Results showed that the web search performed better as results were more likely to be correct, and the search was faster (Jay et al., 2016).

13.6   Clinical document architecture

As emphasised in previous sections, information exchange is very important for health information systems. HL7 was known originally as a messaging standard, but the HL7 group moved on to standards for clinical document architecture, and published the first ANSI standard in 2000 (Dolin et al., 2001), followed by release 2 in 2005 (Dolin et al., 2006). HL7 clinical document architecture is intended to apply to clinical documents that require stewardship, have a definite lifetime, and require legal authentication. Examples include discharge summaries and progress notes. As far as possible the exchange of such documents should not require particular platforms or applications. The clinical document architecture for this HL7 version 3 family of standards is based on a shared reference information model, an object-oriented model (see chapters 1 and 7).

The main premise is that health care can be modelled through three main classes – act, role and entity – linked together using three association classes. For example, a patient encounter is an act, and has attributes such as time, place and an identifier for the encounter. The patient encounter might be a meeting of the multidisciplinary team at the bedside – each act may have any number of participations (by consultant, nurse, occupational therapist, medical student), composed of roles, played by entities (the medical student has a different set of responsibilities from the occupational therapist, and so on). And role is important in differentiating authority for signing off on documents, for example. For a clinical document, we need to specify the originators, authenticators, legal authenticators (all these are service actors) and intended recipients of the document, and the originating organisation. Patients are included in service targets – in other words, a patient is intended to have something done to, or on, them (observation, treatment, therapy etc.), and their family members may also be service targets. This is a very brief example of the way in which HL7 clinical document architecture works. Dolin et al. (2001) note that clinical document architecture structures are very similar to html structures, so transforming clinical document architecture documents to something readable on a web browser is relatively easy – although html will not support the detailed mark-up required of clinical document architecture.

The clinical document architecture release 2 (CDA 2) (Dolin et al., 2006) in 2005 was intended to help code the narrative in many clinical reports. Like the original clinical document architecture, release 2 has a header and a body for each clinical document. The header identifies and classifies the document (providing details about authentication, the patient encounter, the patient and involved providers). The body comprises the clinical report, organised into sections that can be encoded using standard vocabularies. In CDA 2, unlike the first release, the clinical body may be formally expressed in a reference information model. This is important, as it is possible that clinicians may not be responsible for much of the routine coding associated with clinical documents, and that aspects of clinical significance may be hidden within the clinical narrative. Dolin et al. (2006) describe how CDA 2 works with SNOMED CT, for example, and list the relationship entry types in CDA 2, which specify the relationship between two acts. The richer semantic model in CDA 2 allows for more accurate and meaningful linkages to be made. As might be expected, there are parallel approaches to clinical document architecture. Ferranti et al. (2006) discuss how to harmonise HL7 clinical document architecture with the continuity of care record model produced by the American Society for Testing of Materials.

Applications of clinical document architecture include disease surveillance. Reams, Powell and Edwards (2014) describe a case study in Kentucky when a clinical document architecture was successfully transmitted from a physician's office to a state cancer registry. They discuss recruitment of suitable oncology practices for the project, vetting of electronic health record vendors to ensure they could cope with the technical specifications required for the clinical document architecture, and the problems encountered on implementation. The proposition that information exchange should support continuity of care is valid for individual patients, but the practice is often a lot messier. McMurray et al. (2013) describe some of the problems encountered when electronic information systems meet paper-based systems for patients who are being moved from one care setting to another. Despite care providers having electronic record systems, they routinely faxed requests for admission and discharge documentation to each other, and maintained separate paper charts. Despite the theory of the continuity of care record model (Ferranti et al., 2006), practice is more complex, particularly when dealing with community care, nursing homes and social care, and hospital information systems.

13.7   Conclusions

Information technology is increasingly used in healthcare in collecting or processing data from various sources, and organising information for policy making and managing health services. However, there are some difficulties facing health information system developers as different information systems (or modules) are being developed by different developers and/or vendors for particular healthcare units. Rigid information system design, lack of integration of information, and lack of user input during the design duplicate efforts and make information available only at unit level and separated from other functional units. System and module interoperability is an issue to consider.

Data sharing and communication are essential to support clinical research. Collecting data and case reports in a usable format and in time is critical for clinical research and investigation. Healthcare systems are collecting and organising the required data for clinical investigation. Clinical data management involves collecting data from different clinical systems, so data should be collected according to the appropriate protocol. Moreover, data management systems should reflect site workflow and use standards-based system integration where staff are required to enter data correctly and consistently. Electronic data capture into a database is intended to improve data entry, data validation and reporting for clinical trials, which in turn might reduce clinical analysis time. When electronic data is captured data standards are used to ensure that the collected data can be integrated with other data from other resources with different data standards, and make data migration easier – 21 CFR Part 11 (see Section 13.4).

Electronic health records and electronic data capture systems have similar data, for example on medications and test results, but have different workflow and regulatory compliance needs. For instance, electronic health record systems aim to improve healthcare experience and provision, while electronic data capture systems primarily focus on workflow that enables verification of data integrity and validity. However, there has been an emphasis on the need to align data capture and documentation with the clinical team's workflow and to integrate electronic health records and electronic data capture to exchange data. RFD is the proposed method for gathering data within a user's current electronic health record settings in order to prepare it for use in an external source (electronic data capture settings).

Clinical document architecture is important to support information exchange in health information systems. HL7 is an architecture for health care documentation that focuses on messaging requirements to help users know where to look for information they require, under headings they recognise. The structure of clinical document architecture is similar to html structures.

It appears that although healthcare is benefitting from information technology it is not fully exploited in healthcare settings. For example, despite having electronic record systems, care providers still use faxes to exchange admission and discharge documentation. It seems that dealing with the complexity of health care practice is still partly beyond the capability of electronic systems.

References

Al-Sakran, H. O. (2015) Framework Architecture for Improving Healthcare

Information Systems Using Agent Technology, *International Journal of Managing Information Technology*, **7** (1), 17.

Almunawar, M. N. and Anshari, M. (2012) Health Information Systems (HIS): concept and technology, https://arxiv.org/ftp/arxiv/papers/1203/1203.3923.pdf.

Ateya, M. B., Delaney, B. C. and Speedie, S. M. (2016) The Value of Structured Data Elements from Electronic Health Records for Identifying Subjects for Primary Care Clinical Trials, *BMC Medical Informatics and Decision Making*, **16** (1), doi:10.1186/s12911-016-0239-x.

Benson, T. (2011) The History of the Read Codes: the inaugural James Read Memorial Lecture 2011, *Informatics in Primary Care*, **19** (3), 173–82.

Bowker, G. C. and Star, S. L. (2000) *Sorting Things Out: classification and its consequences*, MIT Press.

Bruland, P., McGilchrist, M., Zapletal, E., Acosta, D., Proeve, J., Askin, S., Ganslandt, T., Doods, J. and Dugas, M. (2016) Common Data Elements for Secondary Use of Electronic Health Records Data for Clinical Trial Execution and Serious Adverse Event Reporting, *BMC Medical Research Methodology*, **16** (159), doi:10.1186/s12874-016-0259-3.

Chatterjee, P., Pawse, P. and Gopalani, L. (2016) Data Integrity in Clinical Trials: current trends and future directions, *Pharma Times*, **48** (5), 14–16.

CDISC (2011) CDISC Clinical Research Glossary, Clinical Data Interchange Standards Consortium, https://www.cdisc.org/sites/default/files/members/standard/foundational/glossary/act1211_011_043_gr_glossary.pdf.

Cook, J. A. and Collins, G. S. (2015) The Rise of Big Clinical Databases, *British Journal of Surgery*, **102** (2), e93–e101.

Cusack, C. M., Hripcsak, G., Bloomrosen, M., Rosenbloom, S. T., Weaver, C. A., Wright, A., Vawdrey, D. K., Walker, J. and Mamykina, L. (2013) The Future State of Clinical Data Capture and Documentation: a report from AMIA's 2011 Policy Meeting, *Journal of the American Medical Informatics Association*, **20**, 134–40.

Dolin, R. H., Alschuler, L., Beebe, C., Biron, P. V., Boyer, S. L., Essin, D., Kimber, E., Lincoln, T. and Mattison, J. E. (2001) The HL7 Clinical Document Architecture, *Journal of the American Medical Informatics Association*, **8** (6), 552–69.

Dolin, R. H., Alschuler, L., Boyer, S., Beebe, C., Behlen, F. M., Biron, P. V. and Shabo, A. (2006) HL7 Clinical Document Architecture, Release 2,

Journal of the American Medical Informatics Association, **13** (1), 30-9.

Ferranti, J. M., Musser, R. C., Kawamoto, K. and Hammond, W. E. (2006) The Clinical Document Architecture and the Continuity of Care Record, *Journal of the American Medical Informatics Association*, **13** (3), 245-52.

FDA (2013) Guidance for Industry: electronic source data in clinical investigations, Food and Drug Administration, www.fda.gov/downloads/drugs/guidancecomplianceregulatoryinformation /guidances/ucm328691.pdf.

FDA (2015) Source Data Capture from Electronic Health Records (EHRs): using standardized clinical research data, Food and Drug Administration, www.fda.gov/Drugs/DevelopmentApprovalProcess/FormsSubmissionRequ irements/ElectronicSubmissions/ucm464653.htm.

Franzén, S., Janson, C., Larsson, K., Petzold, M., Olsson, U., Magnusson, G., Telg, G., Colice, G., Johansson, G. and Sundgren, M. (2016) Evaluation of the Use of Swedish Integrated Electronic Health Records and Register Health Care Data as Support Clinical Trials in Severe Asthma: the PACEHR study, *Respiratory Research*, **15** (1), 152.

Gangarapu, P., Reddy, J. P., Sundaram, A. M., Sabareesh, M. and Prabhakaran, V. (2015) Regulatory Considerations in Clinical Data Management, *International Journal of Current Pharmaceutical & Clinical Research*, **5** (3), 143-52.

Garrett, P. and Seidman, J. (2011) EMR vs EHR – What is the Difference?, HealthITBuzz, 4 January, https://www.healthit.gov/buzz-blog/electronic-health-and-medical-records/emr-vs-ehr-difference/.

Goldschmidt, P. G. (2005) HIT and MIS: implications of health information technology and medical information systems, *Communications of the ACM*, **48** (10), 68-74.

Hanauer, D. A., Mei, Q., Law, J., Khanna, R. and Zheng, K. (2015) Supporting Information Retrieval from Electronic Health Records: a report of University of Michigan's nine-year experience in developing and using the Electronic Medical Record Search Engine (EMERSE), *Journal of Biomedical Informatics*, **55**, 290-300, http://doi.org/10.1016/j.jbi.2015.05.003.

ITI Technical Committee (2011) IHE IT Infrastructure Technical Framework – Retrieve Form for Data Capture (RFD), Integrating the Healthcare Enterprise, www.ihe.net/technical_framework/upload/ihe_iti_ suppl_rfd_rev2-2_ti_2011-08-19.pdf.

Jay, C., Harper, S., Dunlop, I., Smith, S., Sufi, S., Goble, C. and Buchan, I. (2016) Natural Language Search Interfaces: health data needs single-field variable search, *Journal of Medical Internet Research*, **18** (1), e13, http://doi.org/10.2196/jmir.4912.

Jolley, R. J., Sawka, K. J., Yergens, D. W., Quan, H., Jetté, N. and Doig, C. J. (2015) Validity of Administrative Data in Recording Sepsis: a systematic review, *Critical Care*, **19** (1), 139.

Kessel, K. A. and Combs, S. E. (2015) Data Management, Documentation and Analysis Systems in Radiation Oncology: a multi-institutional survey, *Radiation Oncology*, **10** (1), 1.

Kush, R. (2006) Electronic Data Capture – Pros and Cons, *BioExecutive International*, **2** (6), S48–S52

Kushniruk, A. and Nøhr, C. (2016) Participatory Design, User Involvement and Health IT Evaluation. In Ammenwerth, E. and Rigby, M. (eds), *Evidence-Based Health Informatics: promoting safety and efficiency through scientific methods and ethical policy*, IOS Press.

Laird-Maddox, M., Mitchell, S. B. and Hoffman, M. (2014) Integrating Research Data Capture into the Electronic Health Record Workflow: real-world experience to advance innovation, *Perspectives in Health Information Management*, **11** (Fall), 1e.

Lopienski, K. (2016) The Beginner's Guide to an Electronic Data Capture (EDC) System, https://forteresearch.com/news/beginners-guide-electronic-data-capture-edc-system/.

Lu, Z. and Su, J. (2010) Clinical Data Management: current status, challenges, and future directions from industry perspectives, *Open Access Journal of Clinical Trials*, **2**, 93–105.

McMurray, J., Hicks, E., Johnson, H., Elliott, J., Byrne, K. and Stolee, P. (2013) 'Trying to Find Information is Like Hating Yourself Every Day': the collision of electronic information systems in transition with patients in transition, *Health Informatics Journal*, **19** (3), 218–32.

Niazkhani, Z., Pirnejad, H., Berg, M. and Aarts, J. (2009) The Impact of Computerized Provider Order Entry Systems on Inpatient Clinical Workflow: a literature review, *Journal of the American Medical Informatics Association*, **16** (4), 539–49.

Reams, C., Powell, M. and Edwards, R. (2014) State Synergies and Disease Surveillance: creating an electronic health data communication model for cancer reporting and comparative effectiveness research in Kentucky, *eGEMs (Generating Evidence & Methods to Improve Patient Outcomes)*, **2** (2), article 4.

Rigby, M. and Ammenwerth, E. (2016) The Need for Evidence in Health Informatics. In Ammenwerth, E. and Rigby, M. (eds), *Evidence-Based Health Informatics: promoting safety and efficiency through scientific methods and ethical policy*, IOS Press, 3-11.

Scheurwegs, E., Luyckx, K., Luyten, L., Daelemans, W. and Van den Bulcke, T. (2016) Data Integration of Structured and Unstructured Sources for Assigning Clinical Codes to Patient Stays, *Journal of the American Medical Informatics Association*, **23** (e1), e11-e19.

SGS (2017) Electronic Data Capture Services, Société Générale de Surveillance, www.sgs.com/en/searchresults?s=EDC&dc=http.

Shah, J., Rajgor, D., Pradhan, S., McCready, M., Zaveri, A. and Pietrobon, R. (2010) Electronic Data Capture for Registries and Clinical Trials in Orthopaedic Surgery: open source versus commercial systems, *Clinical Orthopaedics and Related Research*, **468** (10), 2664-71.

Singh, H., Nugent, Z., Yu, B. N., Lix, L. M., Targownik, L. and Bernstein, C. (2017) Hospital Discharge Abstracts have Limited Accuracy in Identifying Occurrence of Clostridium Difficile Infections Among Hospitalized Individuals with Inflammatory Bowel Disease: a population-based study, *PLoS One*, **12** (2), doi:10.1371/journal.pone.0171266.

Smith, I. L., Nixon, J., Brown, S., Wilson, L. and Coleman, S. (2016) Pressure Ulcer and Wounds Reporting in NHS Hospitals in England, Part 1: audit of monitoring systems, *Journal of Tissue Viability*, **25** (1), 3-15.

Souza, T., Kush, R. and Evans, J. P. (2007) Global Clinical Data Interchange Standards Are Here!, *Drug Discovery Today*, **12** (3), 174-81.

Tan, C., Liu, K. and White, E. (2013) Information Architecture for Healthcare Organizations: the case of a NHS Hospital. In *[Proceedings of] the UK Thirty Fourth International Conference on Information Systems (ICIS2013), Milan, Italy.*

Walther, B., Hossin, S., Townend, J., Abernethy, N., Parker, D. and Jeffries, D. (2011) Comparison of Electronic Data Capture (EDC) with the Standard Data Capture Method for Clinical Trial Data, *PloS One*, **6** (9), doi:10.1371/journal.pone.0025348.

Welker, J. A. (2007) Implementation of Electronic Data Capture Systems: barriers and solutions, *Contemporary Clinical Trials*, **28** (3), 329-36.

CHAPTER 14

Producing systematic reviews and getting evidence to the clinician

Faten Hamad

COMMENTARY: DINA TBAISHAT

This chapter focuses on managing clinical data, to get the research evidence to those who need to use it for decision making. The chapter complements Chapter 13, which discusses electronic data capture and clinical document architecture. Policy makers and clinicians need research evidence to help make health-care-related decisions on behalf of populations or individuals. Therefore, organisations such as the international Cochrane Collaboration work to gather, summarise and synthesise the best evidence from research, making the task of practitioners and policy makers easier. The evidence-based practice movement has moved from medicine to other health care disciplines and further into other areas of social science (including library and information practice). Evidence-based practice has always had its critics, who often note that a rules-based approach was not in accordance with the way professionals practise, denying any value to professional judgement (Pope, 2003) or how clinicians, for example, appear to learn to make decisions quickly, using 'illness scripts', or that the popularity of published case reports and care studies demonstrates the value of the 'story' – just as in knowledge management (Urquhart, 1998). Greenhalgh, Howick and Maskrey (2014), writing on behalf of the Evidence-Based Medicine Renaissance Group, note some current problems. For example, there is too much evidence in the form of guidelines and the possible solution of clinical decision support aids does not help practitioners make decisions for, and more importantly with, individuals who cannot be compartmentalised so easily into neat boxes, and who often have multiple (and interacting) problems.

The chapter explains what a systematic review is and how practitioners use them – or maybe just the summaries – to answer queries quickly. The searching strategy types are then introduced briefly, with the conclusion that subject or keyword searches are used most often, and sometimes simpler strategies across several databases might be as effective as the more comprehensive searches, particularly if there are text mining tools to help with screening. Various tools are suggested to improve the systematic review process, and the pros and cons for these tools considered, which may help in later decisions on when each of these tools is most appropriate. Integration with other systems is another issue that might be of interest, as data management systems should reflect site workflow, a difficult task and an obstacle when attempting to exploit their full electronic system capabilities. Problems such as poor reporting of primary evidence still occur although there have been some improvements. Research should focus on how to tackle problems that might result from poor understanding of statistics, but the emphasis should be on helping clinicians working with patients. The chapter outlines some methods, including those using visualisation and graphical tools. Chapter 2 emphasises the growing importance of these tools in information architecture.

References

Greenhalgh, T., Howick, J. and Maskrey, N. (2014) Evidence-based Medicine: a movement in crisis?, *British Medical Journal*, **348**, g3725, doi:10.1136/bmj.g3725.

Pope, C. (2003) Resisting Evidence: the study of evidence-based medicine as a contemporary social movement, *Health*, **7** (3), 267–82.

Urquhart, C. (1998) Personal Knowledge: a clinical perspective from the Value and EVINCE projects in health library and information services, *Journal of Documentation*, **54** (4), 420–42.

14.1   Introduction

Health policy makers and individual clinicians need syntheses of the research evidence to make decisions about healthcare for populations (should a particular intervention be funded, for example?) or decisions about the care of an individual patient (is this treatment likely to be effective for this particular patient?). The Cochrane Collaboration has led the way in production of systematic reviews of the research evidence on health interventions, but other publishers have experimented with ways of presenting that evidence to busy health professionals. Section 14.2 examines some approaches to incorporating easy access to the evidence in normal clinical workflows.

Cochrane systematic reviews depend heavily on evidence from randomised controlled trials, as the randomised control study design is less susceptible to bias than other designs. Harden et al. (2004, 794) stated, 'Systematic review methodology is well developed for trials, but the debate about systematic approaches to reviewing non-experimental research is in its early stages.' Section 14.3 examines some of the main principles of searching the literature for systematic reviews. Retrieval and management of references for a systematic review is a time-consuming process, and other approaches have been proposed to assist systematic reviewers, and information professionals supporting policy makers. Section 14.4 discusses use of text mining and other tools for assisting the systematic review process. It takes time and effort to produce a systematic review, and keep it updated; hence there is interest in text mining and other tools to speed up the workflow.

One of the underlying themes for this book was to consider the state of the evidence for some of the advice given on information systems architecture. Chapter 9 provided some evidence for design guidelines, and other chapters (chapters 4, 11 and 12 for example) have discussed theoretical frameworks that help in evaluation, and generation of new evidence. Chapters 5–8 examined aspects of workflows, and business process analysis. This chapter takes a slightly different, though related, perspective. It examines aspects of workflows involved in the generation of health evidence – the production of systematic reviews of the health research evidence. Just as important, it suggests that evidence needs to be integrated into normal clinical workflows – what professionals do in and around the electronic health record.

Section 14.2 discusses how clinical data is collected and used, and how to help the process of making clinical decisions become more evidence based. Section 14.3 discusses the workflows in the production of systematic reviews, how the review process is managed, and how it could be assisted. Section 14.4 draws conclusions.

14.2   From clinical data collection to evidence-based care

There is little time for health professionals to research the evidence resources that may be available in large clinical data sets, whether data sets from routine patient data collection or clinical trials, usually (though not always) reported in the journals. Furthermore, these provide population-based evidence that may or may not be relevant to any particular patient and their needs. Sackett and Rosenberg (1995) emphasise that clinical evidence-based practice and other health care decisions should be based on the best 'patient-based' and 'population-based' evidence, as well as 'laboratory-based' evidence, for better evidence-based decisions. In other words, a practitioner has to consider the data (and other knowledge) generated from consumers and their perspectives and preferences beside the external research evidence related to a particular diagnostic tool or treatment approach (Schlosser and O'Neil-Pirozzi, 2006).

Practitioners can save time if experienced people can provide them with pre-filtered evidence, usually through systematic reviews that aim to synthesise the results of multiple original studies by using strategies that identify and account for bias. The international Cochrane Collaboration aims to transform the way health decisions are made by gathering and summarising the best evidence from research for practitioners to use to support informed decision making, and thus improve global health. Cochrane (www.cochrane.org/) is a global independent network of researchers, professionals, patients, and carers, who work together to produce credible, accessible health information that is free from commercial sponsorship and other conflicts of interest.

The main output of the Cochrane Collaboration is the systematic review, but these are (understandably) quite long, and many practitioners rely on the summaries of a review to appreciate the key messages. Cochrane reviews have an abstract and a plain language summary, and some Cochrane reviews have audio podcasts. A small survey randomising participants (university staff) among four different summary formats (abstract, plain language summary, podcast or podcast transcript) found that there were non-significant differences in correct identification of a key review outcome (Maguire and Clarke, 2014). A similar but larger study with student midwives (Alderdice et al., 2016) found that plain language summaries without conclusions had the lowest proportion of correct responses, although the abstracts with and without conclusions generated similar responses. Prior knowledge and belief affected responses, as did the years spent in midwifery education. Murthy et al. (2012) carried out a systematic review of interventions designed to improve the uptake of evidence from Cochrane systematic reviews on managers, policy makers and clinicians. They found that mass mailing a printed bulletin only works when there is a single clear message, if the change is relatively simple to accomplish, and there is a growing awareness by users of the evidence that a change in practice is required. We read what we expect and wish to read, presumably.

Subject or keyword searching is probably the most popular way of information seeking, particularly for practitioners seeking rapid answers (Agoritsas et al., 2012). It is possible that practitioners might benefit from a search interface for MEDLINE with a built-in thesaurus (MeSH terms) and tree browsers, to help searching for topics that are less familiar to them (Mu, Lu and Ryu, 2014), helping to find related terms to their entry terms. PubMed MEDLINE (https://www.ncbi.nlm.nih.gov/pubmed/clinical) offers a set of clinical query filters – searching on a disease name, for example, produces a set of items with choices for type of clinical study and broad or narrow search, alongside lists of systematic reviews and relevant items on medical genetics.

Other medical publishers have produced routes into the evidence for practitioners and clinical decision support tools. For example, the *British Medical Journal* (BMJ) provides BMJ Best Practice (a decision support tool for professionals to use at the point of care); PACK, a clinical practice aid aimed at improving primary health care in lower- and middle-income countries; and Evidence Updates (BMJ, 2016). An evaluation of the quality of point of care information summaries from the 23 products that fulfilled the inclusion criteria for the review and were available for analysis rated each for editorial quality, evidence-based methodology and breadth of coverage (Kwag et al., 2016). The study concluded that BMJ Best Practice, DynaMed Plus and UpToDate scored the highest across all dimensions. Another review (Andrews et al., 2017) compared BMJ Clinical Evidence, DynaMed Plus, Evidence Essentials, First Consult, Medscape and UpToDate, noting that no single resource scores well across all criteria and choice depends on the clinician's need and situation at the time.

Even the best, most comprehensive point of care decision tool may not be used if it cannot easily be integrated into clinical workflows, and the way the electronic health record is actually consulted (McGinn, 2016). Usability testing in the design of a pulmonary embolism clinical decision support tool involved users reviewing various workflow designs with a scenario to help them visualise how the tool would work. Test participants were asked about the appropriate trigger location, and words to use. Workflows were demonstrated through the use of wireframes, web page schematics that may be static or partially dynamic, to show what would happen on clicking through (Press et al., 2015; Khan et al., 2016).

Graphical interfaces may help users for some searching purposes. Doc'CISMeF (Catalogue et Index des Sites Médicaux de langue Française) is a semantic search engine used to find resources in CISMeF-BP (bonnes pratiques), a health gateway, which gathers guidelines available on the internet in French. Visualisation of Concepts in Medicine (VCM) is an iconic language, which was integrated into a semantic search engine for easier information retrieval. The seven graphical components (colour, shape, pictogram etc.) can be built up to represent many medical concepts. Usability studies show that the incorporation of VCM helps users find relevant resources faster (Griffon et al., 2014).

14.3   Managing the systematic review process

The first, preparation, stage of a systematic review involves formulating and refining the research question, checking for other systematic reviews, writing the protocol and formulating the search strategy. Electronic search strategies need to be devised for systematic review searching. These need to be comprehensive but also efficient search statements to be used in the retrieval process, and should be replicable (Yoshii et al., 2009). In order to find all, or at least most, of the relevant studies, searching several databases is usually necessary because of differences between databases' coverage of articles, including selection procedures and indexing processes (McGowan and Sampson, 2005; Goss et al., 2007). Therefore, taking advantage of the differences in indexing across databases will increase the chances of retrieving relevant items that may be in different databases, but easier to find in one database than in another with the chosen search strategy. In other words, to increase the quality of the systematic review and limit the bias, a comprehensive literature search is required to identify as much of the relevant literature as possible (Sampson et al., 2009). Search filters may help to focus on particular research designs (qualitative research, for example) or type of study (diagnostic test accuracy), to make retrieval more efficient (Dixon-Woods, Fitzpatrick and Roberts, 2001). The search interface may affect the retrieval, and searchers need to avoid search errors that may adversely affect sensitivity, specificity and precision of the retrieval (Sampson and McGowan, 2006).

The most usual searches used in retrieval of the medical literature are subject search using medical subject terms or headings to retrieve relevant articles, author search, citation search (searching for an article that cited a specific article) and related or similar article searching (Sampson et al., 2008). Subject searching is the basis of search strategies for professional systematic reviewers, although multiple databases may have to be used (Papaioannou et al., 2009; Relevo, 2012) and a pragmatic search strategy adopted using text words not in the thesaurus and subject terms from the thesaurus (Golder and Loke, 2009). The interface for the same database differs according to search provider – and so does the retrieval, according to Craven et al. (2014), who examined search functions such as truncation, exploded MeSH terms (term plus narrower terms in the subject tree) and variations of adjacency and free text term searching. The search syntax varied across the different interfaces as well. The alternative approach to a highly detailed Boolean logic combination of thesaurus and free text terms, tailored for one particular interface and database, is a search across multiple databases, perhaps combined with some follow-up of references in relevant items retrieved.

Hamad (2013) found that a simple combination of subject terms worked effectively to retrieve clinically related research studies, defined as sibling studies for a randomised controlled trial and its related qualitative, economic, process evaluation research, and any other related randomised-controlled-trial publication. More than one database should be searched, with an appropriate and probably pragmatic choice of databases. Apparently, sibling study retrieval depends on the reporting and indexing (labelling, classification and vocabulary) used in each database. Moreover, information professionals might consider combining similarity search (such as the Similar Articles link on PubMed) and a simple Boolean search on multiple databases, to increase recall. Sometimes it is difficult to assess the degree of kinship between published studies; one solution would be for authors to provide the clinical trial register number of the randomised controlled trial, which in turn would be picked up in the metadata by the database provider (Hamad, 2013).

The searching and sifting (appraisal) stages of a systematic review often run alongside each other. Text mining techniques (Ananiadou et al., 2006) can assist the systematic review process (Ananiadou et al., 2007, 2009), and search engines have been used for screening (Sampson et al., 2006). Tools such as the EPPI Reviewer 4 (http://eppi.ioe.ac.uk/cms/Default.aspx?alias=eppi.ioe.ac.uk/cms/er4) can assist in all types of systematic review, and cover bibliographic management, screening, coding and options for synthesis. A systematic review of the use of text mining tools shows that text mining should reduce workload of screening, by prioritising which studies should be screened. Text mining could be used as a 'second screener'– although some studies might be missed (O'Mara-Eves et al., 2015).

A systematic review of tools to automate parts of the systematic review process lists a variety of tools, and notes their functions and limitations (Tsafnat et al., 2014). The review categorises the 15 tasks involved in the main stages of preparation, retrieval, synthesis and write-up, and examines the potential for automation with each task, what current systems currently provide, and future research needs. For example, for screening titles and abstracts, decision support systems may use natural language-processing techniques (e.g. text mining) to highlight sentences and phrases likely to be of interest (Thomas, McNaught and Ananiadou, 2011). This reduces the possibility that those screening miss potential studies while screening a large number of titles and abstracts. Other tools such as ExaCT use an information extraction engine that searches the article for text fragments that best describe the trial characteristics, together with a web-browser-based user interface that allows human reviewers to assess and modify the suggested selections (Kiritchenko et al., 2010). The information extraction engine uses a statistical text classifier to locate those sentences that have the highest probability of describing a trial characteristic. Another approach is machine learning, based on trying to model what a human screener does when making decisions on include or exclude. The system Abstrackr picks keywords from the title and abstracts and attempts to model the process (Wallace et al., 2010). The task is difficult as the set of relevant (included) items is much smaller than the set of excluded items. Wallace et al. (2010) use an ensemble of support vector machines built over different feature-spaces (e.g. abstract and title text) that are trained interactively by the person doing the screening.

Another systematic review of data extraction techniques found that there was research on this, but – perhaps unsurprisingly – no outstandingly successful tool (Jonnalagadda, Goyal and Huffman, 2015). Data extraction is very time-consuming; one of the problems is that there is no guarantee that funding information (for example) will consistently be mentioned in one section of a journal article. And there is also the problem that there can be inconsistencies between the text and the tables in a paper. Assessing the risk of bias is another tedious part of preparing many systematic reviews. A tool to help with this

(RobotReviewer) is a machine learning system that could help Cochrane reviewers assess the risk of bias and provide snippets of supporting text for the risk of bias tables (Marshall, Kuiper and Wallace, 2016).

14.4   Conclusions

Clinical evidence is important for health practitioners and policy makers for decision making. The Cochrane Collaboration has led the way in producing systematic reviews to support busy health professionals in the decision-making process. Systematic reviews depend heavily on evidence from randomised controlled trials, a bias free clinical design. The production of systematic reviews goes through several defined steps, starting with formulating and refining the research question.

An important principle to consider when producing systematic reviews is the searching process. Search strategies need to be devised to be comprehensive, and often need to be carried out over several databases to get over the differences between databases' coverage of articles, and different indexing processes. Subject search using medical subject terms or headings to retrieve articles is the primary search strategy. Author search, citation search (searching for an article that cited a specific article) and related or similar article searching are also used. Searching on a simple combination of subject terms can be effective to retrieve clinically related research studies, defined as sibling studies for a randomised controlled trial and its related qualitative, economic, process evaluation research, and any other related randomised-controlled-trial publication.

There are suggestions that it would be beneficial to automate the production of systematic reviews, through natural language processing to help in some of the stages. For example, the appraisal process of a systematic review might benefit from text mining tools (decision support systems) by prioritising which studies should be screened. However, not all automation techniques are useful and applicable, and the workflows need to be considered carefully. For some teams collaborative tools may be useful, but there may not be suitable tools for the time-consuming tasks such as data extraction.

References

Agoritsas, T., Merglen, A., Delphine, S., Courvoisier, D. S., Combescure, C.,

Garin, N., Perrier, A. and Perneger, T. V. (2012) Sensitivity and Predictive Value of 15 PubMed Search Strategies to Answer Clinical Questions Rated Against Full Systematic Reviews, *Journal of Medical Internet Research*, **14** (3), e85, doi:10.2196/jmir.2021.

Alderdice, F., McNeill, J., Lasserson, T., Beller, E., Carroll, M., Hundley, V., Sunderland, J., Devane, D., Noyes, J., Key, S., Norris, S., Wyn-Davies, J. and Clarke, M. (2016) Do Cochrane Summaries Help Student Midwives Understand the Findings of Cochrane Systematic Reviews: the BRIEF randomised trial, *Systematic Reviews*, **5**, 40, doi:10.1186/s13643-016-0214-8.

Ananiadou, S., Kell, D. B. and Tsujii, J.-ichi (2006) Text Mining and its Potential Applications in Systems Biology, *Trends in Biotechnology*, **24** (12), 571-79.

Ananiadou, S., Procter, R., Rea, B. and Sasaki, Y. (2007) Supporting Systematic Reviews Using Text Mining. In *[Proceedings of] the Third International Conference on e-Social Science*, Ann Arbor, www.nactem.ac.uk/assert/projectReports2.php.

Ananiadou, S., Rea, B., Okazaki, O., Procter, R. and Thomas, J. (2009) Supporting Systematic Reviews Using Text Mining, *Social Science Computer Review*, **27** (4), 509-23, doi:10.1177/0894439309332293.

Andrews, R., Mehta, N., Maypole, J. and Martin S. A. (2017) Staying Afloat in a Sea of Information: point-of-care resources, *Clevelans Clinical Journal of Medicine*, **84** (3), 225-35.

BMJ (2016) *Products and Services*, British Medical Journal, www.bmj.com/company/products-services/#service15.

Craven, J., Jefferies, J., Kendrick, J., Nicholls, D., Boynton, J. and Frankish, R. (2014) A Comparison of Searching the Cochrane Library Databases via CRD, Ovid and Wiley: implications for systematic searching and information services, *Health Information and Libraries Journal*, **31** (1), 54-63.

Dixon-Woods, M., Fitzpatrick, R. and Roberts, K. (2001) Including Qualitative Research in Systematic Reviews: opportunities and problems, *Journal of Evaluation in Clinical Practice*, **7** (2), 125-33.

Golder, S. and Loke, Y. (2009) Search Strategies to Identify Information on Adverse Effects: a systematic review, *Journal of the Medical Library Association*, **97** (2), 84-92.

Goss, C., Lowenstein, S., Roberts, I. and DiGuiseppi, C. (2007) Identifying Controlled Studies of Alcohol-Impaired Driving Prevention: designing an effective search strategy, *Journal of Information Science*, **33** (2), 151-62.

Griffon, N., Kerdelhué, G., Hamek, S., Hassler, S., Boog, C., Lamy, J.-B. and Darmoni, S. J. (2014) Design and Usability Study of an Iconic User Interface to Ease Information Retrieval of Medical Guidelines, *Journal of the American Medical Informatics Association*, **21** (e2), e270-e277, http://doi.org/10.1136/amiajnl-2012-001548.

Hamad, F. (2013) *Retrieval of Sibling Studies for Clinical Randomised Controlled Trials*, doctoral thesis, Aberystwyth University.

Harden, A., Garcia, J., Oliver, S., Rees, R., Shepherd, J., Brunton, G. and Oakley, A. (2004) Applying Systematic Review Methods to Studies of People's Views: an example from public health research, *Journal of Epidemiology and Community Health*, **58** (9), 794-800.

Jonnalagadda, S. R., Goyal, P. and Huffman, M. D. (2015) Automating Data Extraction in Systematic Reviews: a systematic review, *Systematic Reviews*, **4**, 78, http://doi.org/10.1186/s13643-015-0066-7.

Khan, S., McCullagh, L., Press, A., Kharche, M., Schachter, A., Pardo, S. and McGinn, T. (2016) Formative Assessment and Design of a Complex Clinical Decision Support Tool for Pulmonary Embolism, *Evidence Based Medicine*, **21** (1), 7-13.

Kiritchenko, S., de Bruijn, B., Carini, S., Martin, J. and Sim, I. (2010) ExaCT: automatic extraction of clinical trial characteristics from journal publications, *BMC Medical Informatics and Decision Making*, **10** (1), 56.

Kwag, K. H., González-Lorenzo, M., Banzi, R., Bonovas, S. and Moja, L. (2016) Providing Doctors with High-Quality Information: an updated evaluation of web-based point-of-care information summaries, *Journal of Medical Internet Research*, **18** (1), e15.

Maguire, L. K. and Clarke, M. (2014) How Much Do You Need: a randomised experiment of whether readers can understand the key messages from summaries of Cochrane Reviews without reading the full review, *Journal of the Royal Society of Medicine*, **107** (11), 444-9.

Marshall, I. J., Kuiper, J. and Wallace, B. C. (2016) RobotReviewer: evaluation of a system for automatically assessing bias in clinical trials, *Journal of the American Medical Informatics Association*, **23** (1), 193-201.

McGinn, T. (2016) Putting Meaning into Meaningful Use: a roadmap to successful integration of evidence at the point of care, *JMIR Medical Informatics*, **4** (2), e16.

McGowan, J. and Sampson, M. (2005) Systematic Reviews Need Systematic

Searchers, *Journal of the Medical Library Association*, **93** (1), 74–80.

Mu, X., Lu, K. and Ryu, H. (2014) Explicitly Integrating MeSH Thesaurus Help into Health Information Retrieval Systems: an empirical user study, *Information Processing and Management*, **50** (1), 24–40.

Murthy, L., Shepperd, S., Clarke, M. J., Garner, S. E., Lavis, J. N., Perrier, L., Roberts, N. W. and Straus, S. E. (2012) Interventions to Improve the Use of Systematic Reviews in Decision-Making by Health System Managers, Policy Makers and Clinicians, *Cochrane Database of Systematic Reviews*, **9**, doi:10.1002/14651858.CD009401.pub2.

O'Mara-Eves, A., Thomas, J., McNaught, J., Miwa, M. and Ananiadou, S. (2015) Using Text Mining for Study Identification in Systematic Reviews: a systematic review of current approaches, *Systematic Reviews*, **4** (1), 1.

Papaioannou, D., Sutton, A., Carroll, C., Booth, A. and Wong, R. (2009) Literature Searching for Social Science Systematic Reviews: consideration of a range of search techniques, *Health Information and Libraries Journal*, **27** (2), 114–22.

Press, A., McCullagh, L., Khan, S., Schachter, A., Pardo, S. and McGinn, T. (2015) Usability Testing of a Complex Clinical Decision Support Tool in the Emergency Department: lessons learned, *JMIR Human Factors*, **2** (2), e14.

Relevo, R. (2012) Chapter 4: effective search strategies for systematic reviews of medical tests, *Journal of General Internal Medicine*, **27** (supplement 1), 28–32, doi:10.1007/s11606-011-1873-8.

Sackett, D. L. and Rosenberg, W. M. (1995) The Need for Evidence-Based Medicine, *Journal of the Royal Society of Medicine*, **88** (11), 620–4.

Sampson, M. and McGowan, J. (2006) Errors in Search Strategies were Identified by Type and Frequency, *Journal of Clinical Epidemiology*, **59** (10), 1057–63.

Sampson, M., Barrowman, N. J., Moher, D., Clifford, T. J., Platt, R. W., Morrison, A., Klassen, T. P. and Zhang, L. (2006) Can Electronic Search Engines Optimize Screening of Search Results in Systematic Reviews: an empirical study, *BMC Medical Research Methodology*, **6**, 7, doi:10.1186/1471-2288-6-7.

Sampson, M., McGowan, J., Cogo, E., Grimshaw, J., Moher, D. and Lefebvre, C. (2009) An Evidence-Based Practice Guideline for the Peer Review of Electronic Search Strategies, *Journal of Clinical Epidemiology*, **62** (9), 944–52.

Sampson, M., Shojania, K. G., McGowan, J., Daniel, R., Rader, T., Iansavichene, A. E., Ji, J., Ansari, M. T. and Moher, D. (2008) Surveillance Search Techniques Identified the Need to Update Systematic Reviews, *Journal of Clinical Epidemiology*, **61** (8), 755-62.

Schlosser, R. W. and O'Neil-Pirozzi, T. (2006) Problem Formulation in Evidence-Based Practice and Systematic Reviews, *Contemporary Issues in Communication Science and Disorders*, **33**, 5-10.

Thomas, J., McNaught, J. and Ananiadou, S. (2011) Applications of Text Mining Within Systematic Reviews, *Research Synthesis Methods*, **2** (1), 1-14.

Tsafnat, G., Glasziou, P., Choong, M. K., Dunn, A., Galgani, F. and Coiera, E. (2014) Systematic Review Automation Technologies, *Systematic Reviews*, **3** (1), 74.

Wallace, B. C., Trikalinos, T. A., Lau, J., Brodley, C. and Schmid, C. H. (2010) Semi-Automated Screening of Biomedical Citations for Systematic Reviews, *BMC Bioinformatics*, **11** (1), 55.

Yoshii, A., Plaut, D. A., McGraw, K. A., Anderson, M. J. and Wellik, K. E. (2009) Analysis of the Reporting of Search Strategies in Cochrane Systematic Reviews, *Journal of the Medical Library Association*, **97** (1), 21-9.

Index